THE PERSONS CASE

The Origins and Legacy of the Fight for Legal Personhood

Robert J. Sharpe and Patricia I. McMahon

On 18 October 1929, John Sankey, England's reform-minded Lord Chancellor, ruled that women were eligible for appointment to Canada's Senate. Initiated by Edmonton judge Emily Murphy and four other activist women, the *Persons* case challenged the exclusion of women from Canada's upper house and the idea that the meaning of the constitution could not change with time. *The Persons Case* considers the case in its political and social context and examines the lives of the key players – Henrietta Muir Edwards, Nellie McClung, Louise McKinney, Emily Murphy, and Irene Parlby, the politicians who opposed the appointment of women, the lawyers who argued the case, and the judges who decided it.

Robert J. Sharpe and Patricia I. McMahon examine the *Persons* case as a pivotal moment in the struggle for women's rights and as one of the most important constitutional decisions in Canadian history. Lord Sankey's decision overruled the Supreme Court of Canada's judgement that the courts could not depart from the original intent of the framers of Canada's constitution in 1867. Describing the constitution as a 'living tree' the decision led to a reassessment of the nature of the constitution itself. After the *Persons* case, the constitution could no longer be viewed as fixed and unalterable, but had to be treated as a document that, in the words of Sankey, was in 'a continuous process of evolution.'

The Persons Case is a comprehensive study of this important event, examining the case itself, the ruling of the Privy Council, and the profound effect that it had on women's rights and the constitutional history of Canada.

(Osgoode Society for Canadian Legal History)

ROBERT J. SHARPE is a Justice of the Court of Appeal for Ontario.

PATRICIA I. McMAHON is an associate with the law firm Osler, Hoskin & Harcourt LLP.

THE PERSONS CASE

The Origins and Legacy of the Fight for Legal Personhood

ROBERT J. SHARPE AND
PATRICIA I. McMAHON

Published for The Osgoode Society for Canadian Legal History by
University of Toronto Press
Toronto Buffalo London

Printed in Canada

Reprinted in paperback 2008

ISBN 978-0-8020-9750-7 (cloth)
ISBN 978-0-8020-9628-9 (paper)

Printed on acid-free paper

Cover illustrations: (Front) Nellie McClung, detail from
Women are Persons! by Barbara Patterson, bronze casting
on Parliament Hill. Photography courtesy of Merna
Forster. (Back) Five signatures from the petition for the
admission for women to the Senate of Canada

Library and Archives Canada Cataloguing in Publication

Sharpe, Robert J.
The Persons case : the origins and legacy of the fight for legal
personhood / Robert J. Sharpe and Patricia I. McMahon.

Includes bibliographical references and index.
ISBN 978-0-8020-9750-7 (bound)   ISBN 978-0-8020-9628-9 (pbk.)

1. Famous Five (Canadian women's rights activists).   2. Women's
rights – Canada – History.   3. Women – Legal status, laws, etc. –
Canada – History.   4. Persons (Law) – Canada – History.   I. McMahon,
Patricia I., 1972–   II. Osgoode Society for Canadian Legal History
III. Title

HQ1236.5.C2S49 2007   305.42092'271   C2007-903199-4

University of Toronto Press acknowledges the financial assistance to its
publishing program of the Canada Council for the Arts and the
Ontario Arts Council.

University of Toronto Press acknowledges the financial support for its
publishing activities of the Government of Canada through the
Book Publishing Industry Development Program (BPIDP).

Contents

Foreword

The Osgoode Society
For Canadian Legal History

The *Persons* case is one of the best-known Canadian constitutional cases, both for the fact that it declared women to be 'persons' for the purposes of eligibility for appointment to the Senate, and for Lord Sankey's invocation of the 'living tree' metaphor in interpreting the constitution. Robert Sharpe and Patricia McMahon add enormously to our understanding of the case by a detailed exploration of its context. They analyse the campaign waged in both political and legal circles for the recognition of women as senators, and examine the background and personalities of the major players in the litigation, in particular Lord Sankey, Prime Minister Mackenzie King, and Emily Murphy. Murphy, one of the 'Famous Five' litigants, was the driving force behind the demand for legal recognition, and she is shown here to be a fascinating and complex individual.

The purpose of The Osgoode Society for Canadian Legal History is to encourage research and writing in the history of Canadian law. The Society, which was incorporated in 1979 and is registered as a charity, was founded at the initiative of the Honourable R. Roy McMurtry, formerly attorney general for Ontario and chief justice of the province, and officials of the Law Society of Upper Canada. The Society seeks to stimulate the study of legal history in Canada through supporting researchers, collecting oral histories, and publishing volumes that contribute to legal-historical scholarship in Canada. It has published seventy books on the courts, the judiciary, and the legal profession, as well as on the history of crime and punishment, women and law, law and economy, the legal treatment of ethnic minorities, and famous cases and significant trials in all areas of the law.

Current directors of The Osgoode Society for Canadian Legal History are Robert Armstrong, Kenneth Binks, Patrick Brode, Michael Bryant, Brian Bucknall, David Chernos, Kirby Chown, J. Douglas Ewart, Martin Friedland, John Honsberger, Horace Krever, Gavin MacKenzie, Virginia MacLean, Roy McMurtry, Brendan O'Brien, Jim Phillips, Paul Reinhardt, Joel Richler, William Ross, Robert Sharpe, James Spence, Mary Stokes, Richard Tinsley, and Michael Tulloch.

The annual report and information about membership may be obtained by writing The Osgoode Society for Canadian Legal History, Osgoode Hall, 130 Queen Street West, Toronto, Ontario, M5H 2N6. Telephone: 416-947-3321. Email: mmacfarl@lsuc.on.ca. Website: Osgoodesociety.ca

R. Roy McMurtry
President

Jim Phillips
Editor-in-Chief

Preface

The *Persons* case, more formally known as *Edwards v. Attorney General of Canada*, is one of the best known cases in Canadian constitutional law. The *Persons* case recognized the ideal of universal personhood and is cited for the proposition that Canada's constitution is 'a living tree capable of growth within its natural limits.'

The litigants had a less lofty ambition. Emily Murphy, Henrietta Muir Edwards, Nellie McClung, Louise McKinney, and Irene Parbly sought a judicial ruling that section 24 of the *British North America Act, 1867*, which provides for the appointment of 'qualified persons' to the Senate of Canada, be interpreted to include women. And the case began not in the courts, but in the political arena.

Emily Murphy, the woman behind the petition and the push to appoint a woman to the Senate of Canada, was indefatigable in her attempts to persuade one prime minister after another to appoint a woman, especially her, to the Senate. She met with great resistance. Repeatedly, Murphy was told that section 24 of the *BNA Act* did not permit the appointment of women to the Senate because they were not 'persons' within the legal meaning of the constitution. Without a constitutional amendment, three prime ministers responded, their hands were tied. By the summer of 1927, Murphy came to realize that her efforts to secure a political solution were fruitless. And so she turned to the courts for a legal ruling, hoping that either the Supreme Court of Canada or the Judicial Committee of the Privy Council would agree that women were 'persons' for the purposes of an appointment to the Senate even without a constitutional amendment.

The judges of the Supreme Court of Canada took a traditional and narrow approach to constitutional interpretation when they dealt with the matter in the spring of 1928, finding that women were not eligible for appointment under section 24 of the *BNA Act*, in large part because the Fathers of Confederation had clearly never intended their appointment. Undaunted, Murphy and her counsel, Newton Rowell, appealed the case to the Judicial Committee, where the new Lord Chancellor, John Sankey, reversed the decision of the Supreme Court and declared women to be full persons under the law.

A detailed look at this political battle that became a legal one reveals a number of themes. We see how determined individuals can achieve fundamental legal and constitutional change, even if that change is not fully realized during their lifetime. The *Persons* case litigants never could have imagined that Lord Sankey's admonition that the constitution is a 'living tree' would come to inform the most basic interpretation of the constitution. In fact, most people simply forgot about the case once the decision was rendered. Prime Minister King appointed a woman – not Emily Murphy – to the Senate, but the country became preoccupied by other pressing concerns. The Great Depression was paramount in the 1930s, followed by the Second World War and the great boom of the 1950s. In those decades of turmoil, the rights of women somehow managed to get lost. The *Persons* case marked the end of the first era of women's rights, and was all but forgotten until the 1970s when it was resurrected by a new wave of feminists.

Other themes emerge. It probably is not surprising that the women involved in the *Persons* case were from western Canada, the home of the United Farmers' movement and the Progressives. Devout Christians, ardent temperance advocates, and involved in various efforts to promote and protect the rights of women and children, Murphy, Edwards, McClung, McKinney, and Parlby were, in many respects, the very models of post–Word War I social reformers. Typical, too, were many of their attitudes toward race, immigrants, and the disabled, which rightly shock the modern reader as being antithetical to the very ideal the *Persons* case recognized – that of universal personhood.

The story of the *Persons* case also reflects Canada's colonial past, the tensions of Empire, and the strains between the British Judicial Committee's approach to Canada's constitution, which strongly favoured provincial rights, and the belief of many Canadians that the Fathers of

Confederation had created a system of strong central government. Mackenzie King could not deliver on his promise to Emily Murphy that he would have the constitution amended to allow for female senators, as the Canadian constitution remained in the hands of the Westminster Parliament and Canada's politicians could not agree on an amending formula. Yet it was the Judicial Committee's refusal to be strictly bound by the intentions of those who wrote the constitution that opened the door to a constitutional decision that better reflected contemporary Canadian values than the narrow and formalistic approach of Canada's own judges sitting in the Supreme Court of Canada.

We would like to thank a number of people who have provided invaluable assistance with this book.

The staff and legal professionals at Osler, Hoskin & Harcourt, LLP, have been enthusiastic in their support for Patricia McMahon's involvement in this project, as were Chief Justice Roy McMurtry and Robert Sharpe's colleagues at the Court of Appeal for Ontario.

We thank members of the Toronto Legal History Group and the Constitutional Roundtable at the University of Toronto, Faculty of Law, who heard presentations of draft parts of this manuscript and provided many helpful suggestions. At the Judicial Committee of the Privy Council, Clive Duffield provided tours of the court as well as photographs for the book. At the Supreme Court of Canada, Mario Laurier provided copies of the litigants' submissions.

We owe special thanks to those who took the time to review the manuscript in draft form and provided many constructive and insightful comments and suggestions that made this a better book: Martin Friedland, Jim Phillips, Denise Reaume, Kent Roach, Geraldine Sharpe, and two anonymous referees. We thank Alexa Sulzenko who provided us with valuable research assistance.

A special thanks to Kevin Ackhurst, who not only read the manuscript at all stages with great enthusiasm, but also made a significant contribution with his painstaking review of the penultimate draft.

THE PERSONS CASE

The Origins and Legacy of the Fight for Legal Personhood

Introduction:
'A Relic of Days More
Barbarous Than Ours'

Canadian women became legal persons just days before the stock market crash that ushered in the Great Depression. On 18 October 1929, Lord Sankey, the reform-minded Lord Chancellor, recently appointed to England's highest judicial office by Labour Prime Minister Ramsay MacDonald, ruled that women were legally eligible for appointment to the Senate of Canada, proclaiming, 'The exclusion of women from all public offices is a relic of days more barbarous than ours.'[1]

With Edmonton judge Emily Murphy at the helm, five prominent Western Canadian women had fought to secure the legal right for women to be appointed to the Senate. Newton Wesley Rowell, one of Canada's leading constitutional lawyers, represented Murphy and her four colleagues, Henrietta Edwards, Nellie McClung, Louise McKinney, and Irene Parlby. He convinced the Judicial Committee of the Privy Council, then Canada's court of last resort, to reject the prevailing view of Canada's legal establishment that a woman was not, in the words of the *British North America Act, 1867*, a 'qualified person' for appointment to the Senate.

The Privy Council's decision was a bold legal step, overruling the Supreme Court of Canada's unanimous decision of 1928. Chief Justice Frank Anglin and his four colleagues on the Supreme Court had based their decision on the conventional legal reasoning that the meaning of words in the constitution did not change with time. They reasoned that because women could neither vote nor hold public office when the constitution was written in 1867, the Fathers of Confederation could not have contemplated the appointment of a female senator when they used the words 'qualified persons.' Although most Canadian women had acquired the vote, Canada's Department of Justice held the same view in 1921 when it provided a legal opinion on the subject to Conservative Prime Minister Arthur Meighen. So strong was the department's view that its senior officials advised the prime minister that only a constitutional amendment could render women eligible for appointment to the Senate.

Then, as now, constitutional amendments were difficult to achieve. Legally, all that was required to amend the constitution was an enactment of the British Parliament. The *BNA Act* may have been Canada's constitution, but it was still an imperial statute that could be changed by a simple vote of the Parliament at Westminster. Politically, however, constitutional amendments were a far trickier business. The *BNA Act* contained no amending formula, and the compact theory of Confederation, espoused by provincial leaders and accepted by some federal politicians, held that the union of 1867 was a pact among the colonies that had come together to form Canada. On this theory, amending the *BNA Act* – the initial agreement – required consultation with and the consent of the parties to the original pact. On almost every issue, including a workable amending formula, powerful provincial interests blocked any change.

The fate of the Senate, not just whether women could be appointed to the institution, was also the source of some debate in the 1920s. There were various proposals for Senate reform, including outright abolition, and little chance of achieving a consensus. Ontario's premier, Howard Ferguson, announced his opposition to 'tampering' with the constitution to allow for female senators, and Quebec, which did not allow women to vote until 1940, was also fundamentally opposed to any change that would put women in the upper chamber.

In the face of this constitutional impasse, both Arthur Meighen and his Liberal successor in the prime minister's office, William Lyon Mackenzie King, were flooded with requests to appoint Emily Murphy to the Senate. Neither the Conservatives nor the Liberals were eager to have Murphy's forceful voice intrude upon the slumber of the Red Chamber, as the Senate is often called because of its red carpet and draperies. Both prime ministers relied upon the strict letter of the law to excuse their inaction.

The constitution of the day gave Murphy no legal right to complain of sex discrimination. In the 1920s, women and other minorities could not expect the courts to protect them from discrimination. There was no way to enforce individual rights at the federal level before the 1960 *Canadian Bill of Rights* or the 1982 *Charter of Rights and Freedoms*. Before the *Charter*, constitutionalism focused on jurisdictional issues that addressed the division of powers between the Dominion and provincial governments under the *BNA Act*, with the courts serving as umpire. The issue was which level of government had the power to do what under the constitution; no one doubted that within their respective spheres, governments were unfettered in their ability to act.

The most pressing constitutional issue of the 1920s was not the protection of equality rights but rather the division of powers and the scope of Parliament's residuary power under the Peace, Order and Good Government clause of section 91 of the *BNA Act*. Also known as 'POGG,' the residuary power gave Parliament the authority to legislate with respect to matters not specifically assigned to either the Dominion or the provinces. The interpretation of this authority offered by the British Privy Council created a storm in certain Canadian circles. Sir John A. Macdonald and many of the other Fathers of Confederation saw POGG as the centrepiece of the Dominion's overarching authority in a highly centralized federation, where the provinces were viewed essentially as glorified municipalities. The noble lords of the Judicial Committee had other ideas. In a series of cases decided between 1921 and 1926, the Privy Council had imposed strict limits on the Dominion's authority to act under POGG.[2] Ultimately, in *Toronto Electric Commissioners v. Snider*,[3] the Judicial Committee, with Lord Chancellor Richard Haldane holding the pen, reduced the Dominion's residuary power to little more than an emergency measure to be used in the most limited of circumstances.

Snider embodied the Judicial Committee's approach to Canadian constitutional interpretation. For decades – and to the frustration of many Canadian politicians, lawyers, and legal scholars – the Judicial Committee had rarely felt bound by the framers' intentions to create a strong central government and did not hesitate to expand provincial powers as it saw fit, thus adapting the division of powers to suit changing circumstances within Confederation. Indeed, Viscount Haldane, a leading proponent of provincial rights and the Lord Chancellor behind some of the Judicial Committee's most contentious decisions, made no secret of the fact that the Privy Council had changed the shape of the Canadian constitution. He conceded that the original objective of the

BNA Act was 'to make the Dominion the centre of government in Canada, so that its statutes and its position should be superior to the statutes and position of the Provincial Legislatures.' But as Haldane proudly explained, the Privy Council

> put clothing upon the bones of the Constitution, and so covered them over with living flesh that the Constitution of Canada took a new form. The provinces were recognized as of equal authority co-ordinate with the Dominion, and a long series of decisions were given by [Haldane's predecessor Lord Watson] which solved many problems and produced a new contentment in Canada with the Constitution they had got in 1867.[4]

Many Canadian constitutional scholars took issue with Haldane's 'solution' to the 'many problems' facing Confederation, and rejected the assertion that the Privy Council had 'produced a new contentment in Canada.'[5]

The *Persons* case – as the litigation concerning the appointment of women to the Senate came to be called – added a significant twist to this general pattern of the Privy Council's jurisprudence and its 'adaptive' or progressive approach to constitutional interpretation. In stark contrast to the prevailing opinion in Canada, but in keeping with the approach of their Privy Council predecessors, Lord Sankey and his four colleagues refused to be bound by the original intentions of the constitution's creators. There can be little doubt that women, who could not vote in 1867, were no more welcome to sit in the Senate of Canada at that time. What was particularly notable about the *Persons* case was the Privy Council's decision to apply a progressive approach to defining the legal status of women and to abandon centuries of common law jurisprudence that had systematically excluded women from public office. Striking what has come to be the most powerful and enduring metaphor in modern Canadian constitutional jurisprudence, Lord Sankey announced the doctrine of the organic constitution: Canada's constitution is 'a living tree capable of growth and expansion within its natural limits,' a document that is in 'a continuous process of evolution.'[6] According to the Privy Council, the courts should not treat the constitution as an ordinary statute and give it 'a narrow and technical construction.' Instead, judges should accord the constitution a 'large and liberal interpretation'[7] to allow it to meet the changing needs of Canadian society.

The progressive tone of Sankey's decision in the *Persons* case reflected the spirit of the age, not the conservative thinking of the Canadian legal establishment. The world had emerged from the horrors of the First World War and entered an age preoccupied, however fleetingly, with prosperity and modernity. Canadian women, with the exception of those in Quebec, had won the right to vote. Communication was transformed by radio, movies, and the telephone. Mass-produced Model T's made it possible to go anywhere, anytime; other mass-produced goods fuelled a spirit of consumerism. Popular culture, unbounded by the constraints of tradition, flourished. Jazz and flappers symbolized an age that jettisoned convention in favour of fun, frivolity, and innovation.

Ten days after Sankey announced the *Persons* case judgment, on 29 October 1929, the New York stock market collapsed and the roaring twenties came to an end. Ironically, the recognition of women's rights and the 'living tree' approach to constitutional interpretation met a similar fate. After the success of wartime suffrage, many within the women's movement expected the 1920s would bring great things. Alas, they were sadly mistaken. After gaining the vote in the period from 1916 to 1920, the women's movement simply sputtered. Without a unifying objective, the movement dwindled as women returned to home and household following the Great War. In this sense, the *Persons* case may be regarded as a bright light in the otherwise bleak post-suffrage period of women's rights.

Almost from the moment of its proclamation by the Privy Council, the judgment in the *Persons* case and the principle for which it stood – recognition of full citizenship and personhood for women – were put on hold, only to emerge some forty years later with second-wave feminism in the 1960s and 1970s. Similarly, Lord Sankey's living tree metaphor remained a forgotten footnote until 1982 when, with the enactment of the *Charter of Rights and Freedoms*, Canadian judges responded to the pleas of feminists and others who advocated for the strong judicial protection of fundamental rights and freedoms by resurrecting and embracing the 'large and liberal' approach to constitutionalism as the guiding principle of constitutional interpretation.

The Famous Five and Maternal Feminism

Who were the five women – the 'Famous Five' – who took the *Persons* case all the way to the Privy Council and how did they get there? The legal documents and briefs for the case are cast in technical legal language and say nothing about the women's lives, their beliefs, or their battles for women's issues and social justice. The formal legal citation for the case, *Edwards v. Attorney General of Canada*,[8] ignores all but Henrietta Muir Edwards. The five names, listed in alphabetical order in the title of proceedings and Lord Sankey's judgment, revealed only their formal affiliations, though this was enough to make clear that these were five prominent and successful women from Alberta:

> Henrietta Muir Edwards is the Vice-President for the Province of Alberta of the National Council of Women for Canada; Nellie L. McClung and Louise McKinney were for several years members of the Legislative Assembly of the said Province; Emily F. Murphy is a police magistrate in and for the said Province; and Irene Parlby is a member of the Legislative Assembly of the said Province and a member of the Executive Council thereof.[9]

Henrietta Edwards had been a stalwart member of the women's movement for over fifty years, and although the case bears her name, she was not the most prominent of the five. That distinction belonged to Nellie McClung, well known across Canada as a writer and as a passionate advocate for temperance and women's suffrage. Next to McClung in prominence was Judge Emily Murphy, a well-published author and social crusader, better known to Canadians by her nom de plume, 'Janey Canuck.' In drive and determination, Murphy was the leader, having launched her campaign for a Senate seat shortly after her appointment as a magistrate in 1916; the *Persons* case bore the names of the other four women, but the case was really her battle from the start. Louise McKinney was well known in Alberta as a leading figure in the temperance movement and also as the first woman elected to the Alberta legislature, serving in that body from 1917, the year after Alberta women got the vote. Irene Parlby, a founder of the United Farm Women's Association, was elected to the Alberta legislature in 1921. She was serving as minister without portfolio in the cabinet of the United Farmers Association government when the *Persons* case was argued.

All five women were determined social reformers who had fought to improve the lives of women under Canadian law and to better Canadian society more generally. They were from the West, the home of protest politics and third parties. They thought that maternal virtue would improve Canadian society if only women were permitted to assume their rightful place in positions of power and influence. Their causes included women's suffrage, the improvement of legal rights for women and children, and the prohibition of alcohol.

The Famous Five espoused what modern scholars have called 'maternal feminism.'[10] They believed that the distinctive biological qualities of women made them well suited to play a crucial role in public life. Maternal feminism was a progressive social reform movement that stressed the importance of family and the distinctive role of women as mothers and wives. Maternal feminists believed that the application of female, maternal virtue to issues of social welfare would improve Canadian society and the lot of the disadvantaged, especially impoverished women and children. They advocated the legal equality of men and women but they did not seek to obliterate traditional gender roles. The female role was defined by motherhood, childrearing, and ensuring a happy home life.

In 1915, when Nellie McClung wrote to advance the cause of suffrage, she did so from the perspective of a maternal feminist, explaining 'every normal woman desires children.'[11] Similarly, Henrietta Edwards described motherhood as 'God's greatest gift' and saw a mother as 'a co-worker with God in a way that no man can ever be.'[12] Irene Parlby, too, believed that women had a political role to play in securing better conditions for children, better education, and better public health, but that when a woman was deciding whether to 'desert her home for politics ... one's children should always come first.' Parlby also believed that 'only a limited number of women have qualities which will prove useful' in politics. Most women, she declared, could and should limit themselves to their domestic duties.[13]

Maternal feminists came to realize, however, that predominance in the domestic sphere would only advance their goals so far. Laws and the legal status of women would have to change. In 1902, Henrietta Muir Edwards had described the dilemma facing the Canadian woman: though she reigned as a 'queen in her home,' 'unfortunately the laws she makes reach no further than her domain.' Edwards urged women to enter the political world to make their 'written or unwritten' laws capable of being enforced outside the home.[14]

Nellie McClung expressed similar frustration when she campaigned for female suffrage in 1915: 'One very contemptible bit of "dope" handed to women to keep them quiet was the hoary old lie that "the hand that rocks the cradle rules the world." If the cradle rockers had even a fair share of ruling the world, the world would very soon be vastly improved by the banishing of the bar and the battlefield.'[15]

McClung believed that if the 'instinctive love' of women could be marshalled, 'there [would be] enough of it in the world to do away with all the evils which war upon childhood, under nourishment, slum conditions, child labour, drunkenness. Women could abolish all this, if they wanted to.'[16]

Speaking to the Edmonton Women's Canadian Club in 1912, Emily Murphy contended that giving women the vote would achieve a 'perfectly balanced duality' as 'women will stand to the moral side of all questions, rather than to the economic or scientific.'[17] Likewise, Irene Parlby believed that extending the franchise to women 'will make for righteousness in the public life of the country.'[18]

All five women were strong Christians who believed in societal improvement through the application of Christian morality in public life. Their political agenda was heavily influenced by their religious beliefs.[19] They had fought hard during the early years of the century for the vote and for the right to sit in Parliament and the provincial legislatures. They could not understand how the words of Canada's constitution could now possibly mean that a woman was not a 'person' qualified for appointment to the Senate. They accepted that this interpretation might have been possible in 1867, but after the efforts of so many women during the Great War, surely women had earned the right to full personhood.

These women embraced a vision of the social gospel movement that applied Christian teaching beyond individual faith to reflect the kingdom of God on earth through social renewal. Christian values could eliminate poverty, social inequality, capitalist greed, denominational division, prostitution and sexual impurity, and promote altruism as the dominant public virtue. Social gospel proponents were a mixture of Methodists, Presbyterians, Baptists, and Anglicans. Adherents of the movement spread their message in churches, but they also drew upon science and sociology to identify the causes of social ills, joining with other reformers to promote temperance, minimum hours of work and minimum wage legislation, old age pensions, child welfare, and improved public education and public health.

Temperance and the prohibition of alcohol were central to the maternal feminist agenda and played an early role in the activist life of several of the women. In the early years of the twentieth century, alcohol was cheap in a society with few other diversions. Excessive alcohol consumption was a serious social problem. Louise McKinney and Nellie McClung had belonged to the Woman's Christian Temperance Union (the WCTU), and believed that drunkenness was a primary cause of crime, social unrest, unemployment, disease, immorality, and family violence and breakdown. Alcohol did more than poison private, domestic life; it was also thought to have a corrupting influence on politics. Advocates of temperance believed that the liquor interests based in Ontario and Quebec exerted undue influence in Canadian politics through their major donations to the mainstream Liberal and Conservative political parties, largely at the expense of the West.

The Famous Five are rightly regarded as important pioneers in the struggle for women's equality, but to focus on equality adopts a modern perspective. Their own vision was one of social betterment rather than equality. Maternal feminists were overwhelmingly middle-class, white, heterosexual, Anglo-Saxon Christians with an elitist sense of their own virtue and moral superiority. They viewed women as 'naturally the guardians of the race,'[20] and that race was decidedly white, British, and Protestant. A modern scholar aptly observed that Emily Murphy's work and writing 'reveal a woman with an unshakeable sense of the entitlement of her class to rule over those who are less competent and less worthy.'[21]

Maternal feminists were progressive in a number of ways, but many of their views on race were not. Many shared the racist and xenophobic attitudes that prevailed in the society in which they lived. Their elitism and strong attachment to British culture and values made many maternal feminists unreceptive, even hostile, to other races and cultures. Many promoted eugenics as a means to improve public health. One such strategy involved sterilization laws, like the legislation in Alberta that permitted the sterilization of 'mental defectives.' These views shock the modern reader and quite rightly attract fire from today's feminists, who struggle 'to transcend' what they regard as the 'insensitivity and arrogance' and 'debilitating moral blind spots' of their predecessors.[22] But no matter how wrong these views are from today's perspective, they were not just the views of a few individuals but also the prevailing attitude of an entire era.

Western Pioneers

All five women joined the wave of migration from eastern Canada and immigration from Britain, the United States, and Europe that transformed the Prairies in the early years of the twentieth century. Between the election of Wilfrid Laurier in 1896 and the outbreak of war in 1914, more than two and a half million people arrived in Canada, increasing the Canadian population by one-third. Half of those new-comers settled in the West, lured by the promise of cheap fertile land and the hope of economic prosperity. The women of the *Persons* case were part of this western wave of settlers.

Developing Canada's West required energy, imagination, courage, initiative, and a lot of very hard work. The pioneering spirit that fuelled western growth also generated an idealistic belief that building the Canadian West could serve as a model for the world. As Nellie McClung explained in 1915, revealing a distinctly anti-racist strain in her own thinking, Canada aspired to be known as

> the land of the Fair Deal, where every race, color and creed will be given exactly the same chance; where no person can 'exert influence' to bring about his personal ends; where no man or woman's past can ever rise up to defeat them; where no crime goes unpunished; where every debt is paid; where no prejudice is allowed to masquerade as reason; where hon-est toil will insure an honest living; where the man who works receives the reward of his labor.[23]

In 1919, Louise McKinney spoke to the United Farmers of Alberta con-vention and expressed a similar vision of a free and open land where every man and woman would be treated with respect, 'where no man is asked whether his father was a prince or a peasant, where suspicion gives place to tolerance.'[24]

Despite these views, Canadian immigration policy retained highly discriminatory elements that most citizens, including the Famous Five, failed to perceive as unjust. Asian immigrants suffered severe restric-tions. Although Canada's immigration policy no longer restricted entry to those from Great Britain, and offered entry to southern and eastern Europeans, it was assumed that all newcomers would assimi-late to British culture and habits. From Laurier to the Famous Five, the belief in the superiority of British ways was widespread, and the goal of assimilating immigrants to the English language and to British cul-ture was unquestioned.

The Canadian West gave people a chance at a better life. Hardwork-ing, enterprising immigrants, who assimilated to British ways, could build new lives for themselves as well as a land of fairness and justice. Emily Murphy, Henrietta Edwards, Nellie McClung, Louise McKin-ney, and Irene Parlby, all newcomers to Alberta, shared the ideal that they could build a better world and they all believed that as women, they had a distinctive role to play. First they had to overcome the barriers to their full participation in the political life of the nation and then they had to mobilize the forces of feminine and motherly virtue to realize their vision of a just society.

The Men Who Supported the *Persons* Case

Without the support of some significant men, the *Persons* case would never have come to pass. First and foremost is William Lyon Mackenzie King. King made the *Persons* case possible by agreeing to use the government's statutory authority to refer the question to the courts, and he was the first prime minister to appoint a woman to the Senate.[25] Yet his enthusiasm to see any woman appointed to the Senate was muted at best. From the time of his election to office in 1921 to his defeat in 1930, King deflected Emily Murphy's persistent pleas for a Senate appointment with promises. Of dubious sincerity, King's promises were too weak to overcome the obstacles of constitutional wrangling and the considerations of practical politics.

Next is Newton Wesley Rowell. If it took the power of the prime minister to refer the *Persons* case to the courts, the Famous Five needed a pre-eminent litigator to see the case through to the Supreme Court of Canada and then to the Privy Council in London. For Rowell, the case was more than just another retainer. He was sympathetic to the idea of appointing women to the Senate and supported many of the same causes as the women who hired him. Rowell's wife had helped to found local women's associations within the Liberal Party. As Liberal leader in Ontario from 1911 to 1917, Rowell, a devoted Methodist, had been a staunch proponent of female suffrage and temperance.

Despite Rowell's prowess as an advocate, those skills would have been wasted if not for John Sankey, the Lord Chancellor of England who wrote the Judicial Committee's decision in October 1929. Sankey refused to be bound by a consistent and lengthy line of cases that had stubbornly resisted conferring legal rights on women. He insisted that the *BNA Act* was a constitution, not a mere statute. In addition to permitting the appointment of women to the Senate of Canada, Sankey described a progressive approach to constitutional interpretation that has left an indelible mark on Canadian constitutional law. As he explained, 'Their Lordships do not conceive it to be the duty of this Board – it is certainly not their desire – to cut down the provisions of the Act by a narrow and technical construction, but rather to give it a large and liberal interpretation.'

The *Persons* Case: People and Politics

The *Persons* case is justifiably known as a landmark decision for women's legal rights; its broader legacy is the recognition of Canada's constitution as an enduring document intended to withstand the challenges of time. In the chapters that follow, we take a closer look at the people behind the *Persons* case as well as the social and political forces that produced it. First, we discuss Emily Murphy and her background. How was it that she came to lead the charge to secure the appointment of women to the Senate of Canada and what role did personal ambition play in her activities? Next, we examine the lives of the other four women involved in the litigation. Though Murphy took the lead, the credibility secured through the participation of Henrietta Edwards, Nellie McClung, Louise McKinney, and Irene Parlby was crucial to the success of the case.

This book also seeks to provide some context for the fight to secure the right to appoint women to the Senate. Chapter 3 outlines how the rights of women changed both legally and politically in the years prior to the *Persons* case, especially during the First World War.

A book about the *Persons* case would be incomplete without a discussion of the politics of the era as well as the politics of the women's movement. Chapter 4 discusses Emily Murphy's personal campaign to secure her own appointment to the Senate. No matter that she was a Conservative by inclination and upbringing, Emily Murphy set out to persuade William Lyon Mackenzie King not only to appoint women to the Senate but also to appoint *her* to the upper chamber. Only when that political campaign failed did Murphy decide to try her luck in the courts. In chapter 5, we detail the various steps Murphy took to get her case – a reference by the government, not an action against it – before the Supreme Court of Canada. These activities have been the subject of a number of myths and inaccuracies that we hope to correct.

In chapter 6, we deal with the first legal decision in the litigation and the men of the Supreme Court of Canada who determined that women were not persons under the *BNA Act*. Next, we provide some context for the relationship between Canada and the Judicial Committee of the Privy Council, the debate surrounding the Judicial Committee's role as an appellate body, and some of its constitutional decisions in the 1920s that caused particular consternation among Canadian scholars. In chapters 8 and 9, we discuss Newton Rowell's preparation to appear before the Judicial Committee as well as the argument and the outcome. The influence of Lord Sankey is especially noteworthy. Finally, we close this book by examining the legal and cultural legacy of the *Persons* case and the Famous Five who sought to transform the Senate and ended up changing the fundamental tenets of Canadian constitutional interpretation.

We hope that this case study will shed light on Canada's constitutional history and the process of constitutional decision-making. There are many advantages to taking a close look at the people and the politics behind a specific case. One sees that individuals do make a difference and that a landmark ruling can be driven by unpredictable personal and political combinations. In retrospect, we can agree that the Privy Council got it right, yet at the time, there was nothing inevitable about the result. But for the unlikely coincidence of Emily Murphy's unquenchable thirst for a Senate appointment, William Lyon Mackenzie King's fondness for referring difficult questions to the courts, and John Sankey's determination to make his mark as a reforming Lord Chancellor, the result could easily have been quite different.

Our case study also demonstrates why the law must be constantly changing and why it does not and cannot operate in a vacuum isolated from political and social forces. In 1928, the Supreme Court, stuck in the mores of another age, had failed to move with the times. Women worked, voted, and held public office, yet Canada's highest court refused to recognize them as persons. A year later, the Privy Council's decision broke the centuries-old mould of exclusion because John Sankey saw that a way had to be found to permit the law to accommodate the change that social forces demanded.

Finally, one sees how the symbolic importance of a constitutional decision can transcend the specific issue it decides. Even her closest friends could not understand why Emily Murphy was fighting so hard to secure an appointment to a body that most Canadians regarded as outdated and irrelevant. But almost eighty years later, we embrace the ideal of universal personhood as lying at the core of our ideal of a just and democratic society.

1

First of the Five

But for the determined efforts of Emily Murphy, the *Persons* case would not have occurred. Despite her lack of formal legal training, Murphy – an author, social activist, and judge – had a significant impact on the fabric of Canadian law beyond the case that permitted women to be appointed to the Senate. From the bench of the Woman's and Children's Court in Edmonton, where she sat as the presiding magistrate from 1916 until her retirement in 1931, Murphy challenged the traditional approach of Alberta's legal profession. Likewise, in her quest for a seat in the Senate and her bold fight to gain recognition for women as persons with full citizenship rights, Murphy challenged the narrow constitutional vision of Canada's political and legal establishment.

The third child of six in the Ferguson family, Emily was born in March 1868, in Cookstown, Ontario, a town of some two hundred inhabitants in Simcoe County, a few miles north of Toronto. The Fergusons were a prosperous family with strong ties to the Conservative Party; Canada's first prime minister, Sir John A. Macdonald, was once a houseguest, and Emily's uncle, Thomas Robert Ferguson, was the local Member of Parliament for the five years following Confederation. The Ferguson family was also prominent in the legal community. A cousin, another Thomas Ferguson, was a judge on the Supreme Court of Ontario. Three of Emily's brothers became lawyers and one of them, William Nassau Ferguson, was appointed to the First Appellate Division of the Supreme Court of Ontario in 1916.

When Emily was fifteen, her parents sent her to board at Toronto's elite Bishop Strachan School for Girls, while brothers Tom and Gowan attended Upper Canada College. It was Tom and Gowan who introduced their sister to Arthur Murphy, an Anglican theology student at Toronto's Wycliffe College. In 1887, nineteen-year-old Emily Ferguson married thirty-year-old Arthur Murphy.

Arthur's first parish was in Forest, Ontario, followed by stints in Watford, Chatham, and Ingersoll. Emily gave birth to four daughters, though only three survived early childhood. After ten years of parish work in southwestern Ontario, Arthur answered the evangelical calling of his Wycliffe training and turned to missionary work. He agreed to live the nomadic and financially uncertain life of a missionary, and his assignments took the Murphys first to remote corners of Ontario, and then, in 1898, to England.

Freed from her duties as a rector's wife, Emily Murphy began her literary career, writing loosely autobiographical sketches describing the people she met and the places she saw. Emily adopted the nom de plume of 'Janey Canuck,' and in 1901 published *Impressions of Janey Canuck Abroad*, a poorly edited, badly printed, but well-written collection of lively and vivid impressions of life in England.

Shortly after their return to Canada in 1901, the Murphys' life took a sudden and unexpected turn. Arthur contracted typhoid fever and Doris, the couple's youngest daughter, died of diphtheria. Physically and mentally drained, Arthur decided to give up the ministry to work on a timber lot he had acquired in Manitoba. In 1903, the Murphys moved to Swan River, Manitoba, just three years after the remote town had been established, and two years before it was linked to the Canadian Northern Railway.

Emily Murphy's literary career flourished in her new surroundings. She wrote book reviews for the *Winnipeg Tribune* and published a series of magazine articles about life in the West for *National Monthly*. She wrote articles on housekeeping and fashion under various pseudonyms – 'Lady Jane,' 'The Duchess,' and 'Earlie York.'[1] At the same time, Arthur's timber business prospered. He also profited from his speculative real estate deals. However, in 1907, after four years in Manitoba, Arthur decided to move the family further west to Edmonton, a rapidly growing city of about 18,000. There, Arthur got into the coal mining business and bought and sold real estate.

Emily continued to write in Edmonton. Her most successful book, *Janey Canuck in the West*, describing immigrant cultures, was published in 1910. *Open Trails*, a book comparing Canadian and American life, followed in 1912, and *Seeds of Pine*, a book describing native legends, appeared in 1914. Murphy's books were a collection of light, amusing, and often self-deprecating sketches, criticized by some modern scholars for their racism.[2] In *Open Trails*, long before she entertained the ambition to be appointed to the Senate, Murphy described her visit to Ottawa when she was initially refused entry to the Senate Chamber because she was not 'in full dress.' After whispered discussion with a cabinet minister, the Black Rod allowed Murphy to enter, allowing her to claim 'the distinction of being the first woman to hold a seat on the floor of the Senate Chamber in a street suit.'[3]

Emily Murphy became president of the Canadian Women's Press Club in addition to her various activities in many other women's organizations. In 1914, she met fellow writer Nellie McClung, a prominent suffragist and a newcomer to Edmonton. Together, they worked in the campaign for suffrage. Murphy also took a strong interest in public health issues and, as a member of a ladies hospital committee, captured front-page headlines with her unladylike report disclosing unsafe conditions and inadequate management.[4]

Murphy's interest in women's rights was inspired by a series of lectures given by British suffragist Emmeline Pankhurst in Edmonton in 1911. Pankhurst's talk motivated Murphy to get involved in the Canadian women's suffrage movement. At the same time, Murphy also took up the struggle to reform Alberta's property laws. Although the common law rule prohibiting married women from owning property had been abolished in the nineteenth century, the legal right to own property was a hollow one for most pioneer women; it meant little to women who had no property before marriage and little hope of acquiring any after marriage.

Formal legal equality also meant little to women who were deprived of property by social custom. A husband could hold title to all property to the exclusion of his wife, and most husbands did just that. The law gave a married woman no entitlement to a share of the matrimonial home or the family farm, and there was nothing in the law to require a fair division or equalization of property upon breakdown of the marriage or death of the husband. Women who had migrated or immigrated to Canada's West to work alongside their husbands – breaking the land, feeding the animals, building a home, and raising children – had no legally enforceable right to be compensated for their efforts or to claim their fair share of the family farm. A husband could sell the family property or give it all away in his will, and a wife was left with no legal recourse. Matters were further complicated by the version of the land titles system adopted in the Western provinces that denied women even the minimal common law right of dower that gave widows a one-third life interest in the lands owned by their husbands during marriage. When combined with social attitudes that a woman's proper place was in the home, the lack of affirmative legal protection meant that most women had no resources and were entirely dependent upon their husbands.

Emily Murphy joined Henrietta Edwards in trying to help these women.[5] One of these women was a mother of seven who feared her husband might deprive her of any right to the farm she had worked to build, doing 'all kinds of work' outdoors 'in all kinds of weather,' chopping wood, feeding livestock, 'besides all the baking, cooking washing and housework for a large family.' She wrote to Murphy with a simple plea for justice:

> It would be a great comfort and security for most women to be assured that if her husband died, something would be hers ... I think if a wife got one half of all her husbands [sic] property ... it would only be her due ... I really think that if we women had a law compelling men to go equal shares with their wives there would be more home comforts and true happiness, less bachelors, less race suicide, as wives would not fear for having to provide and educate their children if left with a big family. Shame on the Farmers of Western Canada. They cry for Equity Associations ... But how few of them would ever think of being Even and Equal with the wife of his bosom.[6]

It was not just farm women who were at risk. Women who lived in towns and cities were also vulnerable. In the decade between 1901 and 1911, the population of Alberta ballooned from just over 70,000 to almost 375,000, while that of Saskatchewan grew even faster, rising from just over 90,000 to almost half a million. During the same period, Edmonton's population grew almost eight-fold from just over 4,000 in 1901 to 31,000 in 1911. The population of Calgary grew even more, from 4,400 to 44,000. In the early years of the century, the land booms associated with rapidly expanding urban centres provoked speculation with all of the attendant hazards, and the call for law reform spread across the Prairies.[7] As one judge explained, 'The wives in Alberta said ... where this speculation affects our homes, we want it stopped. We have a home in the morning but it is sold or mortgaged at night.'[8] Murphy worked on a bill presented by future prime minister R.B. Bennett, then a young opposition member in the legislature, but the bill died after second reading. Nevertheless, in 1915, the province enacted the *Married Woman's Home Protection Act*, which allowed a married woman to file a caveat precluding her husband from transferring or encumbering the 'homestead' or matrimonial home. The caveat could only be vacated upon application to a Supreme Court judge who was authorized to 'make such order ... as may seem just.'[9]

This legislative reform had clear limits. The statute did not confer upon a married woman any right to a share of her husband's property and the extent of a woman's entitlement was left to the discretion of the court. Further lobbying by Murphy and Edwards, together with Irene Parlby's support in the legislature, produced the *Dower Act* in 1917. That act prohibited a husband from disposing of the 'homestead' without his wife's consent. The legislation also guaranteed a widow's life interest in her husband's property after his death.[10] But, as women soon learned, even this reform had limited impact: a wife received no more than a life interest and had no entitlement to the furniture or equipment she would need to actually run the farm.

Emily Murphy: Magistrate

In March 1916, a group from the Edmonton Local Council of Women went to court to observe the trial of several women whom the police had arrested as common prostitutes. The prosecuting counsel insisted that respectable women should not hear the evidence he intended to call, and asked the women to leave the courtroom. Angered, the women left and turned to Emily Murphy for advice. She suggested that they ask the government to establish a special woman's court and to appoint a female judge to try cases involving women and children. The women agreed and asked Murphy to make the proposals to Charles W. Cross, Alberta's Liberal Attorney General. She wrote to Cross to convey the Local Council of Women's formal resolution urging him to establish the court, adding that if he thought it advisable to establish the court, 'I shall be pleased to accept your instructions.'[11] To Murphy's surprise, Cross liked the idea and immediately asked her if she would serve as the court's first judge. With little hesitation, Murphy's friends and family urged her to accept. Three months later, Cross wrote to confirm Murphy's appointment 'as Police Magistrate in and for the Province of Alberta, and as a Commissioner under the Children's Protection Act.'[12] With that letter, Murphy became the first woman to be appointed as a magistrate in the British Empire.

The Alberta government made a conscious effort to bring a fresh approach to judging, especially in cases involving women and children. Murphy's prominence as a writer and social activist were important factors leading to her appointment to the bench. An admirer from Toronto congratulated Murphy, and 'the fortunate Edmontonians who were wise enough to avail themselves of our Janey Canuck's heart and head.'[13] The *Edmonton Morning Bulletin* boasted that when Murphy took her place on the bench, 'Edmonton will have its first woman police magistrate and Alberta will have taken another step in the path of social reform, leading every other province in the Dominion.'[14] The *Edmonton Journal* proclaimed, 'Edmonton will make a step which will lead the whole Dominion in the matter of social reform.'[15] These claims were only partly correct: a women's court had been established in Toronto in 1913, but until 1922, a male magistrate presided.[16] Similarly, in England, women sat as justices of the peace and lay magistrates after a 1919 law eliminated gender disqualification.[17]

Murphy, forty-eight years old when appointed to the bench, was not unduly concerned about her lack of formal legal training. She insisted that life experience and common sense were equally important preparation for the bench: 'I find that all I ever thought about people, what they are or should be, and living conditions comes in useful ... Legal knowledge one needs and must acquire, but many women who have adjudicated for a family or club have as good a training for the bench in some particulars as lawyers.'[18] Murphy's brothers – Thomas, William, and Harcourt – were all lawyers, and they had encouraged her to accept the appointment, as had her husband Arthur.

Despite the seriousness of her task, Murphy also had a sense of humour about judging. Her long-time literary friend, William Arthur Deacon, described her as 'quite short and stout, and [she] walked with the lusty, sea-going roll of a sailor ashore. She was abundantly blessed with a love of humor. Her laughter, which was frequent, was no ladylike titter but something spontaneous and free and full-throated.' Emily Murphy insisted: 'A sense of humor to act as a kind of shock absorber is one of the most necessary adjuncts of the woman judge.'[19] Murphy regaled Deacon with her stories of incidents in the courtroom: 'William, it was dreadful! I was on the bench and had to keep a straight face!'[20]

Courts as Casualty Clearing Stations

Emily Murphy rejected the prevailing view of the legal establishment that the criminal law was a system of formal rules applied objectively by neutral judges to identify and punish wrongdoers. Instead, Murphy took a 'scientific' approach to criminal law, which focused on the social history of the offender, and encouraged other magistrates to do the same. She liked to describe the work of her court in medical terms and thought judges should adopt a therapeutic approach to crime and criminals. They should be 'magistrate-physicians.' The courts should be viewed as 'casualty clearing stations where the offender's case shall be carefully diagnosed and the proper remedy applied,'[21] 'where the X-ray is turned on, looking towards a cure.'[22] In Murphy's view, crime was often the product of mental or physical illness, including 'feeble-mindedness, venereal disease, and drug addiction, a trinity of evils greater than any scourge that ever afflicted mankind.' Murphy also approached the criminal law with an eye towards social justice, going so far as to argue that the *Criminal Code* ought to be renamed 'The Code of Social Justice.' Similarly, Murphy thought the criminal law should change its penal focus to 'coincide with justice as a specific and curative force in social life.'[23] To Murphy, far too much attention was paid to punishment and far too little paid to prevention and reformation. She urged her fellow magistrates to make use of their powers to do good – 'to strive for the amendment of laws,' 'to assist in the redemption of criminals' and 'the starting of things which would eradicate the evil' – and to concern themselves less 'with the punishment of evil-doing.' 'Reformation,' Murphy believed, 'ought to be our chief object, and not punishment. We are not required to blister accused persons so much as to locate the cause of their disease and remove it.'[24] Notwithstanding these reform-minded views, Murphy did not ignore the law, nor did she refrain from imposing stiff sentences when she was convinced that stern punitive measures were necessary. However, Murphy's most notable characteristic was her empathy for the unfortunate individuals who appeared before her. Her first instinct was to lend a helping hand rather than to inflict punishment. She was, in her own way, compassionate, caring and determined to get at the root causes of crime. To her close friends, Murphy immodestly claimed that no one 'has done more in the Dominion to domesticate (or should I say 'humanize'?) the administration of criminal law than myself – to show how penal justice may be made to coincide with social justice.'[25]

'To Exercise a Motherly Influence over Them'

Murphy's method combined a progressive, scientific approach of therapeutic jurisprudence with a kind of maternal feminism that was especially pertinent to her specific mandate as a magistrate presiding in the Woman's Court. John McLaren, in his study of Murphy's work as a magistrate, argues that 'her personal frame of reference was that of the intelligent, successful maternal figure, who, through her familial role; strength of character, and moral insight, could lead the less fortunate to a recognition of the error of their ways and personal reformation, and society to a new and more moral tomorrow.'[26] Murphy believed that the pursuit of reformation and rehabilitation came naturally to the female magistrates. She realized that many men would reject rehabilitation as a model for dealing with matters in the criminal law, but thought that 'no decent woman could sit, day after day, coldly passing judgment upon persons of her own sex, without making some attempt, however slight, to sting them awake; to pull them out of the slough and generally back them up at repairing their broken lives.'[27]

Although Murphy's legal methods were unorthodox, she nevertheless enjoyed the support of the provincial government. In 1921, an Alberta report praised the woman's court initiative as a 'great advance' in dealing with the cases of dependant and delinquent children. Female judges, the report argued, 'naturally take a greater interest in the members of their own sex who get into difficulty, and are able to exercise a motherly influence over them.'[28]

Murphy's courtroom procedures coincided with her therapeutic approach to adjudication, which was more akin to the practices of a social worker than those of a judge. As Murphy explained, 'In the Woman's Court we have no dock. The prisoner sits in an armchair in front of the magistrate, standing to be sworn and to hear the minute of adjudication.'[29] Murphy thought this difference in setting was important, and resisted an effort in 1922 to require her to sit in other courtrooms. She told the Deputy Attorney General that her court ran differently: 'I sometimes hear the case in my private office or in a private room upstairs. This is also advisable in the case of very young children who will give evidence more readily if seated in a chair beside the magistrate.'[30] Murphy tried to create a welcoming atmosphere for the women who appeared before her. Almost every member of the court staff was female and most of them brought a piece of needlework with them to ensure that women coming before the court felt themselves to be among peers, 'free from the leering, lecherous "rounders" who frequent these places to satisfy their odious curiosity, or to lay plans of luring them back into their old haunts.'[31] Murphy and her female court staff also coordinated their efforts with the female police officers assigned to 'the cabarets, dance-halls, and on the streets after theatre hours,'[32] and with the women probation officers attached to the Department of Neglected Children.

Murphy clearly refused to be bound by the conventional idea that the judge should only act within the confines of the courtroom. She believed that a magistrate 'is closer to the human side of his city than anyone in it – or ought to be – and sees all phases of its life.' From this unique perspective, she believed that magistrates could and should advocate legal and social reforms to deal with the problems paraded before the courts.[33] Magistrates should actively promote temperance and the measures needed to prevent 'the exploitation of girl-children' and venereal disease. Murphy deplored the tendency in the superior courts to see criminal cases 'as abstractions to which purely legal methods are applied' as well as the inclination in the lower courts to view the successful magistrate as the one who generates the most fines. She quipped sarcastically that some magistrates 'easily fall into the habit of drawing their opinions and salary from the same source.'[34]

Murphy spent a great deal of her time doing what many would regard as social work. Her files are full of letters written in her capacity as a magistrate but having nothing to do with the actual cases that came before her in court. She helped unmarried mothers arrange for adoption and advised them how to go about collecting support from the father.[35] She helped children find places for their elderly and disabled parents, and she helped parents to deal with their unruly children.

Despite her propensity for reform, Murphy held some traditional views. She firmly believed that the institution of marriage was sacrosanct and that nothing should be done to weaken those bonds. She strongly opposed 'companionate marriages' – the cohabitation of unmarried couples or trial marriages: 'The acceptance of a system of companionate marriages must end in social chaos. Promiscuity belongs to fish, reptiles and insects. Monogamy belongs to the higher forms of life.'[36] Murphy also deplored serial monogamy – she described it as 'progressive polygamy' – and warned against the perils of a lengthy separation of husband and wife. The experience of the First World War showed that 'it is disastrous to separate a man and his wife over a period that runs into months or years. It is easier to nail the spouses to a cross than to keep them there.'[37] So strong was Murphy's desire to maintain the bonds of matrimony that she feared that liberal alimony awards in favour of a separated spouse could encourage wives to leave their husbands.[38]

Murphy's instinct was to maintain the integrity of the family unit at virtually any price, even in cases of spousal violence. She dissuaded women from proceeding with assault charges against their spouses and urged them to reconcile to avoid the harm of publicity and destitution that would follow a criminal conviction. If a recalcitrant husband refused to cooperate, Murphy threatened him with a trial before her hard-nosed colleague Magistrate P.C.H. Primrose, whom she described as 'the positive terror of one-sided or rancorous reasoning.'[39]

Murphy felt unconstrained by her judicial office from taking public stands on political issues affecting women and children. By the 1920s, along with Irene Parlby and Henrietta Edwards, Murphy was pushing for fundamental reforms to the property rights of married women. 'The relations of the sexes can never be really wholesome,' she wrote, 'until woman achieves complete economic independence. The partnership in marriage is one of soul and body and should include that of property.' She continued, espousing a vision of matrimonial equality: 'Upon marriage, woman should become equal shareholder in the home, renouncing the so-called "privileges" of the past. The husband and wife should be of equal rank both in law and in fact and, therefore, seized of a joint responsibility for the maintenance of their home and children.'[40]

In 1925, Parlby presented a bill in the Alberta legislature to establish a community property regime, but the bill was defeated.[41] Alberta's United Farmers government felt the pressure for change and appointed Parlby along with Murphy and Edwards to an advisory committee to consider and report on the matrimonial property rights of women. In one of her articles on the subject of marriage and property, Murphy invoked the idea of a 'living jurisprudence': 'If our law is to remain a living jurisprudence – that is to say, if it is to pursue its never ceasing task of applying old principles to new circumstances,'[42] the courts should enforce marriage contracts and strive for the recognition of a more equal division of matrimonial property. However, despite their enthusiasm for community property, Murphy and Parlby signed the committee's report in March 1928, which recommended a watered-down reform that guaranteed married women the more limited right to 'matrimonial necessaries.'[43] Murphy's plea for the equal division of property went unanswered for more than half a century, until the revolution in family law that occurred in the 1970s and 1980s.

Murphy was also a strong proponent of mediation and reconciliation for domestic disagreements. Family law disputes of all kinds and from all corners of the province came to Murphy. She did her best to resolve difficult domestic disputes. Pleas for help from deserted wives trying to get support were promptly answered with practical suggestions. She often acted as a marriage counsellor, giving freely of her advice, often at long distance by correspondence. In other cases, where reconciliation was out of the question, Murphy assumed the role of lawyer, giving a distressed spouse advice on how to bring the case before the courts.[44]

Murphy dealt regularly with single mothers and issues of child support, child welfare, and adoption. Her approach to these questions was one of social betterment, and her views on this issue, like so many others, were strongly influenced by her attitudes to social class and ethnic origin. Correspondence between Murphy and Charlotte Whitten, then at the Social Service Council of Canada,[45] about 'illegitimacy' illustrate the point. When Whitten asked Murphy for her views on the subject, Murphy replied that in her experience, most cases involved 'girls' in domestic service, including hotels and cafeterias, where 'there is little supervision of the conduct of the girls, and in which they are subject to unusual temptations.' Most single mothers were under twenty years old and either foreign born or first generation Canadian. She explained: 'The crowded conditions of the country homes and lack of moral instruction are also responsible for much illegitimacy.'[46]

Murphy believed that single parents and their children should be encouraged to become self-sufficient, useful members of society. The state should assume responsibility for obtaining child support from fathers, and allowances should include something to pay for the child's education and job training as well as a modest allowance for the mother one month before and one month after the birth of the child.

Murphy also supported adoption, although she described the separation of mother and child as 'a vexed question.' In most instances, Murphy favoured separation for a number of reasons:

First, because where an infant is adopted into a home, it is adopted because the people wish to make it their own child. No one can possibly exploit an infant, in this way the child gets a better start in life. Second, it is removed from any stigma of illegitimacy. Third, the mother does not fall so easy a prey to other unscrupulous men, who, seeing her with a child feel she was special game. Fourth, the mother is not so handicapped as a wage earner. Fifth, she has a better opportunity of marrying.[47]

Murphy's views on other women's issues were unusually progressive for her time. For example, she attacked a decision from Manitoba that banned married women from teaching.[48] She argued that the word 'obey' should be removed from the marriage vow,[49] and urged the abolition of the right of action for breach of promise to marry.[50] Murphy also supported sex education and birth control, ridiculing religious arguments that promoted celibacy as a means of birth control on the grounds that the sole object of sex was procreation.[51] However, she opposed abortion, which she viewed as 'murder in embryo,' and would have permitted abortion only for those that were approved by a committee of doctors in cases of serious disease or insanity.[52]

'Flower-like Faces of Young Girls Who Have Fallen into Wrong-Doing'

Many of the cases Murphy dealt with involved prostitution, which she regarded as a scourge to be eradicated through law enforcement. She saw young prostitutes as innocent girls lured into doing evil by pimps, poverty, and drugs. She dealt with these cases as a stern, concerned mother, not as a judge preoccupied solely with the legal niceties of the case. 'The flower-like faces of young girls who have fallen into wrong-doing' touched her. Murphy was less sympathetic to experienced sex-trade workers whom she viewed as a corrupting influence on men who were vulnerable to their own sexuality and unable to restrain their sexual urges.

Murphy believed that domestic service, broadly defined to include work in restaurants and cafes, rendered women vulnerable to sexual exploitation. She urged governments to establish places where homeless girls could sleep to prevent their exploitation, and advocated raising the age of sexual consent. Murphy observed that many prostitutes were impoverished women who came to the city from rural communities in search of work. They were easy prey, and Murphy offered a bit of homey advice to their fathers: 'It is high time the farmers woke up and put trespass notices and scarecrows on their homes instead of in their fields.'[53]

Murphy worried about the sexual exploitation of domestic workers, often victimized by the 'hired man' and the sons of employers. 'Many people look upon the Indian girl or the immigrant girl as legitimate prey. The immigrant girl is far from her country; she does not know of our child protection laws; she has no friends. We can seldom go after the real criminal in these cases because you cannot [secure a] conviction on the unsupported evidence of a girl.'[54]

As in other aspects of the criminal law, Murphy's approach was therapeutic, but she found the effort to rehabilitate prostitutes 'discouraging in the extreme ... largely due to the fact that women who lead immoral lives almost invariably become addicted to the use of habit-forming drugs.' Sometimes, prostitutes fell prey to drugs because 'they would be wholly unequal to the physical strain without taking opium or cocaine.' Others succumbed to 'panderers, who prey upon them' and pushed them into drugs 'in order that the women may be kept steadily to their evil practices.' Murphy blamed 'those blackguardly persons who are responsible for the white slave traffic' for the evil of prostitution. They convinced the innocent 'girl' that 'she is an outcast and irretrievably lost, and that no respectable occupation is open to her.' Rehabilitation required an effort to 'root from her mind' these impressions of unworthiness.[55]

The Black Candle

One of Emily Murphy's greatest passions was her fight against the illicit drug trade in Canada. In 1922, based on a series of articles she had previously published in *Maclean's* magazine,[56] Murphy published a full-length book on the subject: *The Black Candle*.[57] She was convinced that Canadians were unaware of the lurking evil of drug purveyors and the devastating effects of illicit drug use, and set out to alarm the country into action with a sensationalized account of depravity. She viewed drugs as a dire threat to the moral health of the nation, and, with characteristic fervour, launched a vigorous anti-drug campaign.

Murphy's own awareness of the issue came from her time as a magistrate. Although she had used morphine to relieve pain,[58] like most Canadians she regarded illegal drug use as an isolated problem affecting certain areas of Vancouver. On the bench, Murphy was shocked by the extent of illicit drug use and drug-related crime and prostitution in Edmonton. *The Black Candle* was based on her extensive research on the subject, in which she interviewed drug users in her court, searched libraries, and read everything she could find on the topic. She even sent hundreds of questionnaires to police and drug enforcement officials across North America.

Murphy wrote as a strict moralist with a zeal for social reform. The book also reveals her racialized vision of the world with language and imagery that shock the modern reader. In Murphy's account, Asian and black drug dealers predominate, seducing and corrupting white women and threatening the Anglo-Saxon and Christian way of life. She recounted stories of innocent, well-educated white women being seduced into drug use and 'consorting with the lowest classes of yellow and black men' sometimes deserting their 'half-caste' children.[59] She described 'opium ghosts' as being predominantly Chinese, 'ashy-faced, half-witted droolers ... unfortunate cringing creatures who are so properly castigated by the whips and scorpions they have made for themselves.'[60]

She wrote about an alarming and growing trade in illicit drugs and the surreptitious methods used by sophisticated 'drug rings' of greedy white men with links to Chinese suppliers and black traffickers, reaping enormous profits while seducing innocent white women into lives of prostitution. She condemned lawyers and businessmen who profited from the trade and strongly criticized doctors and pharmacists for recklessly prescribing and dispensing narcotics for profit.

Murphy also feared the moral debasement and impotence that she attributed to drug use would contribute to the decline of the British Empire. 'Within a generation or so,' she wrote, 'prolific Germans, with the equally prolific Russians, and the still more fertile yellow races, will wrest the leadership of the world from the British.'[61] She worried that 'the white race lacks both the physical and moral stamina to protect itself, and that maybe the black and yellow races may yet obtain the ascendancy,' and warned that 'this seems possible – even probable –unless the enslavement which comes from these abhorrent and debasing narcotics can be strongly and speedily dealt with.'[62]

Murphy was certainly not alone in linking illicit drug use to Chinese immigrants, about whom she wrote, 'it is quite certain that we do not understand these people from the Orient, nor what ideas are hid behind their dark inscrutable faces.'[63] Murphy's language and imagery reinforced racial stereotypes that were in common circulation.[64] The prohibition of opium in Canada was directly linked to the rise of virulent anti-Chinese sentiment that culminated in anti-Asian rioting in Vancouver in 1907, and anti-Asian racism was more potent in British Columbia than in Alberta. Although many prominent British literary and public figures consumed opium, in Canada the practice was seen to be restricted to Chinese labourers who had been brought to Canada to build the railways. The *Opium Act* of 1908 prohibited the sale of opiates, except for medical purposes, and was strengthened by the *Opium and Drug Act, 1911*. Enforcement, however, remained weak.

As a magistrate, Murphy urged a 'get tough' strategy on drugs. She argued for stiffer sentences, especially for traffickers. She approved of using undercover informers and urged statutory changes to make it easier for the police to obtain search warrants. She approved a policy (apparently followed in Edmonton) whereby the investigating officer would be rewarded with half the fine levied upon conviction. Murphy regarded non-whites as 'visitors,' whose right to remain in Canada depended upon their behaviour.[65] In her view, non-white offenders, particularly those engaged in the drug trade, deserved to be deported.[66]

Yet Murphy did not abandon entirely her social betterment approach to judging. She also supported a coordinated treatment strategy as an integral part of her proposed war on drugs. She believed that governments should make treatment facilities available and the courts should see themselves as 'casualty clearing stations,' isolating for remedial treatment those victims of the drug trade who were capable of being redeemed.[67]

The Black Candle was widely read and had a significant impact on public opinion. Reviewers described the book in glowing terms,[68] and editorial writers praised Murphy for bringing a serious social issue to public attention. Already something of a celebrity, Murphy accepted invitations from across the country to speak about the ills of illicit drug use.[69] She was so proud of her work in this area that she nominated herself for the Nobel Prize in 1923.[70] Moreover, the work itself left a legacy in the form of Canada's drug laws. Some have credited Murphy's book as being 'extremely influential in shaping Canadian drug laws,' which changed significantly in the 1920s.[71] Her suggestions for closer supervision and regulation of doctors and pharmacists were put into effect and 'writs of assistance' were introduced to give police great latitude to search for illegal drugs without prior authorization. Longer prison sentences, corporal punishment, and the deportation of aliens engaged in the drug trade were encouraged as penalties. Parliament also heeded Murphy's fear of the evils of 'marahauna' by adding it to the list of prohibited drugs. Regrettably, no heed was paid to Murphy's recommendations for the creation of appropriate treatment facilities.[72]

Murphy's views were not without controversy and led some to

question whether she was fit to sit in judgment over cases involving accused persons of Chinese origin. In 1924, the case of *R. v. Mah Doon and Mah Ling* appeared on Murphy's docket. Lawyers for the accused, who were charged with trafficking in drugs, sought to have Murphy removed for bias.[73] The written application to the superior court insisted upon trial by a male magistrate. In oral argument, Hugh C. Macdonald, QC, counsel for the accused, relied on Murphy's published description of the drug trade and those who promoted it. Macdonald read to the presiding judge those passages from *The Black Candle* that described drug dealers and users as liars. Justice Ives was unmoved. He concluded that there was nothing to show that Murphy was biased against the two accused before her court, and added: 'I am biased against those who unlawfully deal in narcotics as I am biased against those found guilty of murder, but that is not enough to prevent a fair trial.' Having lost the bid to exclude her, the defence tried to use *The Black Candle* to its advantage at trial. The chief Crown witness was a drug user, and counsel tried to discredit his evidence by reading a passage from the book asserting that drug addicts could not be believed. The tactic drew a laugh from everyone in the courtroom, including the accused and Murphy, who chortled: 'A week ago you were using it in an attempt to prove that my views on the narcotic evil have prejudiced me and rendered me unfit to give an impartial verdict in a narcotic case.'[74]

Juvenile Delinquency

Emily Murphy also had strong views on the subject of juvenile delinquency, a problem she attributed to inadequate mothering. She described the typical mother who bothered to come to her court as 'a shilly-shally person either utterly ignorant or utterly indifferent to the life led by her own daughter ... thickly stupid ... apparently unmoved and uninterested ... all marrow and no bone.'[75] Juvenile offenders needed mothering and Murphy thought it was her responsibility to provide it. She worked 'to secure the entire confidence' of children appearing in her court. 'You must re-tie her hair; admire her new shoes, discuss the stitches in her sweater, and find out her standard at school.'

Murphy also blamed poverty and a lack of education for delinquency. As she put it, theft by juveniles 'is largely due to their living in flats and other places as tenants' and a consequent 'lack of property-sense.'[76] For her, the juvenile court was the most important of all courts. Murphy's description of the aims of the juvenile court reveal the strong influence of maternal feminism on her conception of her role as a judge. The court should 'preserve the home as a unit' and 'provide good homes for children who are without them.' The judge should act as 'a real parent to the neglected or delinquent child' and 'punish those beasts in the human jungle who destroy children.'[77]

Although Murphy's religious beliefs were less than fervent, she was influenced by social gospel ideals and believed that secularism was another significant source of delinquency. At a 1925 conference in Ottawa, Murphy railed against secular education: 'The point we have to consider as a child welfare conference is whether in view of the increasing delinquency among children in Canada we are justified in debarring from our public schools the spiritual tenets of the gentle Christ.' Even worse, in Murphy's view, were what she described as many 'soviet or communistic Sunday schools in Western Canada.' There, children were 'taught terrible blasphemy and other disregard of law and order.'[78]

Modern entertainment was another of Murphy's bêtes noires: 'We have to face the fact that the sex instinct is being commercialized in songs, literature, drinks, pictures, vaudeville and jazz,' she wrote. 'Nowadays children learn all about birth control at a shocking age.'[79]

'The Clang of Prison Doors'

Murphy was sympathetic to the plight of prisoners. She was a regular visitor to prisons and when 'passing through the cells,' she felt 'their chill in my soul.' She described 'the clang of prison doors' as the 'awfullest sound in the world.'[80] Murphy also undertook extensive correspondence with many people she had sent to prison, and often did what she could to help them. In addition, she visited prisoners and patients in mental hospitals, encouraged the Red Cross to send them sewing supplies,[81] and helped them to track down belongings lost in the turmoil of arrest and incarceration. Sometimes, Murphy sent books, magazines, or fabric for sewing.[82] She also wrote articles to officials, urging them to pay wages to prisoners to help them support their families or to give them money upon their release.[83]

Murphy was concerned about the conditions prisoners faced. She deplored the treatment of those held in pre-trial custody. Murphy had visited the institutions and knew quite well that the conditions for those held in pre-trial custody were often worse than those reserved for convicts. On one hand, she observed that most accused persons held in custody 'are compelled to remain in jail because they are poor and cannot get bail.' On the other hand, delay benefited the rich or sophisticated accused, giving them 'the opportunity of either spiriting away the informant or tampering with witnesses.'[84]

Murphy urged that those held awaiting trial 'should be securely detained in a special home at least as comfortable as a soldier's barracks.' If not convicted, they should be indemnified for their lost time. She recommended that women convicted of offences related to prostitution be separated from other female prisoners,[85] and urged the provincial police to rescind a rule that prohibited insane prisoners held in a police lock-up from having access to a window: 'In my opinion they should be encouraged to look out of the windows, and where any insane persons are concerned they should be made as happy and comfortable as possible, for only in this way can we reasonably expect their recovery.'[86]

Murphy also objected to the publication of an offender's name because it labelled the individual as a criminal and impaired reformation and rehabilitation. Instead, she advocated 'a merciful shielding of the offender from all curious, critical, or calculating eyes.' Despite the absence of the modern-day equivalent of a publication ban, the newspapers cooperated and refrained from mentioning names.[87]

Murphy's concerns about the criminal justice system extended well past the conditions of incarceration to the sentences imposed for various offences. She generally opposed capital punishment.[88] After seeing a condemned man on one of her prison visits who 'did not seem like a murderer' but had cracked under the strain of rural poverty, Murphy wrote to the minister of justice asking him to commute the sentence.[89] Yet her opposition to capital punishment was not universal. Her views on gender equality led her to urge Prime Minister Mackenzie King to refuse requests to commute the death sentence imposed upon a woman convicted of murdering a police officer. 'I desire to protest against the pernicious doctrine that because a person who commits a murder is a woman that person should escape from capital punishment,' she wrote. 'As women we claim the privilege of citizenship for our sex, and we accordingly are prepared to take upon ourselves the weight of those penalties as well.'[90]

'Insane People Are Not Entitled to Progeny'

In keeping with her scientific approach to law enforcement and social justice, Emily Murphy was a strong proponent of eugenics and the forced sterilization of the mentally ill and those she described as 'feeble-minded.' Theories of eugenics emerged in the late nineteenth century and gained considerable currency among social reformers in the early twentieth. Inspired by discoveries in genetics and biology, many social workers, social reformers, and health care professionals become persuaded that the human race could be improved through scientific breeding. Diseases, both physical and mental, could be eliminated and the social ills of poverty, crime, prostitution, alcohol, and drug addiction could be reduced. Eugenics theory resonated with those who harboured xenophobic fears over Eastern European and Asian immigration and the relative decline in the birth rate among those of British origin.[91]

'Feeble-mindedness' was thought to be the root cause of a significant proportion of crime and other forms of deviant behaviour. For Murphy, and for many otherwise enlightened progressive thinkers of her age, 'feeble-mindedness' was thought to be a scientifically established medical condition passed on from one generation to the next. 'We should not allow the imbecile or the feeble-minded to become a burden upon the workers lest the nation become weak. We must segregate these people till they become less numerous, making them as happy as circumstances permit, and, if possible, self-supporting.'[92] The scientific veneer of eugenics theories played into Murphy's therapeutic, 'casualty-clearing-station' approach to judging. A remarkable proportion of Murphy's judicial work involved dealing with those offenders who had been classified as insane, and she sent a significant number of them to mental hospitals. Murphy took a special interest in these prisoners, and frequently wrote to authorities at the prison or mental health facility to explain why she was sending an individual into their care, offering suggestions for the care of the prisoner patient.[93] These letters reveal Murphy's strongly held views about the interconnectedness of heredity, crime, and feeble-mindedness.

Emily Murphy's motto in this area was simple: 'Insane people are not entitled to progeny.'[94] She estimated 30,000 individuals, or 4 per cent of the population of Alberta, to be either feeble-minded or insane, of whom only 1,700 were receiving 'treatment.' Murphy complained that the state housed only those who were 'dangerous' and left the rest 'to roam at large and to propagate their kind whether in wedlock or out of it.' Reproduction was a significant concern. 'In this connection,' she explained, 'it must be borne in mind also, that the feeble-minded propagate somewhere from four to six times more rapidly that normal people.' Murphy believed that genetic factors were responsible for 90 per cent of the patients in mental health facilities, though it is by no means clear where she got that figure. Equally mysterious is the source for her assertion that 75 per cent of Alberta's mental patients were immigrants or settlers from other countries.[95]

Murphy drew on dramatic stories from her work as a magistrate to make her point that sterilization, a measure she described as 'not punitive, but corrective,' was the best way to deal with this pressing social problem. She recalled committing a mother of three children three times, her last child 'having to be removed from her arms in the padded cell where she had been placed awaiting removal' to the provincial institution at Ponaka. Another woman, she reported, had nineteen children 'in all stages from idiocy to imbecility.' A regular visitor to the home in Red Deer, Murphy reported on the 'hopelessness' of the children kept there: 'A large proportion of these patients could not be taught to chew gum without swallowing it.'[95]

Murphy identified three objectives that were served by forced sterilization: the prevention of sexual crimes against women and children committed by feeble-minded males; the reduced cost of keeping the feeble-minded; and 'the mental and physical betterment of our racial life.' Murphy was persuaded that 'the science of genetics shows to us that where both the husband and wife are feeble-minded, all the children are feeble-minded.' Thus, 'some families ... should become extinct – parenthood is not for all, but is a privilege which should be denied to those who are biologically unfitted to it.' In this context, Murphy regarded 'social necessity' as being 'of infinitely greater moment' than 'private liberty.'[97]

Murphy's views on eugenics had a racist and xenophobic hue. She advocated sterilization of the insane as an 'attempt at salvaging the human wreckage which has been dumped from foreign lands.'[98] In her assessment, the quest for genetic purity justified requiring those planning to marry to provide a medical certificate guaranteeing the absence of certain diseases, including venereal disease, feeble-mindedness, and epilepsy. Those who could not satisfy the authorities of their fitness to procreate should be permitted to marry only if they were first sterilized.[99]

However misguided Murphy's unwavering belief in the merits of eugenics may now seem,[100] they were widely – though not universally – shared by other progressively minded social activists of the era.

2

The Other Four

Emily Murphy may have taken the leading role in litigating the *Persons* case, but she knew that the battle could not be hers alone. She enlisted the aid of four other accomplished women: Henrietta Muir Edwards, Irene Parlby, Nellie McClung, and Louise McKinney, each of whom had played a distinctive role in the promotion of women's legal rights and equality. The formidable Famous Five represented all the major concerns in the women's reform movement of the day: the struggle for suffrage, the fight for prohibition, the effort to apply Christian values to public issues, and the promotion of improved legal and social rights for women and children.

Henrietta Muir Edwards and Legal Rights for Women

Henrietta Muir Edwards, for whom the case is officially named in the law reports – *Edwards v. Attorney General of Canada* – was a leading advocate for the reform of property laws, a major legal concern confronting Canadian women in the early years of the twentieth century.

Henrietta Muir was moved by the plight of hardworking women. She shared the experience of many newcomers who had left comfortable lives elsewhere to endure the hardship of life on Canada's western frontier, though she herself was a woman of great privilege. Born to a prosperous Montreal family in 1849, Henrietta Muir enjoyed many opportunities as a young woman. She travelled to Europe, studied art in New York, and was a sufficiently accomplished artist to have paintings exhibited in the Royal Canadian Academy. She was known for her miniatures and was commissioned by the Dominion government to paint a set of china for the Canadian Art Exhibit at the World's Fair in Chicago in 1893.

Yet, fuelled by her evangelical Christian beliefs, Henrietta Muir decided at an early age to devote her life to her family and to women's causes. She persuaded her father to buy a house in Montreal where she established the Working Girls Association to provide single women with rooms, training, and legal advice. A reading room provided a space for gospel meetings and educational classes. Circulating library materials along with daily papers and magazines were available. 'Fancy work' was taught. Employers who needed female workers to serve as clerks, domestics, and do other 'women's work' were invited to apply by letter, and on Tuesday evenings 'girls seeking employment [were] requested to call.'[1] Henrietta Muir ran the operation on subscriptions from donors. When the Young Women's Christian Association (YWCA) opened in 1889, it assumed the work of the Working Girls Association. At the same time, she acquired a printing press and began publishing *The Working Woman of Canada*, a magazine that she financed by doing job printing and selling her miniature portraits of prominent public figures.

Henrietta Muir moved to the West because of her husband's work. She married Dr Oliver Edwards in 1876, and followed him to Indian Head, Northwest Territories (now Saskatchewan), in 1883. There, Dr Edwards served as the government doctor for the local Indian Reserves.[2] In addition to his medical duties, he travelled with the government treaty party to the Peace River district. Here, Henrietta Muir Edwards had extensive contact with Aboriginal communities, an experience that shaped her views on race in a way that was quite different from Emily Murphy's view.[3]

While raising three children, Edwards continued to work to improve conditions for women, corresponding with fellow activists and studying laws that affected women and children. She was a devout Christian who believed that one's life should be devoted to the service of God and the community. She feared that materialism and the 'luxury of modern life' produced 'self-indulgence,' which in turn engendered 'indolence and indolence selfishness, the worst of all sins, for from selfishness spring nearly all other sins.'[4]

Oliver Edwards became ill in 1890 and the Edwards family returned east to Ottawa. There, Henrietta took up the cause of female prisoners and worked with Lady Aberdeen, wife of the Governor General, to establish the National Council of Women of Canada (NCWC) in 1893. The NCWC was a federation of Local Councils of Women and various other women's groups, including the Girls' Friendly Society and the Women's Art Association, and came to surpass the Woman's Christian Temperance Union as the largest women's group in Canada. Lady Aberdeen, herself a staunch proponent of suffrage, insisted that the NCWC appeal to a broad national base, whether English or French, Protestant or Catholic. As a result, the NCWC had a moderate agenda, even on women's suffrage, which it did not endorse until 1910.

Edwards also worked with Lady Aberdeen to establish the Victorian Order of Nurses (VON). Created in 1897, the VON sought to provide better obstetrical and maternal care for western and working-class women in an attempt to combat alarming rates of infant and maternal mortality. In addition, Edwards served as president of the Ottawa YWCA, an organization that provided single women with accommodation and recreational opportunities.

Edwards was also interested in peace and international affairs. For this reason, she studied Esperanto, a constructed international language invented in the late nineteenth century, with the hope that it would serve as a universal second language that would foster peace and international understanding.

Oliver Edwards returned to the West on his own, making two arduous trips with a government treaty party, but had no permanent position and struggled to make a living. With the help of Henrietta's connections in the Liberal Party,[5] he was appointed in 1901 as the medical officer for the Blood and Peigan Reserves near Fort McLeod, in the southwest corner of what was then the Northwest Territories. Henrietta joined him there with their children in 1903, two years before Alberta became a province.

Although she lived in what was then a remote corner of the country, Edwards maintained her close relationship with the National Council of Women of Canada, belonged to the Woman's Christian Temperance Union, and worked for women's suffrage and with women's missionary societies. Despite her lack of formal legal training, which was hardly surprising in an era when women were denied entry into the legal profession, she was appointed by Lady Aberdeen in 1893 as the convener of the NCWC's standing committee on laws, a position she held until her death forty years later. In that capacity, Edwards compiled summaries of federal and provincial laws affecting women and children. Her first book, *Legal Status of Canadian Women*, published in 1908,[6] set out the statutory provisions dealing with marriage, divorce, property rights, custody and support, wills and estates, and criminal laws relating to rape, abortion, neglect in childbirth and concealing dead bodies, abduction, and seduction. A second book, *Legal Status of Women in Alberta*, was published in 1921.[7] For years, Edwards worked with Louise McKinney, Irene Parlby, and Emily Murphy to lobby the Alberta government for recognition of dower and matrimonial property rights. Ultimately, Edwards became the equivalent of in-house counsel to the NCWC, advising on the status of laws, drafting resolutions, and developing strategies for various legal reforms.

Henrietta Edwards faced her share of tragedy. In 1915, two members of her immediate family died: her husband, Oliver, and her daughter, Margaret, who died in childbirth. Then sixty-five years old, Edwards moved from the reserve to Fort McLeod, where she lived on a very modest income with her sister. Three years later, Edwards suffered another heartbreak when her son, Muir, died in the influenza epidemic of 1918.

By the time the *Persons* case was launched in 1927, Edwards was almost eighty years old. She was a revered and respected figure in the women's movement and she had political connections to boot. Her brother-in-law, W.C. Edwards, a wealthy lumber baron and life-long Liberal, had been appointed to the Senate in 1903 by Wilfrid Laurier, and died in office in 1921. When the possibility of appointing a woman to the Senate was discussed, Edwards was often mentioned as a possible candidate. She eagerly accepted Emily Murphy's invitation to come to Edmonton in late August 1927 to discuss the petition asking Prime Minister Mackenzie King and his cabinet to direct a reference to the Supreme Court of Canada to decide whether a woman could be appointed to the Senate.

Nellie Mooney McClung and Women's Suffrage

Nellie Letitia Mooney was born on a farm in Grey County near Chatsworth, Ontario, in 1873, the youngest of six children. The Mooneys moved to southern Manitoba in 1880 to take up a homestead on the Souris River. Nellie did not start school until she was ten, but she graduated from the Winnipeg Normal School when she was sixteen, taking a job as a teacher in Manitou, a southern Manitoba town a few miles from the American border. In 1896, Nellie married Wesley McClung, a pharmacist. They had five children.

Nellie McClung produced a steady stream of popular books and magazine articles reflecting her natural sympathy for the voiceless and downtrodden. Her first novel, *Sowing Seeds in Danny*, was published in 1908. It was an amusing portrayal of life in a small western town seen through the eyes of a twelve-year-old girl. It was a sensational success, selling over 100,000 copies. The book launched McClung's literary career and from that platform, she stepped into the world of public affairs.

McClung's public readings to promote *Sowing Seeds in Danny* attracted large audiences. She was a witty and engaging performer with charismatic appeal. Soon, McClung turned her oratorical skills and personal charm to the causes of women's suffrage and the prohibition of alcohol. Introduced to the Woman's Christian Temperance Union as a child by her mother, McClung remained a stalwart prohibitionist all her life.

The McClungs moved to Winnipeg in 1911 after Wesley gave up his career as a pharmacist to become an insurance salesman. Already a prominent author (her second book, *The Second Chance*, was published in 1910), Nellie joined the Canadian Women's Press Club, and continued to play an active role in the WCTU. Like Emily Murphy, McClung was inspired by the English suffragist Emmeline Pankhurst, who visited Manitoba on her trip to Canada in 1911. As a result, McClung joined the Winnipeg Political Equality League, created to promote the vote for women and to defend the interests of female factory workers. She quickly became a passionate proponent of suffrage, promoting women's suffrage with the same fervour that she devoted to prohibition.

McClung was also an active member of the Methodist church, and worked with J.S. Woodsworth, the future member of Parliament and founder of the Co-operative Commonwealth Federation (CCF), at his 'All People's Mission.' She shared Woodsworth's evangelical vision that linked politics and social betterment with a crusade against greed and immorality.[8] In the words of a modern feminist scholar, McClung's feminism 'reflects the evangelical social reformer's perception of a civilization in need of redemption. She is a feminist because she believes that only women can be the redeeming agents.'[9]

McClung's dedication to women's suffrage and her concern over the appalling wages and working conditions of female factory workers set her on a collision course with the Conservative premier of Manitoba, Sir Rodmond Roblin. Somehow, McClung managed to convince Roblin to accompany her on a tour of Winnipeg sweatshops, though he rejected McClung's suggestion that he appoint a female factory inspector on the grounds that no woman should have to see such conditions. Roblin's patronizing responses only strengthened McClung's resolve to promote suffrage.

McClung was convinced that laws protecting women and children would never be enacted until women were given the vote. In one famous effort to dramatize the importance of the vote, the Political Equality League organized a mock parliament restricted to women. McClung, in the role of premier, derided Roblin's anti-suffrage stance and moved a successful resolution denying men the vote. After a corruption scandal forced Roblin from office, McClung saw an opportunity as the Liberals, led by T.C. Norris, prepared to fight the 1915 provincial election. She vigorously campaigned on behalf of the pro-suffrage, pro-temperance Liberals, an effort that is described by her biographers as 'the pinnacle of her public career,'[10] and helped to defeat the Conservatives.

In 1916, to McClung's delight, Manitoba became the first province to give women the vote. The Liberals also delivered on prohibition, as well as on laws to improve working conditions, and introduced a minimum wage for working women. The progressive agenda of the Manitoba Liberals announced the arrival of a reform spirit that began to spread across the West.

In 1914, Wesley McClung's employer transferred him to Edmonton. Despite her strong political ties in Manitoba, Nellie did not question the move (although she managed to play a significant role in the 1915 Manitoba election). She soon met fellow author and feminist activist Emily Murphy, and joined the fight for temperance and female suffrage in Alberta. In 1915, the Liberal government of Premier Arthur Sifton presented a prohibition referendum. McClung campaigned for six weeks and led a massive march down Jasper Avenue the day before the vote. She was gratified by a significant victory for the 'drys.'

In 1916, Premier Sifton yielded to the pressure for suffrage and the women of Alberta got the vote with only one member of the legislature voting against the measure. Henrietta Edwards travelled to Edmonton for the occasion. She described the event to her daughter as 'the great day for women at the legislature,' and added that she 'had a delightful time' at Government House the next day at a reception to mark the event.[11] Alice Jamieson and Emily Murphy, both recently appointed by the Sifton government as magistrates to preside in special courts for cases involving women and children, joined Nellie McClung in buying new hats and having their photograph taken to celebrate. McClung formed a Provincial Law Committee composed of prominent women to discuss the legal issues to be addressed by Alberta's newly enfranchised female voters. The committee brought four of the Famous Five together. Henrietta Edwards served as the organizing chair and Irene Parlby was first vice-chair. At the committee's first meeting, Emily Murphy presented a motion urging the provincial government to proceed 'without delay' to enact laws 'dealing with the matters of a woman's interest in her husband's estate; equal parental rights; red light abatement; and proportional representation.'[12]

McClung used her oratorical talents to promote women's suffrage to the masses. She was active on the suffragist speaking circuit in both Canada and in the United States, gaining a reputation as an effective speaker and campaigner. In 1915, she published her speeches in a collection entitled *In Times Like These*,[13] a powerful feminist polemic, described more than a half a century later as 'the best feminist writing Canada has yet produced.'[14] McClung used wit, humour, sarcasm, storytelling, and logic to rally complacent women and combat conservative men who stood in the way of temperance and women's suffrage.

McClung's vision of equality was founded on the belief that all human beings, whether male or female, were entitled to the same basic rights of citizenship. Like Edwards, McClung held more progressive views on race than Murphy or many other maternal feminists.[15] However, she also passionately believed in a distinctive female virtue that could transform society. 'Men and women,' she wrote in 1916, 'have two different spheres when considered as men and women, but as human beings' they share a 'common field of activity' in which women demand equal rights.[16] While she believed that women had a distinctive role to play as mothers, she lamented the complacency 'of the happily married woman ... who has a good man between her and the world, who has not the saving privilege of having to work,'[17] and who politely demurred at claiming her full rights of citizenship.

McClung believed that male resistance to women's suffrage was nothing more than the fear of yielding power and control. She dismissed 'tender-hearted and chivalrous gentlemen who ... cannot bear to think of women occupying public positions' as hypocrites. 'Their tender hearts shrink from the idea of women lawyers or women policemen, or even women preachers,' yet they are quite content to have poorly paid domestic workers clean their offices at night. 'The tender-hearted ones can bear this with equanimity. It is the thought of women getting into comfortable and well-paid positions which wrings their manly hearts.'[18]

The enormous contribution of female workers during the First World War undermined the dominant vision of the sheltered female, unsuited and unable to take her place beside her husband at work. Women, like men, could be economically productive nation-builders. Their wartime efforts bolstered the cause of women's suffrage. Manitoba gave women the vote in 1916,[19] Alberta,[20] Saskatchewan,[21] and British Columbia[22] all followed later that same year. Irene Parlby attributed the relatively easy spread of the female franchise across the Canadian West to the fact that men recognized and respected the courage and hard work of pioneer women.[23] Ontario enacted women's suffrage in 1917,[24] Nova Scotia followed in 1918,[25] New Brunswick in 1919,[26] and Prince Edward Island in 1922.[27] Only Quebec denied its women the vote through the 1920s and 1930s, finally yielding to pressure in 1940.[28]

Female suffrage at the federal level was complicated by wartime politics, xenophobia, and the issue of conscription. Prime Minister Robert Borden's Conservative government reluctantly accepted female suffrage but feared that newly naturalized voters would oppose Canada's war effort and support the anti-conscription Laurier Liberals. McClung decided that half a loaf would be better than none, and at first supported Borden's plan to enfranchise British and Canadian-born women, but deny the vote to foreign-born women. The suggestion provoked a furor of opposition from McClung's fellow suffragists, and she quickly withdrew her support for Borden's limited reforms.

Fearing defeat at the polls over the introduction of conscription and to ensure victory for Conservatives and pro-conscription Liberals in the 1917 election, Borden was determined to press ahead with partial enfranchisement. The Conservatives introduced the controversial *Wartime Elections Act*,[29] disenfranchising conscientious objectors and anyone born in an enemy country and naturalized since 1902, while enfranchising all women who had close relatives serving in the overseas forces. Borden formed a Union coalition government of Conservatives and pro-conscription anglophone Liberals. Alberta's Liberal premier Arthur Sifton and Ontario's Liberal opposition leader Newton Wesley Rowel resigned their provincial positions to join the Borden government. With the help of those women who were entitled to vote, the Union government won the bitter conscription election of 1917, but the country was seriously divided between pro-conscription English and anti-conscription French.

Nellie McClung supported the Union government, but she did not campaign for it nor did she approve of partial enfranchisement. She feared it would 'make a cleavage in the ranks of our women citizens who are today bearing their full share of the burdens of life whether they happen to have relatives at the front or not.'[30] In 1920, the vote was extended to all female British subjects over twenty-one years of age who had resided in Canada for twelve months.[31] There were, however, some glaring omissions from this legislation. Men and women of Asian and Aboriginal origin would have to fight another world war to gain their enfranchisement.

Towards the end of the First World War, Nellie McClung and Emily Murphy decided that women should be mobilized to do more to contribute to the war effort and to fill the gaps left by the men fighting overseas. Of particular concern were the hundreds of rural schools that lay empty because they had no teachers. They proposed a mobilization plan to Prime Minister Borden.[32] In February 1918, Newton W. Rowell, minister of health and vice-chair of the War Committee, sent a telegram to McClung, Murphy, and scores of other prominent Canadian women, including Henrietta Edwards, inviting them to attend a conference in Ottawa:

> You are invited to attend a conference in Ottawa. Representative women from all parts of Canada to confer with war committee of cabinet on plans for wider participation of women in necessary war work, including national registration, increased production, commercial and industrial pursuits, conservation of food, the further development of spirit of service and sacrifice among the Canadian people, and other war problems in which women are particularly interested.[33]

The conference produced a list of general resolutions on industrial activity, agriculture, public health, 'thrift and economy,' women's organizations, and national registration. Rowell reported to Borden that the conference 'on the whole, I think ... was very satisfactory,'[34] yet the results had little, if any, impact on Canadian politics or the position of women. However, Murphy and McClung managed to attract attention to women's issues and they met Newton Rowell, who ten years later would go to court for them to argue that women were 'persons' in the eye of the law.

In her vigorous campaigns for temperance and suffrage, McClung avoided party involvement and backed whichever party supported her cause. She resisted the idea, promoted by some feminists, of a women's party and maintained a non-partisan, issue-by-issue strategy, refusing to become embroiled in party politics.

Over time, however, McClung was drawn to the Liberal Party. The provincial Liberals gave women the vote in Manitoba and in Alberta and, from 1919, were led federally by William Lyon Mackenzie King. McClung was alarmed by the violent confrontation provoked by the 1919 Winnipeg strike, and King's book, *Industry and Humanity*,[35] mapped out a gentler vision of social welfare that appealed to her Christianity, her humanity, and her instinct for reconciliation and cooperation. By 1921, McClung overcame her opposition to female involvement in partisan politics and ran in the provincial election as a Liberal candidate in Edmonton. She won her seat, but the Liberals were defeated by the newly formed populist political arm of the United Farmers of Alberta (UFA).

The rise of the UFA was not ideologically troubling for McClung, who probably would have been comfortable sitting with a party that was politically amateur and staunchly prohibitionist. Instead, she found herself sitting on the opposition benches, beside a man, one of the oldest members of the legislature, who did not believe women should be able to hold public office. By contrast, McClung sat opposite the only other woman in the legislature: fellow feminist reformer Irene Parlby, minister without portfolio in the UFA government. McClung and Parlby had much in common, especially on social issues. As McClung later explained: 'We united our forces when questions relating to women were under discussion.'[36] McClung also admitted, 'I was not a good party woman ... I could not vote against some of the government measures which seemed to me to be right and proper.'[37]

To McClung's 'deep regret,'[38] Louise McKinney, an independent and the first woman elected to the Alberta legislature in 1917, was defeated in the 1921 election. McKinney congratulated McClung, despite McClung's decision to run as a Liberal, telling her in a letter to do a good job, 'even if I shall not be there to work with you!'[39]

During her term as an opposition member of the Legislative Assembly (MLA), McClung supported the causes she had espoused for more than a decade: improved legal rights for women and children; a minimum wage; mothers' allowances; improved public health and education. Like Emily Murphy, McClung also championed the causes of birth control and sterilization of the mentally unfit.[40] McClung's unrepentant support for a return to prohibition – which had been repealed after the UFA held a mid-term referendum that revealed a 'wet' majority – and a move to Conservative Calgary (again to accommodate her husband's work) were fatal to her career in politics. Defeated in 1926 after only one term in the legislature, McClung never again ran for public office despite the hyperbolic urging of Prime Minister King in 1930 that she take on Conservative leader R.B. Bennett.[41]

Murphy had a serious, albeit temporary, falling out with Nellie McClung in the summer of 1926. Temperance was at the heart of the dispute. In her early years, Murphy supported prohibition, as did McClung. Over time, however, Murphy came to believe that the only practical way to deal with alcohol was through regulation, not prohibition. 'So long as liquor is manufactured it cannot be eliminated,' she argued. Murphy also had proof that regulation could work, citing the regulation of alcohol in Alberta as an example.[42] When Murphy expounded her pro-regulation, anti-prohibition views in a 1926 press interview, she found herself in the middle of a political maelstrom.

The Ontario Conservatives, led by Premier Howard Ferguson, were running for re-election in 1926 on an anti-prohibition platform. They pounced at the chance to enlist the support of a prominent feminist. Murphy's interview with John Willison, a well-known Conservative journalist, was published as a campaign pamphlet, 'Alberta Liquor Law; One Woman's View.'[43] Murphy argued that Canadians would be better off without alcohol, 'but as long as these are produced for consumption we must regulate them in the best manner possible. To argue otherwise would be imbecility.' As for women frequenting beer parlours, Murphy promoted a 'separate but equal' approach to the subject: 'I am not in favor of a double standard. If it is unfitting that women should drink in beer parlors, it is equally unfitting that men should do so. I think, though, that in large cities, a separate parlor, in a separate building, should be provided for women.'

McClung attacked Murphy for betraying what she regarded as a fundamental tenet of the women's movement.[44] Murphy pleaded with her friend that she had given the interview in Alberta, before the Ontario election was called, and did not intend to meddle in politics:[45] 'I am quite sure that you did not mean to intimate that politics has anything to do with my convictions on these matters, for strictly speaking, I have no politics.' Murphy tried to reassure McClung that her intentions were sound: 'It is my desire from the Gospel standpoint to see all the world wise and sober so that they will not want distilleries and breweries.' Murphy was convinced that the strict enforcement of liquor control laws was the best way to combat the abuse of alcohol.

> I am enforcing [the law] myself – ruthlessly too, if you will – and I intend to enforce it for all that is in me. I am interdicting men and women whenever called upon to do so, with a very great deal of satisfaction. If the Gospel has not reached them, I'm going after them with the law to the very limit. Of course, I pour the Gospel into them too – in every case – but nevertheless, I warn them that I'll see that the Law gets them for sure if they attempt to evade it.[46]

McClung and Murphy quickly reconciled, and McClung became one of Murphy's staunchest promoters for an appointment to the Senate. Although she lost her taste for politics, McClung remained committed to the cause of women's rights. She believed in Murphy and shared her outrage at the suggestion that women were not 'persons' under the constitution. So it was that McClung travelled quite happily to Edmonton in late August 1927 to sign Murphy's petition urging Prime Minister King and his cabinet to direct a reference to the Supreme Court of Canada to determine whether a woman could be appointed to the Senate.

Louise Crummy McKinney and Temperance

Louise McKinney was the same age as Emily Murphy and Irene Parlby. Born in 1868 in Frankville, a small town in eastern Ontario, McKinney was the seventh child in a family of ten. Her parents were Irish immigrant farmers. An excellent student, Louise wanted to become a doctor but her limited resources and her gender effectively excluded her from medical school. Instead, McKinney went to Ottawa Normal School and became a teacher. After teaching for six years in Ontario she took a teaching job in North Dakota where she became deeply involved in the temperance movement. She married James McKinney, a fellow temperance worker who had also been born in Ontario, in 1896. Seven years later, the couple moved to Claresholm, a town about 100 km south of Calgary.

Louise McKinney had her doubts about the move to the Canadian West, but she soon caught the 'contagious ... charm of the new country ... the country is developing; things are moving and I am helping them grow.'[47] Louise and James McKinney devoted themselves to their church and to the cause of temperance. Devout Methodists, the McKinneys helped to organize and build the town's first church. Their only son, Willard, was named after Frances E. Willard, an American temperance leader and founder of the Woman's Christian Temperance Union.

The temperance movement was a focal point for social and intellectual interaction between conscientious women who faced the daily challenge of subsistence existence in the villages and towns on Canada's frontier. Many progressively minded women joined Louise McKinney, Nellie McClung, and other early feminists in the temperance movement as the best way to improve society and to establish a better world for women and children. The Woman's Christian Temperance Union (WCTU), founded in the United States in 1874, became one of Canada's most important women's organizations in the early years of the twentieth century, and sought to achieve this objective. Its members were middle-class evangelical Protestant women who blamed many of society's ills on excessive alcohol consumption. In one of her early speeches, McClung described the WCTU as 'organized motherhood' in which 'women banded together to make life easier and safer,' to fight 'whatever seeks to destroy our homes,' and to help 'every agency whereby men are made better and Christ's kingdom extended.'[48] Over time, the agenda of the WCTU expanded to promote female suffrage and sexual hygiene, to oppose the evils of tobacco, and to lobby for improved property rights for women. Louise McKinney eventually gave up her career as a teacher and devoted herself entirely to the WCTU. She became the superintendent of the WCTU's Department of Scientific Temperance Instruction and served as the president of the Alberta WCTU from 1908 and vice president of the Dominion WCTU from 1909. Her goal, only partially achieved, was to ensure that temperance was taught in every classroom. After all, the 'fight for prohibition' necessarily involved the use of 'propaganda against drinking itself.' In her view, 'a continuous educational campaign' would produce 'a growing sentiment in favor of total abstinence.' Such a campaign would also raise public consciousness regarding the perils of 'continuing a traffic ... attended by so much that [is] evil and demoralizing.'[49]

It was in her role as superintendent that McKinney got her first taste of politics. She wrote letters and petitions, lobbied members of the legislative assembly, officials at the Department of Education, and linked forces with other organizations, including the United Farm Women of Alberta. She even met with the premiers of Alberta and Saskatchewan.[50]

Prohibitionists sought to criminalize the manufacture and sale of alcoholic beverages. They succeeded in the United States when the eighteenth amendment to the constitution was adopted in 1920, prohibiting 'the manufacture, sale, or transportation of intoxicating liquors.' Enforcement, however, was impossible, and the illicit trade in alcohol spawned organized crime. Popular opinion quickly turned against what became known as the 'noble experiment,' and prohibition was repealed in 1933 with another constitutional amendment.

In Canada, prohibition was a highly contentious issue pitting the pro-temperance moral crusaders against those who saw the right to drink as a matter of individual choice. The issue also divided the country on linguistic and ethnic lines. A national referendum in 1898 asked Canadians: 'Are you in favour of passing an Act prohibiting the importation, manufacture, or sale of spirits, wine, ale, cider, and all other alcoholic liquors for use as a beverage?' The result produced a 'dry' majority. The country, however, was divided: the urban population, immigrant population, and Quebec all voted 'wet.' Prime Minister Laurier and other elected politicians decided to take the 'sunny middle road' and to allow the issue to be resolved by local referenda.

Between 1915 and 1917, the temperance forces scored many triumphs. In 1916, the year women won the vote in Alberta and the year before her election to the legislature, McKinney and the WCTU won a major political victory when the province became the first in Canada to enact prohibition. The other provinces followed suit and an uneven patchwork of provincial anti-alcohol laws emerged. The issue was sold as a patriotic wartime measure, but temperance advocates rightly claimed partial credit for what appeared to be a growing tide against alcohol. Louise McKinney, writing in 1918, described 'a new wave' that had 'swept the country.' She recognized that some regarded prohibition only as a war measure, but as she confidently saw it, 'the probability is that the open bar will never return ... we rejoice in the wonderful advancement made both in sentiment and legislation.'[51]

The time for rejoicing was short lived. Quebec quickly abandoned any pretence at prohibition and, as production for the export market was not banned, liquor interests reaped enormous profits derived from selling alcohol illicitly in the neighbouring 'dry' but very thirsty United States. Ontario grape growers successfully lobbied for an exception for wine. As in the United States, domestic enforcement was notoriously difficult and ineffective. As soon as the war ended, the temperance cause faltered completely. To the dismay of Louise McKinney and the WCTU faithful who thought they had won the day, public support for Canada's uneven and porous temperance laws eroded. Referenda in British Columbia (1920), Alberta (1923), Saskatchewan (1924), and Ontario (1927) all went 'wet,' and liquor control legislation replaced prohibition.

In 1917, the year after women won the vote in Alberta, McKinney was asked to run as a Non-Partisan League candidate for the provincial legislature. Temperance remained her preoccupation, and at first she refused. Then, 'a combination of circumstances seemed to indicate a call to duty,' and she agreed to run, 'though the chances of winning seemed very small.'[52] No doubt McKinney decided that if she were elected, she could push for prohibition. As her son explained, 'she met so many pitiful cases of wives abused by drunken husbands' and 'she grew impatient of the archaic property laws and the inertia of the Alberta government in amending them.'[53]

The Non-Partisan League had a populist, pro-farmer, pro-labour platform with links to the United Farmers of Alberta.[54] McKinney and her colleagues at the Non-Partisan League refused to join either the Liberal or the Conservative Party because each one accepted donations from liquor companies. The Non-Partisan League advocated gradual nationalization of the major utilities; limiting contributions to political parties; compulsory public insurance for accident, old age, and illness; direct legislation and recall by popular initiative; and reforms to the banking system to make credit more freely available.

To McKinney's surprise, she won her seat. Only one other woman was elected at that time. Roberta McAdams, a wartime nurse, was elected as one of two representatives of those serving overseas, running on the slogan 'after you give your vote to the man of your choice, give your other vote to the sister.'[55] McAdams' nursing duties in England prevailed over attendance at the opening of the legislature, which meant that McKinney was the first to be sworn in, thus becoming the first female legislator in the British Empire.

As the enthusiasm for prohibition waned, so too did McKinney's political career. Indeed, the focus of McKinney and other early feminists on the WCTU and temperance probably undermined their ability to appeal to a wider audience and to gain acceptance for women as true equals in politics, business, and the professions.[56] McKinney survived for only one term as an MLA, but during that time she worked with Henrietta Edwards and Emily Murphy to draft, introduce, and enact Alberta's *Dower Act* to improve property rights for married women.[57]

Following her defeat in the 1921 election, McKinney withdrew from politics, but remained actively involved in the affairs of the WCTU and her church, serving as one of only four women to sign the United Church Basis of Union in 1925. In August 1927, when Murphy asked McKinney to lend her name to the petition that would launch the *Persons* case, she did so without the slightest hesitation.

Irene Marryat Parlby and the United Farmers of Alberta

Irene Marryat was the daughter of an English colonial officer. Born in London, England, in 1868, she lived there until the age of thirteen, when she joined her father in British-ruled India, where he held the post of manager of the Bengal and Northern Railways in Rawalpindi. The family returned to England three years later, in 1884. When she was eighteen, Irene made her debut into adult society as an eligible female with a traditional 'coming out' party in London. Irene rejected out of hand her father's suggestion that she attend university to become a doctor. Instead, she drifted aimlessly until 1896 when, at the age of twenty-six, she accepted an invitation from a family friend to visit their ranch near Buffalo Lake, Northwest Territories (now Alberta). There she met Walter Parlby, an Englishman and an Oxford classics graduate with a rowing blue, whose path to the remote Canadian West seems to have been as unlikely as Irene's. After three years in India on a tea plantation, Walter had joined his brother Edward, who had farmed in the Buffalo Lake district some five years earlier.

Walter established a home in Alix in 1896. The following year, Irene Marryat and Walter Parlby were married. Their son, Humphrey, was born on a return trip to England in 1899. The Parlbys were prominent citizens in Alix. Walter served as the local justice of the peace and game warden. He was also involved in the affairs of the United Farmers of Alberta and served as one of the original members of the Alberta Wheat Pool and the Central Dairy Pool. An enthusiastic polo player, he played with the Alix polo team in Edmonton on 1 September 1905 before Sir Wilfrid Laurier as part of the celebration to mark the creation of the new Province of Alberta.

It would have been difficult to predict from her genteel upbringing that Irene Parlby would become a strong advocate for the rural women and children of the Canadian West. She retained the manner and accent of a well bred and sophisticated English woman whose 'air of refined gentility did not diminish her fierce advocacy of social reforms.'[58] No doubt her activism on behalf of those less fortunate than her had an element of noblesse oblige. Parlby always insisted that she was more interested in her garden than in politics, and she did not enjoy the rough and tumble of partisan political debate. With her strong moral conscience, she was gradually drawn into politics as a member of the women's arm of the United Farmers of Alberta.

Elected as the president of the Women's Auxiliary of the United Farmers in 1916, Parlby transformed the organization into the United Farm Women's Association (UFWA) and used her position to promote legislation that would improve the lot of women and children. The establishment of municipal hospitals and a system of public health nurses were high on her list. The UFA also supported women's suffrage. Although she was a reluctant campaigner and did not consider herself to be a feminist, Parlby proclaimed:

The day has forever fled when a woman can confine her interests within the four walls of her home. Our duties are ever pushing us further into the great world. We cannot work there alone. We must have the whole hearted cooperation of the men, to bring about the sane and Christian civilization for which the world is today in travail.[59]

By 1920, Parlby had resigned from the presidency of the UFWA intending to retreat to her garden, her books, and her love of music. UFA party organizers, preparing for the 1921 election in which they hoped to topple the governing Liberals who had held power since the founding of the province in 1905, challenged Parlby to live up to her own rhetoric regarding women in public service. The challenge was persuasive. Although Parlby 'had no desire for public life,' as president of the UFWA, she had 'urged women to live up to their responsibilities and take a greater share in public life.' Now, she felt that she could not 'shirk and repudiate all my preachings to other women.'[60] Parlby considered it to be her duty to run 'if only to make the men realise that women are, after all, a fairly important section of our population.'[61] Parbly did not expect to win the nomination, nor did she enjoy the nastiness of the campaign:

Practically the only issue that seemed to interest the electorate or the opposition, was that I was a woman, and worse an English woman at

that, who although she had been in the country from 1896 when the country was still an undeveloped wilderness, could not possibly know anything about Canada.[62]

When Parlby won, she 'didn't know whether to laugh or cry!'[63] She
did not attribute her victory by a healthy majority to the support of
female voters because 'women will not stand as a solid unit behind a
woman' candidate. Instead, Parlby claimed that she was elected 'not
by women as a women's representative, but by those people, men and
women, who felt that I understood something of their problems; something, also, of the ideals for which they stood.'[64]

The UFA was a populist, progressive movement that had the support of organized labour. Much to Parlby's surprise, not only was she
elected but also the long-governing Liberals were swept from office.
The UFA had much in common with the Progressives with whom
Mackenzie King had to cooperate to stay in power following the 1921
federal election. The UFA refused to accept corporate donations, advocated the use of referenda, and insisted that elected members provide
their constituency organization with a signed letter of resignation that
could be used to recall the member who strayed from the populist
cause. More generally, the UFA reflected the grievances of the West.
Frustrated by the combination of high prices for goods and equipment
resulting from tariffs to protect eastern manufacturers and falling
post-war prices for wheat, the West was angry and disillusioned with
the traditional political parties. Farmers' demands for lower tariffs,
public ownership of transportation and utilities and regulation of the
grain trade shaped western politics at both the provincial and national
level.

The UFA did not expect to win the election and was unprepared for
power. The party had no leader and only two members with legislative
experience. After the surprising victory, Herbert Greenfield was
selected as premier and Irene Parlby was appointed to the provincial
cabinet as minister without portfolio, the second woman in the British
Empire to hold cabinet office.

The main plank in the party platform was 'Cooperative Democracy.'
Parlby explained:

I envisage the time when we will not only be marketing our grain and
livestock through cooperative channels, but we will be milling our grain
into flour in our own cooperative mills, processing our livestock in a great

packing plant, and eventually selling these products in our own stores, and even sending them across the seas in our own cooperatively owned ships ... When consumers in the cities become more enlightened as to the advantages of the cooperative principles from the consumers' point of view they will set up their own wholesale houses and stores. Then we shall have gone up a long way towards a Cooperative Democracy.[65]

Parlby saw the cooperative movement as having spiritual rather than economic roots and her vision had a decided feminist bent. She believed that women were 'by nature greater cooperators than men,' and had a special role to play. Cooperation required female idealism, intuition, and the willingness to sacrifice individual interests, and men had to realize that they could not achieve the greatest good for society 'by continuing to use women as a kind of external Ladies Aid.'[66]

Prevailing attitudes precluded a gentleman of His Majesty's Loyal Opposition from challenging a female government minister, and the task of questioning or responding to Minister Parlby was assigned to Liberal Nellie McClung, even though McClung supported many of Parlby's legislative initiatives. Parlby was quickly disillusioned in the legislature. She found the legislative process to be slow and even tiresome. As she explained, 'If the mills of God grind slowly, the mills of Parliament sometimes seem as if they stopped grinding altogether.' [67]

Parlby did, however, succeed with a number of initiatives. She sponsored legislation imposing a minimum wage for women.[68] She promoted legislative changes relating to the support of children of unmarried mothers to meet the often heard defence that the putative father was only one of several possible fathers – the amendment provided the trial judge with the authority to find all possible fathers liable.[69] The *Dower Act* was strengthened[70] and mother's allowance grants were improved.[71] Parlby sponsored the *Official Guardian Act*.[72] Another law provided that children born to unmarried parents should be declared 'legitimate' upon their parents' subsequent marriage.[73]

Another 'progressive' UFA measure, fully supported in the legislature by Parlby and McClung, and, from the bench, by Judge Emily Murphy, was the 1928 legislation providing for the sterilization of 'mentally defective' children.[74] A committee appointed in 1926 to investigate conditions in Alberta's mental hospitals reported that there were 1,300 insane and feeble-minded persons in Alberta's institutions. That number had doubled in the previous five years and the cost of $7.5 million per year was alarming. The committee suggested sterilization as the solution: 'Insane persons are not entitled to progeny and the only way we can ever hope to master the menace is to put a stop to reproduction.'[75]

Proponents of eugenics were not far from the mainstream. They cited the judgment of the esteemed justice of the Supreme Court of the United States, Oliver Wendell Holmes, who upheld the constitutionality of a Virginia sterilization law in *Buck v. Bell*. He explained, 'It is better for all the world if instead of waiting to execute degenerate offspring for their crime, or to let them starve for their imbecility, society can prevent those who are manifestly unfit from continuing their kind.' Holmes believed that utilitarian benefits could be gained from forced sterilization. He reasoned that if citizens could be conscripted and forced to give their lives for the public good in war, 'it would be strange if we could not call upon those who already sap the strength of the state for these lesser sacrifices, often not felt to be such by those concerned, in order to prevent our being swamped with incompetence.' As Justice Holmes notoriously concluded, 'Three generations of imbeciles are enough.'[76] In the early twentieth century, eugenics was an idea that appealed to well-intentioned people as a scientific means to improve society and relieve the suffering of the disadvantaged.

Maternal Feminism in Decline

By the late 1920s, Henrietta Muir Edwards, Nellie McClung, Louise McKinney, Irene Parlby, and Emily Murphy were no longer young women. Edwards was almost eighty, McKinney, Parlby, and Murphy all turned sixty in 1928, and McClung was in her mid-fifties. Their maternal feminist causes like prohibition had faltered. They had achieved the vote for women, but ten years of female suffrage had made little impact on politics and social policy. Few women ran for office, fewer still sat in the provincial legislatures and only Agnes Macphail sat in Parliament as an opposition MP.

The decline of maternal feminism coincided with a general disillusionment with progressive idealism that followed the cataclysmic Great War. Never before had the world suffered such losses or witnessed such destruction. Thought to be over by Christmas of 1914, the war lasted until late 1918. The 'war to end all wars' began with a spirit of romantic optimism and most people believed it would bring about an era of lasting peace and prosperity. But after four years of unprecedented death and destruction, the world was not a better place, and the post-war depression did not make it any more likely that it was about to become so.

The modern world seemed to be headed in a new direction and maternal feminists lacked broad appeal. The moralistic, missionary zeal of agrarian women who were advocates of suffrage and temperance had little attraction for the modern, urbanized women of the late 1920s. Eighty-year-old Edwards and her sixty-year-old colleagues were horrified by the 'flappers,' whose smoking and sexually provocative dress and dance marked the gaping generational divide. 'The suffragists, their organizations and their causes, had committed the ultimate cultural crime – they weren't modern. Flapper Jane simply stopped listening.'[77]

McClung was distressed by the unwillingness of women to pull together and take full advantage of their citizenship. She often said that 'women are enfranchised, but not emancipated.'[78] From her lonely seat in the Alberta legislature, Irene Parbly agreed with this sentiment. As she reported one day to McClung: 'About women – I long ago came to the conclusion that we need never count on them to support women.' Parlby thought that her women's causes would attract support from men – 'the best and finest type of men, or from the type of men who see a political advantage in standing by a woman.' The majority of women, Parlby complained, 'will for a long time to come be indifferent or jealous!! ... There are also still many women who think it is almost indecent for a woman to go into politics!'[79] Shortly after her defeat in the 1921 provincial election, Louise McKinney declared that the 'greatest enemy there is and ever has been to progress is the comfortable woman ... she accepts as her right, her sheltered, pampered position and she uses it to minister to her own comforts rather than to those of others.'[80]

Women seemed to have squandered their full rights of citizenship and failed to take advantage of the leap they had made during the war years when they had been a potent force in the workplace. Nellie McClung complained that instead of seizing upon enfranchisement and their proven capacity as nation-builders, women returned to their homes. They abandoned church duties, had smaller families, and turned to golf, bridge, and tennis rather than to politics and public engagement where they could bring their female and maternal virtue to bear upon public policy. 'A great many women are wandering in a maze of discontent and disillusionment. Idle hands and empty minds make an explosive mixture. Having nothing to do, they do nothing; and doing nothing, they miss that sense of work well done which sustained their grandmothers.'[81]

The temperance movement had suffered major setbacks as province after province repealed prohibition laws. The dream of a society free from the ravages of alcohol was more or less dead. Prohibition survived in the United States, but from the Canadian perspective, American prohibition only served to line the pockets of the enterprising Canadian liquor interests who had managed to penetrate the porous border with their illicit wares.

Social gospel idealism survived with J.S. Woodsworth to preach its message in the House of Commons, but for the time being, it seemed to be swamped by the rise of a consumer-driven secular popular culture and the huge profits reaped by corporate and financial interests in the booming years of the late 1920s.

By the late 1920s, then, the organized women's movement had 'lost its way.'[82] The Famous Five were disappointed that women's suffrage and social gospel had failed to bring about fundamental social change. They were equally frustrated by the lack of support for temperance. The quest to secure a declaration from the courts that women were persons within the meaning of the constitution gave these five women the cause they needed to revive the spirit of feminist action, a cause that would transcend the limits of maternal feminism.

3

Women and the Law:
The Trials of Legal Personhood

Canadian women achieved a number of firsts during the Great War, and Emily Murphy was already able to count herself among these Canadian pioneers. She was very proud of 'being the first woman' appointed as a magistrate 'in the British Empire,'[1] but she quickly learned that not everyone welcomed her presence on the bench. Some lawyers regarded Murphy as an interloper invading their exclusively male domain, and they did what they could to humiliate her and to undermine her authority. Shortly after her appointment, Murphy handed down a stiff sentence. After she left the courtroom, the prisoner's lawyer exclaimed: 'To hell with Women Magistrates, this country is going to the dogs because of them. I would commit suicide before I would pass a sentence like that.' The court staff advised Murphy of the lawyer's outburst and she immediately wrote him a terse letter of rebuke: 'Unless I receive from you an unqualified apology in writing, I shall regretfully be obliged to henceforth refuse your admittance to this Court in the capacity of Counsel.'[2] A reluctant but humble apology followed.

The antipathy between the bar and Murphy was mutual. Murphy found the methods and manners of criminal lawyers to be trying. She complained that the 'chief culpability' of the typical defence lawyer was a 'desire to persuade the criminal that he is earning his fee, by protesting, cross-questioning, repeating, denying, forbidding, objecting and quoting so that he not only "takes time, but trespasses upon eternity." Some day, an irate Judge is going to kill a lawyer for this, at least, it is so anticipated.'[3]

Murphy thought very little of the lawyers who came before her to defend prostitutes. In her view, they were nothing better than pimps. The 'girls' were often owed money by 'the man who was responsible for her fall.' The lawyer would charge the same amount as the 'girl' was owed by her pimp who would pay the lawyer's fee. 'Personally, I cannot but feel that these high fees charged to the frightened girls ... is just the same offence as what is described by the *Criminal Code* as "living on the avails of prostitution."' Murphy did not believe that all defence counsel were 'rascals,' but she did think 'that among the number who "defend" them (you will notice I put the word defend in italics), there are quite a few who only need fur and hoofs to make them beasts.' [4]

Alberta's Persons Case: Can a Woman Be a Judge?

Several lawyers who appeared before Murphy regarded her appointment not only as unprecedented and unwelcome but also as illegal. As Murphy later recorded: 'On my initial appearance as a Police Magistrate in and for Alberta ... my jurisdiction was sharply challenged by counsel for the defence ... It was then argued in almost every case upon which I sat that women were not eligible to hold this office.'[5] She rejected these challenges to her authority, and she was deeply offended by the assertion that her gender rendered her unfit to hold public office.[6] Murphy regarded this challenge to her right to sit on the bench as an affront to her personal dignity under Canadian law, an insult that reverberated in her mind for years to come.

Alice Jamieson was appointed as a magistrate of the Woman's Court in Calgary a few month's after Murphy's appointment in Edmonton. Jamieson, who had previously served as a justice of the peace in the juvenile court, faced similar challenges to her authority to hold judicial office. In June 1917, J. McKinley Cameron, a determined and well-regarded Calgary defence counsel, decided to take the argument to the higher courts.[7] Cameron represented a woman named Lizzie Cyr on a charge of vagrancy, a vaguely worded provision of the *Criminal Code*, commonly used against prostitutes: 'Every one ... a loose, idle or disorderly person or vagrant' who without 'any visible means of subsistence' and found 'lodging in any barn or outhouse ... and not giving a good account of himself, or who, not having any visible means of maintaining himself, lives without employment.'[8] A man had complained to the police that he had paid Cyr for sex and contracted gonorrhea as a result. The police followed their usual practice and charged Cyr with vagrancy, even though they arrested her in her own home.

Cameron presented a double-barrelled gender-laden defence that Jamieson dismissed summarily. First he argued that Jamieson was unqualified to hold judicial office because she was a woman. Cameron's second point was that Lizzie Cyr could not be convicted of vagrancy because she was a woman. The section of the *Criminal Code* creating the offence required the alleged vagrant to give 'a good account of *himself*' or have 'visible means of maintaining *himself*.' Cameron argued that the use of the male pronoun meant that the offence could only apply to men. Cameron's third point was that the law was too vague. It said nothing about prostitution and if it applied to Cyr, who had been arrested in her home, 'it would follow that many women of good repute would be liable to conviction under it.'[9]

The implications of these arguments were significant. If successful, Cameron's reasoning would eliminate Jamieson and Murphy from the bench and knock a huge hole in the legal arsenal then deployed against prostitutes. There were other offences related to prostitution, such as keeping a common bawdy house and living off the avails of prostitution, but acts of prostitution did not themselves constitute an offence. In practice, the police relied almost exclusively upon vagrancy laws in the prosecution of prostitutes.[10] Emily Murphy was all too familiar with Cameron's second argument. She was eager to use the full force of the law to rid society of the moral scourge of prostitution, but she worried that the use of the male pronoun 'himself' made the vagrancy offence inapplicable to women. Shortly after her appointment to the bench, she had urged Alberta's Deputy Attorney General to request an amendment to the *Criminal Code* to clarify the matter and to ensure that prostitutes could be prosecuted for vagrancy.[11] This, Murphy argued, could be accomplished by adding the words 'or herself' after 'himself' to the definition.

Had Cameron made his arguments in Emily Murphy's court, she certainly would have dismissed the assertion that women could not be appointed to the bench. However, given the views she had expressed to the Deputy Attorney General, one wonders how she would have disposed of the vagrancy argument. Alice Jamieson, however, did not share Murphy's doubts as to applicability of the vagrancy laws to women. She summarily dismissed the argument and, without even asking Cameron if he had any defence to present on the facts of the case, convicted Cyr, sentencing her to a term of six months imprisonment with hard labour.

Cameron complained that he had not been fully heard, and Jamieson offered to hear his defence. Cameron refused, arguing that Jamieson had already made up her mind. No doubt protection of the public from venereal disease was a strong motivating factor behind the severity of the sentence, yet Jamieson expressed no concern about protecting the public from infection by Cyr's male client,[12] leading a modern scholar to suggest that Jamieson's sentence was 'based on the same biases and discrimination that the political elevation of reform-minded women – such as Alice Jamieson – had been intended to overcome.'[13]

Cameron went before Justice David Lynch Scott of the Alberta Supreme Court to challenge the legality of Cyr's conviction.[14] A graduate of Ontario's Osgoode Hall, Scott became a proud westerner.[15] He was Regina's first mayor in 1882 and he prosecuted Louis Riel for treason following the Northwest Rebellion in 1885. Justice Scott paid little heed to Cameron's vagueness argument, dismissing as obviously untenable the contention that the section could ever be applied to men and women of 'good repute.' He could see nothing wrong with a law that would allow the police to arrest suspicious females who were unable to give a good account of their means of livelihood. Applying the principle of statutory interpretation that 'words importing masculine gender include females,' Justice Scott ruled that Lizzie Cyr could be prosecuted for vagrancy despite the fact that she was a woman. However, Justice Scott refused to apply the same principle to the argument that a woman could not be appointed as a magistrate. Indeed, he admitted that he entertained 'serious doubt whether a woman is qualified to be appointed'[16] as a magistrate. Ultimately, Justice Scott dodged the issue on procedural grounds, invoking the common law *de facto* authority doctrine that the propriety of the appointment of a person exercising judicial authority cannot be used to challenge the correctness of a decision. This was hardly a ringing endorsement for the appointment of female magistrates.

Undaunted, Cameron appealed Scott's decision to the Appellate Division where it was heard by a panel of four judges.[17] The Appellate Division recognized that Justice Scott's procedural manoeuvre on the legality of the appointment of female magistrates left them and their courts in legal limbo, and decided to tackle the issue head on. The court refused to follow a long line of English decisions holding that there was a common law rule disentitling women from holding public office.[18] This unusually progressive judgment was written by Justice Charles Allan Stuart, a scholarly judge who had enjoyed an interesting career path to the bench.[19]

Stuart graduated with double honours in classics and political economy from the University of Toronto in 1891 where he was described as 'a brilliant student, indeed more so perhaps than any other graduate of the University.'[20] Stuart took a position as a lecturer in modern history at New York's Columbia University and then returned to Toronto where he obtained a law degree from Osgoode Hall in 1896. He then went to Mexico for health reasons where he practised law before moving to Calgary in 1897, where he practised law with future premier A.L. Sifton. Stuart was also interested in politics, running unsuccessfully as a Liberal against future prime minister R.B. Bennett for the Territorial Legislative Assembly, before securing election to the first Alberta legislature in 1905. The following year, he was appointed to the Supreme Court of Alberta.

Stuart was a strong and independent-minded judge. Shortly after his appointment, R.B. Bennett, his old political rival, appeared before him carrying a brief for a large corporation. Stuart savaged Bennett's argument, declaring that two-thirds of the 'almost innumerable authorities' Bennett cited were irrelevant and those that were not favoured   the other side.[21] In *R. v. Trainor*,[22] Stuart wrote a powerful judgment reversing a sedition conviction in the midst of the 1914–18 war. The accused had laughed at the sinking of the British ocean liner *RMS Lusitania* by a German U-boat in 1915 and stated that 'war is war' and that England had killed as many women and children as Germany had. Stuart insisted that the mere expression of disloyalty did not amount to sedition: 'I detest such an opinion as strongly as any one, but my present duty is to decide the law, not to express moral or patriotic sentiments.' Although the words used were 'detestable,' they were not calculated to promote ill-will between subjects of the Crown, nor to incite disaffection against the government, hence they could not amount to sedition.[23] Stuart concluded: 'What I fear in this case is that the accused is being punished for his mere opinions and feelings and not for anything which is covered by the criminal law.'[24] Another Stuart judgment, which recognized the Aboriginal right to hunt and take game, was considered to be so controversial that the federal authorities managed to keep it from being published in the law reports. The case was finally resurrected and published in 1981.[25]

Although a transplant from Ontario, Stuart strongly believed that his judgments should be crafted to reflect the particular conditions of the West. He proclaimed in one decision that Alberta courts were not bound by the decisions of other provinces, adding: 'I doubt if eastern Courts of Appeal will generally be found very ready to bow to decisions from the west.'[26]

A similar distrust of English precedent influenced Stuart's judgment in *Cyr*. Writing for the court, Stuart reviewed the English cases and concluded that they fell short of establishing an iron-clad rule of female disability. Even if they did, Stuart proclaimed, 'the Courts of this province are not in every case to be held strictly bound by the decisions of the English courts.' He continued, 'we are at liberty to take cognizance of the different conditions here, not merely physical conditions, but the general conditions of our public affairs and the general attitude of the community in regard to the particular matter in question.'[27] Stuart applied what he described as 'the general principle upon which the common law rests, namely that of reason and good sense as applied to new conditions,' and declared 'that in this province and at this time in our presently existing conditions there is at common law no legal disqualification for holding public office in the government of the country arising from any distinction of sex.' He concluded: 'I am strongly of [the] opinion that we are returning to the more liberal and enlightened view of the middle ages in England [when instances of women holding public office could be found] and passing over the narrower and more hardened view, which possibly by the middle of the nineteenth century, had gained ascendancy.'[28]

Stuart had little difficulty concluding that a woman could be convicted of vagrancy. He was not persuaded by the vagueness argument, nor by Cameron's assertion that Cyr should be acquitted on the ground that she was not a vagrant because she was able to support herself through prostitution. Yet this point exposed the glaring inadequacy and unfairness of the vagrancy provision: it was not illegal to engage in prostitution or to hire a prostitute, yet the police had carte blanche to round up prostitutes as vagrants. Stuart imposed a moralistic gloss on the strict letter of the law. He held that the words 'visible means of maintaining himself' referred 'to a source of livelihood that is not only lawful ... but also honest and reputable, that is, such as is generally recognized as not subject to condemnation by the ordinary standards of the community.' Parliament could not possibly have contemplated, he ruled, that a woman who admitted that she had no other livelihood but prostitution should be found to have a visible means of supporting herself.

The Alberta Appellate Division's decision in *Cyr* is noteworthy for its approach to gender equality as well as its refusal to be bound by English precedents that bore no relation to the conditions and legal culture of the Canadian West. Yet the decision was a mixed one for women. Although it was a victory for Jamieson and Murphy and other middle- and upper-class women who aspired to public office, it was a serious loss for Lizzie Cyr and other women who earned their livelihood from the sex trade. Modern scholars have attacked the legal treatment of prostitutes like Cyr as being discriminatory.[29] If the law found Cyr worthy of punishment for engaging in prostitution, why should her male customer be immune from prosecution, treated as a mere victim who had yielded to natural temptation? In 1917, these arguments were rarely heard and never heeded, even by feminists like Emily Murphy and Alice Jamieson.

The Exclusion of Women: The English Persons Cases

The legal recognition of women as persons capable of holding judicial office in Alberta was unprecedented in Canadian and English law. In a series of historical decisions known as 'the persons cases,'[30] the English courts had steadfastly denied that a woman could vote, hold public office, or gain admission to universities or the professions. The leading decision, *Chorlton v. Lings*,[31] was decided in 1868 and dealt with the *Representation of the People Act, 1867*, which was debated and enacted the same year as the *BNA Act*. More commonly known as the 'Second Reform Act,' this legislation extended the vote to 'every man' of full age who was a householder and not 'subject to any legal incapacity.' The proposition was not without controversy; a year earlier, Prime Minister William Gladstone's more modest proposal to extend the franchise to all males who could meet a property qualification had divided the Liberal Party and led to the defeat of the government in the House of Commons. The Conservatives took office, and Benjamin Disraeli, Chancellor of the Exchequer and chief government strategist, decided that the way to win the inevitable election was to outdo Gladstone and to enfranchise all male householders.

When the bill was debated in Parliament, John Stuart Mill, an ardent supporter of female suffrage – who sat as an independent member – urged the House to amend the government's bill to include women.

Although Disraeli hoped to enfranchise a new class of electors who would gratefully return the Conservatives to office, he was not prepared to go so far as to give the vote to women. Mill's amendment was defeated, but another pro-suffrage member pointed out that the cause was not lost. The *Interpretation Act* of 1850 (also known as *Lord Brougham's Act*) provided that 'words importing the Masculine Gender shall be taken to include Females ... unless the contrary as to Gender ... is expressly provided.'[32] Disraeli refused to concede that even without Mill's amendment female householders would also be enfranchised. Confident that the nation's judges would rule against a woman's right to vote under this law, he simply dismissed the issue as one for the courts to decide.[33]

More than 5,000 women from Manchester were more than willing to oblige. Determined to test the issue, they put their names forward to be included on the list of voters. When their names were struck, the women appealed to the courts. John Duke Coleridge, QC, an eminent barrister and prominent Liberal member of the House of Commons, argued their case in November 1868, a month before the general election at which one and a half million newly enfranchised voters would cast their ballots for the first time. Coleridge tried to convince the courts to expand the franchise to include female voters. His junior counsel was Richard Pankhurst, a radical lawyer, who later married Emmeline Goulden, the leading figure in the suffrage movement who inspired both Emily Murphy and Nellie McClung when she visited Canada in 1911.

Coleridge and Pankhurst contended that the law extending the vote to 'every man' had to be read in light of the *Interpretation Act* stipulation that masculine words presumptively included females. The result, they submitted, was that women were every bit as entitled as men to vote. But as Disraeli had predicted in Parliament, the judges rejected the argument, deciding the case a mere two days after it was argued.

Chief Justice Bovill insisted that the common law rendered women incapable of voting, and held that explicit, gender-specific legislation was required to overcome the disability. He conceded that the word 'men' included women in some statutes, in others, the proposition was 'ridiculous.'[34] So far as he was concerned, enfranchising women fell into the latter category. Justice Willes insisted that female disenfranchisement arose not from a lack of female intellect or fitness, but 'chiefly out of respect to women, and a sense of decorum ... they have been excused from taking any share' in public affairs.[35] Justice Keating acknowledged Coleridge's 'eloquent appeal as to the injustice of excluding females from the exercise of the franchise,' but insisted that the courts were powerless to grant a remedy: 'It is for the legislature to consider whether the existing incapacity ought to be removed' and to do that would require 'the use of language very different from anything that is to be found in the present Act of Parliament.'[36]

Gladstone's Liberals, not the Conservatives, were returned to office in the 1868 election with a majority. The following year, they enfranchised women for municipal elections.[37] However, it was not until twenty years later that a woman tested the limits of that reform by running for a seat on the London County Council. The candidate, Lady Sandhurst, won the election but the defeated male candidate went to court to challenge her victory. He claimed the seat as his own arguing that a woman was not legally qualified to sit.[38]

When the case was argued in the Court of Appeal, John Duke Coleridge, by then the Lord Chief Justice, presided over a six-judge court. Since arguing *Chorlton v. Lings*, Coleridge had progressed from Liberal MP to Solicitor General, then Attorney General, followed by Chief Justice of the Court of Common Pleas, and finally, Lord Chief Justice of England. Despite his former record as an eloquent proponent of suffrage, Coleridge insisted on adhering to the precedent set by the very case he had fought so hard against and lost. He ruled that although women were allowed to vote, they were not qualified to sit on a local council. Parliament had specifically given women the limited right to vote in local elections and nothing more. In so ruling, Coleridge upheld the common law disability he had failed to displace as an advocate in *Chorlton v. Lings* to exclude Lady Sandhurst's right to be elected.

The women's movement refused to give up and within a year, another woman was elected to the same council. Despite the ruling in Lady Sandhurst's case, this time no one challenged her right to run for office and she took her seat. The statute provided that if an election went unchallenged for a year, it 'shall be deemed to have been to all intents a good and valid election.'[39] The female councillor participated in the work of the council on behalf of her constituents and, after a year went by, she assumed that she was safe. She was mistaken. Despite the fact that the limitation period had expired, proceedings were brought under another section, which provided that if 'any person' acts in office without being qualified, 'he' shall be liable to a fine.[40]

Once again, John Coleridge presided in the Court of Appeal as the Lord Chief Justice, and once again, adherence to precedent prevailed

over whatever remained of his support and sympathy for female suffrage.[41] The female councillor argued that since the statute imposing
the fine used the masculine gender, as a woman, she could not be held
liable. If the *Interpretation Act*, which provided that words importing
the male gender included females, could not permit the enfranchisement of women, how could the courts rely on that same provision to
impose a penalty for election matters? Coleridge agreed that the election itself could not be challenged because the one-year limitation
period had passed. However, he held that the expiration of a limitation
period did not render a female councillor qualified to sit and upheld
the substantial fine imposed by the trial judge. The voters who had
been foolish enough to elect a woman were now left without any representation on the local council. The judicial declaration that women
could be 'non-persons' for the purpose of legal rights but 'persons' for
the purposes of legal disabilities was precisely what the suffragists had
been ridiculing as unfair and absurd.[42]

There were many other 'persons cases' that followed the same line of
reasoning – women were legally presumed to be incapable of public
duty and only explicit legislation could overcome that disability. Scottish courts upheld the expulsion of women from the University of
Edinburgh solely on the grounds of gender.[43] A 1908 decision of the
House of Lords reiterated the exclusion of women from the franchise
and from public office.[44] A statute gave the vote to 'all persons' who
had graduated from certain universities, but not to women. The tone of
the Lord Chancellor's judgment is revealing. Lord Loreburn explained:
'It is incomprehensible to me that any one acquainted with our laws or
the methods by which they are ascertained can think, if any one does
think, there is room for argument on such a point.'[45]

The English courts upheld the right of the legal profession to exclude
women from the bar[46] and from practice as solicitors.[47] Women fared no
better in the United States.[48] There, the courts also refused to grant
women legal personhood and upheld the denial of the right to vote[49] or
be admitted to the professions on grounds of gender.[50]

Canadian courts did not differ, and refused to allow women to be
admitted to the practice of law on the ground that they were not 'persons' within the meaning of the provincial legislation that governed
the legal profession.[51] It was left to Mabel Penery French, who sued
unsuccessfully, first in New Brunswick,[52] then in British Columbia,[53] to
gain admission to the bar. Chief Justice Tuck of New Brunswick
observed that he had 'no sympathy with the opinion that women

should in all branches of life come into competition with men.' It was not the competition that Tuck feared but the inappropriateness of their participation: 'Better let them attend to their own legitimate business,' he explained.[54] British Columbia's Court of Appeal agreed with Tuck's colleague, Justice Barker, who held that the provision of the *Interpretation Act* providing that words denoting the male gender were to be read as including females 'could not be used to bring about so radical a change' as the admission of women to the practice of law.[55] Annie Macdonald Langstaff met a similar fate in Quebec, where she was solemnly informed that 'her ambition in life should be directed towards the seeking of a field of labor more suitable to the sex and more likely to ensure for her the success in life to which her irreproacheable [sic] conduct and remarkable talents give her the right to aspire.'[56]

It was the legislatures not the courts that resolved the matter when French managed to persuade the legislatures of both New Brunswick and British Columbia to overrule these decisions by passing statutes admitting women to legal practice.[57] As with female suffrage, Quebec lagged badly behind in the recognition of women's rights, and it was not until 1941 that the National Assembly passed legislation to admit female lawyers to the practice of law in that province.

Women and the House of Lords

The English Parliament appeared to end any debate about whether women could hold public office when it enacted the *Sex Disqualification (Removal) Act, 1919*.[58] The Act provided that 'a person shall not be disqualified by sex or marriage from the exercise of any public function' or from being appointed to any civil or judicial post or from entering any civil profession or vocation. However, three years later in 1922, the House of Lords decided that this general language was still not explicit enough to overcome the age-old exclusion of women from its membership.[59] Margaret Haig Thomas, a woman who had been active in the suffrage movement, inherited her father's peerage conferred only fourteen days before his death and became Viscountess Rhondda in 1918. Four years passed before she asked for the formal writ required to admit her to the House of Lords. The matter was referred to a special committee comprised of three judges and four non-lawyers. The Attorney General, Sir Gordon Hewart, soon to be appointed Lord Chief Justice, appeared before the committee and advised that the plain words of the 1919 statute made it impossible to argue that Viscountess Rhondda could be excluded from membership in the House of Lords. The committee voted accordingly. But Lord Birkenhead, the Lord Chancellor, was alarmed by the prospect of admitting female members to the Lords. He refused to accept the committee's decision. In his capacity as speaker of the House of Lords, Lord Birkenhead referred the matter to a larger committee, which debated the question. Over the objections of several members who had been on the first committee, Lord Birkenhead brought the matter to a quick vote. The original committee's decision was reversed by a strong majority and Viscountess Rhondda was denied entry to the House of Lords.

Written opinions in the style of judgments followed the vote and, although this was not a judicial proceeding, the opinions were published in the law reports. Lord Birkenhead wrote that the words used by Parliament where so 'vague and general' that 'when dealing with a constitutional question of the utmost gravity' they could not be interpreted as 'effecting a revolutionary change in the privileges of this House.'[60] The legislature, he explained, 'cannot be taken to have employed such loose and ambiguous words to carry out so momentous a revolution in the constitution of this House.'[61]

Richard Haldane, who had served as Lord Chancellor a decade earlier, strongly disagreed with Lord Birkenhead's legal analysis and took him to task for his high-handed tactics in forcing a quick vote before the opinions could be prepared and considered. Lord Birkenhead was also vilified by feminist writer Virginia Woolf.[62] Lord Astor, whose wife was the first female elected to the British House of Commons, introduced several bills in the 1920s to admit women to the House of Lords but these proposals were defeated, and women were not admitted to the House of Lords until the *Life Peerages Act, 1958*[63] allowed for the appointment of females as life peers and the *Peerage Act, 1963*[64] allowed for their admission as hereditary peeresses.

The Legal Rights of Women in Canada

The reader of Henrietta Muir Edwards' surveys of the laws affecting women and children in Alberta and Canada is struck by many glaring inequities. Divorce was socially condemned and, in any event, legally difficult to obtain, especially for a woman. Until 1925, a man could get a divorce for adultery, but a woman had to prove misconduct in *addition* to adultery. The criminal law also did not apply with an even hand to the sexes. Certain offences – abortion and neglect of the newly born

– singled out women. It was also an offence to harbour a woman who had left her husband without her husband's consent. As the *Cyr* case demonstrated, prostitution-related offences fell into the same category in the manner of their enforcement if not under the letter of the law. Other offences, such as seduction under promise of marriage, were premised on stereotypical portrayals of women as sexual objects, incapable of making appropriate choices on their own.

The *Criminal Code's* sexual offences continued to discriminate against women until 1982. For example, the legal definition of rape made it impossible to convict a man of raping his wife. Under the letter of the law, a man could be convicted of assaulting his wife, but as a practical matter, acts of spousal or other forms of familial violence were rarely prosecuted as the police and the prosecuting authorities deemed it inappropriate to intrude into the 'privacy' of the home. Various legal doctrines and rules of evidence made it difficult to prosecute sexual offences, even those committed outside the home. A man could not be convicted unless there was some independent evidence to corroborate that of the complainant. If the woman did not complain of the assault at the earliest opportunity, her evidence was discounted. When a woman testified in the prosecution of a sexual offence, she opened herself to the humiliation of being cross-examined on her sexual past. Needless to say, most women simply did not file a complaint. What is perhaps more surprising to the modern reader is that most women, including Edwards, appeared to accept the stereotypical sexist thinking underlying the criminal law and it was not until well into the later half of the twentieth century that women recognized and fought these sexist aspects of the criminal law.

Discrimination on the grounds of gender was the social norm and the law did not intervene to protect the equality of women. The limited property rights of women have already been noted. Married women had no legal right to a share in the family home and enjoyed, at best, only limited rights of dower. Other laws were overtly discriminatory. For example, as Henrietta Muir Edwards reported, a woman could not serve on a jury and women who married aliens lost their status as British subjects and could not regain their British citizenship even after divorce or the death of the foreign husband.

Women in the Workforce

In the early years of the twentieth century, women were routinely discriminated against in the workplace. Women who worked as school-teachers could not continue in the classroom if they married. This reflected the prevailing social norm that married women had no place working outside the home. Male workers feared that if the other half of the population worked outside the home, there would not be enough jobs for men and that competition would drive down wages. Male-dominated trade unions were also ambivalent – at best – to female workers. In 1907, the Trades and Labour Congress of Canada passed a resolution 'to abolish ... female labour in all branches of industrial life.'[65] Moral reformers, including many well-intended women, did not resist these attitudes as they thought that allowing wives and mothers to work would weaken morality and family values. Women who did work typically found employment in factories, mills, and clothing 'sweatshops,' or in menial domestic jobs where benefits and protections regarding minimum wages and working conditions were essentially non-existent. Maternity leave was unheard of.

These attitudes were challenged during the First World War as women entered the workforce in large numbers to fill the places left by men fighting overseas and to take up the new jobs in munitions so essential to the war effort. However, even during the war organized labour resisted the entry of women into the workforce. In 1917, the Trades and Labour Congress of Canada protested to the federal government about 'the unnecessary dilution of labour by the introduction of female labour' and the 'substitution of cheap semi-skilled labour ... because of their willingness to accept less than trade union rates.'[66] As soon as the war ended, women were expected to give up their jobs and return to the home to make way for the frustrated veterans who could not find work upon their return to Canada after four years of fighting. Most women seemed to accept this state of affairs. Even Louise McKinney wrote in 1919 that it would be 'a double tragedy' for women who had entered the workforce during the war to remain there and turn their backs on home life and take needed jobs from men.[67] Females who tried to earn a wage did not fare well in the post-war depression that led to high levels of labour strife and produced violent confrontations, most notably the Winnipeg General Strike of 1919. To the extent women did enter the post-war workforce, teaching and nursing were favoured as professions involving nurturing and maternal values.

A Female Senator?

Soon after her appointment as a magistrate, Emily Murphy aspired to another office – she wanted to be the first woman to sit in the Canadian Senate. Maternal feminism had achieved female suffrage, but prevailing social attitudes still saw a woman's place as being in the home. With the notable exception of the Alberta Court of Appeal's decision in *R. v. Cyr*, judicial hostility to the recognition of women as full persons was the norm. As the law stood, it was difficult to see how a woman could be considered, in the words of the constitution, a 'qualified person' eligible to sit in the upper house. It was not only social attitudes and the law that stood in Emily Murphy's way: as the next chapter illustrates, there were political obstacles as well.

4

Emily Murphy's Senate Campaign

The coalition Union government of Prime Minister Robert Borden led in the House of Commons, and the Conservatives held the majority in the Senate, when Emily Murphy began her quest to secure the appointment of a woman to Canada's upper chamber.[1] It all began in 1919, when Murphy was elected the first president of the Federated Women's Institutes of Canada at its inaugural meeting in Winnipeg in February of that year. The Federation brought together hundreds of local Women's Institutes from across Canada that had been formed to advance the interests of rural women, to promote domestic science, and to curb rural depopulation. Murphy's resolution urging the appointment of women to the Senate was adopted and forwarded to the minister of justice.[2] In a 1920 letter to the editor of a women's magazine, Murphy continued her public campaign, urging the appointment of a woman to the upper house, adding: 'I am sure that you will find a woman in the East who would be an ideal appointee.'[3]

Murphy initially concealed her own aspirations but she certainly harboured personal ambitions for the post and others agreed that she would make a fine senator. Gertrude Budd, a feminist originally from Alberta who had moved to Montreal and was familiar with Murphy's work, wrote to Murphy on behalf of the Montreal Women's Club, asking her to stand as their nominee for the Senate.[4] Murphy regarded the letter from Budd as the beginning of it all, actually indicating as much on the letter itself. Murphy was also quick to distance herself from her personal ambition. 'You will see that it didn't emanate from me,' she wrote. 'They just knew I had fought the "person" disability in Alberta and had won out.'[5] Assuming Murphy's protestations to be true, even if she did not start the campaign herself, she was easily persuaded to accept the draft. And given her accomplishments, why should she have refused?

The Department of Justice Opinion

The death of Liberal senator Peter Talbot from Alberta in December 1919 created a vacancy in the Senate, and Budd urged Prime Minister Robert Borden to appoint Emily Murphy in Talbot's place. Borden responded coolly to the suggestion, replying that the constitution did not permit him to appoint a woman to the Senate.[6] Borden's response did not bring the matter to an end.

More than a year passed before Mrs J.F. Price, the publicity convener of Murphy's Federated Women's Institutes of Canada, asked Justice Minister Charles Doherty a variation of the question begged by Borden's response: Could a woman be appointed to the Senate under the *British North America Act* absent a constitutional amendment?[7] Days later, an MP from Saskatchewan, who supported an elected Senate, pointed out the incongruity of permitting the election of women to the Commons but not their appointment to the Senate: 'I see no reason why they should not be enabled to sit in the Upper Chamber of this Parliament.'[8] Doherty, uncertain about the response to Price's question, referred the subject to W. Stuart Edwards, the assistant deputy minister of justice.

Edwards was the nephew of Henrietta Muir Edwards' husband Oliver and sympathetic to the idea of appointing women to the Senate. He was inclined to give an opinion that there was no constitutional impediment to such an appointment. However, Edwards' research in the department's files turned up a problem. There he found a memorandum that had been prepared in 1916 by William Francis O'Connor, KC, who practised in Halifax.[9] O'Connor had aspired to judicial office before the war and when writing to Prime Minister Borden to make his case as the one to fill what he described as 'a Roman Catholic vacancy,' was immodestly driven 'to "admit" in my own favour, that there is no Roman Catholic lawyer of equivalent standing at the Bar.'[10] Judicial office was not offered, but O'Connor served instead as a legal adviser to the minister of justice and solicitor general, becoming the presiding officer for Canada during the 1917 general election.[11]

In 1916, O'Connor was asked for an opinion on whether women were included in the word 'person' in the *Dominion Elections Act*.[12] The issue was complicated by the fact that the *Dominion Elections Act* adopted by reference the existing list of provincial voters. By 1916, only Manitoba, Alberta, and Saskatchewan had extended the provincial franchise to women. In addition, while Manitoba came under Part One of the *Dominion Elections Act*, which adopted provincial 'qualifications necessary to entitle any person to vote,' Alberta and Saskatchewan fell under Part Two, which gave to vote to 'every male person' who, 'not being an Indian,' was otherwise qualified to vote under provincial law. As O'Connor explained: 'A first impression can hardly fail to be that women voters qualified under Manitoba law can vote at Dominion elections, but that women voters of Alberta and Saskatchewan cannot.' This produced a result that was both awkward and uneven, though it was inevitable because the federal law incorporated provincial standards which varied. Some provinces gave women the vote that other provinces denied. However, in the case of female suffrage, O'Connor decided that Parliament could not possibly have intended to depart in such an indirect way from the long-standing general disqualification of women.

O'Connor's view was

> that when, in 1906, the Dominion Parliament enacted ... the words 'the qualifications necessary to entitle any "person" to vote at a Dominion Election,' Parliament had in mind the same class of 'persons' as it had in mind in 1886 when it used the same word and defined it elsewhere as meaning 'male person.' In other words, the use of the word 'person' in 1906 and the coincident dropping of the definition clause the scope of the word 'person' was not in any way *deliberately* intended to include women.[13]

O'Connor based this rather tortured opinion – that 'the names of women voters on provincial lists will be regarded for Dominion purposes [as] those of legally incapable persons' – on the long-standing common law principle that women were excluded from the franchise and from holding any public office. The English courts had consistently insisted that explicit statutory language was required to extend rights of franchise or public office to women. O'Connor thought it impossible to imagine that Parliament could have intended to enfranchise 'prospectively a then unqualified and incapable class.' As he put it: 'A settled and uniform constitutional practice and principle ought not to be held to have been departed from by implication or by the operation of words of reference. We should look for an express declaration of intent.' O'Connor 'admit[ted] that the word "person" *can* include women,' but he was not prepared to conclude that legislators had intended in this instance to have it apply to women in the absence of explicit statutory language.[14]

The Department of Justice had accepted and acted on O'Connor's opinion, but Stuart Edwards' own personal view was different; he believed 'that the question was exceedingly doubtful.' However, because the department had adopted the previous opinion as correct in law, Edwards did not think he could now reach a different conclusion.[15] For that reason, despite his own misgivings, Edwards prepared an unqualified opinion for Minister Doherty, quoting liberally from O'Connor's opinion, withholding any expression of his own personal doubts on the question.[16]

Although Edwards did not refer to other opinions, his advice coincided with a statement made by Doherty in the House of Commons in 1917.[17] It also coincided with the opinion of Francis H. Gisborne, KC, parliamentary counsel, who advised the government in 1919 that while the vote could be extended to women by a simple act of Parliament, it would 'be necessary to get the *British North America Act* amended so as to allow women to be summoned to the Senate.'[18]

Doherty, a former law professor and judge of the Quebec Superior Court, had resigned his judicial office to run for the House of Commons in 1908, and had served as the Conservative Party's minister of justice since 1911. When Doherty replied to Price, he explained to her that it was 'not customary, nor indeed [was] it properly the function of the Minister of Justice to give opinions upon law questions such as you [have] put.' Nevertheless, having asked Edwards to examine the question, he enclosed a copy of the memorandum.[19]

Justice William Ferguson's Opinion

Mrs Price sent a copy of the minister's discouraging response to Emily Murphy, who promptly enlisted the services of her brother, Justice William Nassau Ferguson, a judge of the Supreme Court of Ontario. Known to his close friends as 'Pat,' Ferguson was a year younger than

Emily. A graduate of Upper Canada College and Osgoode Hall, Ferguson had been called to the bar in 1894, appointed King's Counsel in
1911, and elected as a Bencher of the Law Society of Upper Canada in
1915. He was named after William Nassau, Prince of Orange, a reflection of the high office his maternal grandfather held in Ontario's
Orange Lodge. In legal practice, Ferguson became an expert in railway
law. He was appointed to the First Appellate Division of the Supreme
Court of Ontario in 1916. He was an active member of the Conservative Party before his appointment to the bench and counted Ontario
premier Howard Ferguson (no relation) among his close personal
friends. Ferguson had a solid reputation as a courteous, personable,
and common-sense judge who took particular interest in encouraging
the younger lawyers who appeared in his court.

Judges are not entitled to step outside their judicial functions to provide legal opinions on controversial legal subjects, but Ferguson's concern for his sister seems to have prevailed over any concern he might
have had about the propriety of injecting himself into the controversy.
Ferguson wrote Murphy a 'dear sister' letter that she could – and did –
use to promote her cause.[20]

Ferguson argued that the Department of Justice's opinion overlooked
the *Interpretation Act*, which provided 'that in every Act of the Parliament of Canada, unless a contrary intention appears, words importing
masculine gender shall include females.'[21] Ferguson told his sister that
because the *BNA Act* used ambiguous language and did not express a
contrary intention, 'I am of the opinion that there is no legal impediment
to your appointment.' As a matter of 'practical politics,' he added, the
government was free to act. The prime minister could simply make the
appointment to the Senate 'and either allow the Senate to question your
right to sit by reference to the Privileges Committee ... and if they refuse
to admit you to leave you to resort to the Courts.'

A copy of William Ferguson's letter found its way to Gertrude Budd.
Insisting that she was acting 'on her own initiative and without the
knowledge of Judge Murphy,' Budd pressed the new prime minister,
Arthur Meighen, for action on Murphy's appointment.[22] The protestations of Murphy's lack of personal involvement in the campaign ring
hollow. In her letter to Meighen, who had succeeded Borden in July
1920, Budd observed: 'Many Women's Clubs and Societies throughout
Canada are greatly interested in the candidature of Judge Emily Murphy of Edmonton.' She explained to the prime minister that 'women,
interested in politics, cannot see, that since the present government has

granted the franchise to the women of Canada, thereby acknowledging their political equality with men, that there is any logical reason why they should not be admitted to the Senate.' Meighen hardly needed to be reminded that he was only a few months away from a general election in which he would face the new leader of the Liberal Party, William Lyon Mackenzie King, but Budd added this carrot for good measure: 'Women members of the national Liberal and Conservative Party feel that if this government appoints a woman to the Senate, it will be a big factor in gaining the woman vote of Canada in the next general election.'

Murphy's close friend Nellie McClung also went to see Meighen to urge him to appoint Murphy to the Senate. This was almost certainly with Murphy's approval.[23] For her part, Mrs Price also tried to convince the justice minister that his officials had given him incorrect legal advice. She sent Doherty a copy of William Ferguson's letter together with the decision of the Alberta Court of Appeal in R. v. Cyr that held that women were qualified to be appointed as police magistrates. In the name of the National Council of Women, she urged the government to appoint a woman to the Senate 'forthwith as the Council felt strongly that there should be no delay and that the present vacancies be not entirely filled with men.'[24] Doherty replied, promising Price that he would 'look carefully into what is said in these different documents and give them my best consideration.'[25]

Doherty and Meighen decided to ask the Department of Justice to revisit the issue. Despite his own misgivings, Stuart Edwards was not persuaded by Justice Ferguson's letter. Neither was the deputy minister and future justice of the Supreme Court of Canada, Edmund Newcombe, who expressed his views in a handwritten annotation on Edwards' memorandum: 'In the absence of any precise authority to the contrary I hold they are not qualified. There is no Latin word to describe a Senatress, tho' the latter is a good English word. The consistent name "Senator" does not describe a woman.'[26] Edwards duly advised Prime Minister Meighen that there was 'nothing in [Ferguson's letter] which would lead the department to vary the conclusion expressed' in his earlier memorandum. Edwards explained Newcombe's views in more tempered language than the deputy minister had used: 'I may add that I submitted the matter to Mr. Newcombe in order that you might have the benefit of his personal view and he holds that, in the absence of any precise authority to the contrary, women are not qualified.'[27]

More Petitions

The negative opinions from the government's lawyers did nothing to dampen the desires or actions of Murphy's supporters. Prime Minister Meighen was flooded with petitions from various women's societies urging him to appoint Murphy to the Senate. Yet the Conservative government refused to take action. *The Grain Grower's Guide*, a pro-farmer, progressive Winnipeg publication, suggested that this unprecedented public campaign for a Senate seat might actually hurt Murphy's chances, though the report acknowledged that the campaign was so public – there were even petitions in shops for people to sign – that Murphy had to know about it. Because Murphy did not deny her ambition, one could presume that she was actively seeking the appointment.[28] Another report, more partisan in tone, stated optimistically: 'It is sincerely hoped that news of Mrs. Murphy's admittance to the next vacancy will be an early announcement.'[29]

Murphy's campaign for the Canadian Senate had considerable steam. Editorial writers from across the country supported her appointment,[30] as did Nellie McClung, who insisted that 'men and women all over Canada, east, west, north and south, are asking for her appointment.'[31]

'A Superfluous Fossil Institution'

The only publicly expressed scepticism came from those who questioned the utility of the institution itself. The debates surrounding the nature, even the existence, of the Senate of Canada in the 1920s will sound familiar to modern readers. Many criticized the Senate as a useless body, and proposals were made to reform the institution by limiting the term of office or by transforming it into another elected chamber. Still other reformers called for the institution's outright abolition.

The Progressive Party, for one, called for the abolition of the upper chamber as did the *Grain Growers Guide*. The *Grain Growers Guide* called Canada's unelected Senate 'an anachronism,' and complained that 'it does not look well, to say the least, to see women, directly [after] they become enfranchised, playing the game just as men played it and hunting for special favors and privileges presumably at the price of their votes.' The problem was not that Emily Murphy was unqualified to sit in the Senate; rather, 'as nobody ever knows what goes on in the Senate or cares to read the speeches of Senators, Mrs. Murphy would only waste her time and eloquence in that Chamber.' Instead, the *Grain Growers Guide* urged, 'she should get out and tell people what reforms she wants to see established and if they approve she will have no difficulty in persuading them to send her to the proper place for the enactment of the required legislation – the House of Commons.'[32]

The *Grain Growers Guide* could not understand why Murphy would seek a Senate seat, but if she wanted one, it was not opposed to her appointment. The Senate, the *Guide* explained, 'is such a superfluous fossil institution' that it would be 'the last place an able-bodied, alive and alert person could wish to be sentenced.' The *Guide* failed to understand why Murphy wanted to belong to such an institution, but conceded that 'if she is anxious to go there, and the women of Edmonton are of the opinion that it is a good place for her, most of us will not be disposed to object very strenuously.'[33]

Reflecting a general ambivalence about the Senate of Canada, some of Murphy's friends also expressed surprise that someone of her vitality would even think of seeking an appointment to the upper chamber. As William Arthur Deacon, a Manitoba lawyer who gave up his practice for a literary career and who became one of Murphy's favourite correspondents, told her, 'Of course if you want the senatorship, a friend can only hope you will get it, though why an otherwise sane person should desire to be a Senator ...'[34] Deacon was more than just a friend. He became a champion for her appointment, penning a flattering portrait of Murphy that was published in the *National Pictorial*. Deacon sent Murphy a copy of the manuscript with a note: 'And when the Dominion Parliament decides that the time has come for the nomination of women to the Senate we shall be all very happy if "Janey Canuck" becomes Canada's first woman Senator.'[35] Murphy replied in a jocular fashion: 'Really, I don't think I am going to get that Senatorship but you can deceive the public on it if you care to.' She did, however, hint that she had some support within the backroom of the Conservative Party. 'We are having lots of fun out of it and not saying anything to anyone,' she wrote to Deacon. 'I am leaving this to [the prime minister's] own henchmen who proposed me.'[36]

Murphy realized that she would be an unwelcome addition to the Senate, but relished the prospect. To Deacon, she joked about what might happen to her if she were appointed: 'Can you think of how I would wither up under the disapproval of 62 of them – or whatever the number is? Maybe, that amount of hatred directed to one person would poison her straight off.'[37]

Welcome or not, Murphy's hopes were dashed on 15 September 1921 when the Meighen government appointed William Antrobus Griesbach to fill the Senate vacancy for Alberta. A Unionist MP first elected to Parliament in 1917, Griesbach was a prominent Edmonton lawyer who had also been the city's youngest mayor. He had served in the Boer War and had reached the rank of major general in the First World War. Arthur Meighen made the appointment for shrewd political reasons. With a federal election around the corner, the Conservatives had to shore up their political support. Murphy had lost out to a popular local politician with a distinguished war record. In basic political terms, despite the support she had garnered, Murphy did not stand a chance.

Although it is unclear whether Arthur Meighen wanted women to sit in the Senate, he nevertheless promised to amend the *BNA Act* to permit their appointment if he won the general election of December 1921. Murphy was not persuaded, and accused the prime minister of hiding behind a mere technicality to refuse her appointment while holding out the promise of a constitutional amendment to garner the political support of Canadian women. As she explained to Deacon: 'The Hon Arthur had taken the grounds that "the sex" are not qualified under the *BNA Act* because, apparently, he wants us all to work for his election in anticipation of an amendment to the Act.' Murphy also accused the prime minister of ignoring the precedent set by the Alberta Court of Appeal that upheld a woman's right to sit on the bench.[38]

Murphy was undaunted. When she learned that redistribution might produce new Senate seats from Alberta, she wrote once more to Deacon to urge him not to 'change the propaganda for the *Pictorial* ... If Mr. Meighen is returned he is pledged to send a petition from the House of Commons to the British House asking for the amendment of the *BNA Act*. He will hardly fill these vacancies pending the amendment, so my friends are hoping that Alberta will have the first woman senator yet.'[39] Yet Deacon was not optimistic about Murphy's chances or Meighen's willingness to honour his pledge, and warned Murphy not to rely on the promise of a constitutional amendment. He knew of what he spoke. J.T. Haig, the leader of the Manitoba Conservatives and someone Deacon described as 'very close to the Right Honorable Gentleman,' had confided in Deacon that 'he has no personal faith whatever in the amendment to the *BNA Act* which you spoke of and does not believe that it will ever come to pass.'[40]

The Lafleur Opinion

Murphy and her supporters realized that the government's legal opinion effectively blocked the appointment of a woman to the Senate. However, they also understood that a constitutional amendment was bound to be difficult, if not impossible, to obtain.

When Ferguson's opinion failed to change the views of the Department of Justice, Murphy decided to enlist the services of a senior counsel, Eugene Lafleur, KC. A lawyer from Montreal, Lafleur was described by his student and future senator, Eugene Forsey, as 'the leading constitutional lawyer of his day.'[41] A gold medal graduate of McGill's Faculty of Law in 1880, Lafleur combined his practice with a professorship that he assumed at his alma mater in 1891. He was a pioneering scholar of conflict of laws, writing a book on the subject,[42] though later, he shifted his focus to public international law, a subject he taught until the early 1920s. Lafleur's origins were unusual for Quebec. He was of Swiss Protestant ancestry, bilingual, and a master of both civil and common law. Moreover, Lafleur had a sufficient global reputation to be selected as an international arbitrator to resolve a significant border dispute between the United States and Mexico in 1911.

Lafleur was sympathetic to the cause of women's rights. He had supported the right of women to become members of the bar in Quebec and had appeared before the province's bar council in favour of their cause.[43] Lafleur was also highly regarded in government circles, and was often retained to argue difficult constitutional cases on behalf of the federal government and several provincial governments. For that reason, Murphy hoped that Lafleur would provide a positive legal opinion that could carry enormous weight with the Department of Justice.[44] Lafleur had a reputation for courtesy and integrity, and, perhaps more importantly, was known to turn down briefs he believed had no merit. As he told the Lord's Day Alliance in 1923 when he declined a retainer to argue an appeal to the Privy Council that he thought had little chance of success: 'I would find it difficult to do justice to your side of the case.'[45]

To Murphy's disappointment, Lafleur divorced his personal views from the legalities of the issue and reluctantly concluded that a court could not be persuaded to interpret the *BNA Act* to permit the appointment of women to the Senate.[46] He thought that a strict literal approach, based on established rules of statutory construction, might yield a favourable result. After all, the word 'persons' in the *BNA Act* imported no gender qualification and, in Lafleur's opinion, the use of the masculine pronoun 'he' in section 23, describing the qualifications of a senator, did not necessarily exclude women. As William Ferguson had already pointed out to his sister, Lafleur advised that the word 'he' had to be interpreted in light of the *Interpretation Act*. This English act, originally enacted in 1850 and known to lawyers as 'Lord Brougham's Act' after the Lord Chancellor who was responsible for its enactment, set out general principles for the interpretation of statutes. It stipulated that 'words importing the masculine gender shall be deemed and taken to include females.'[47] It followed, Lafleur argued, that 'the mere fact ... that Section 23 of the *British North America Act* refers throughout to a Senator as "he" would not itself prevent a woman from acting as a Senator.'

The problem was not the wording of the constitution, but with the attitudes of the judges who would hear the case and their adherence to 'the long line' of English decisions 'which has whittled away the general terms of Lord Brougham's Act, particularly in cases hinging upon the right of women to vote at elections and to hold public office.' Lafleur emphasized the English Court of Appeal's 1868 decision in *Chorlton v. Lings*[48] rejecting the argument that the Second Reform Act extending the vote to 'every man' had also enfranchised women.

Lafleur pointed out that the House of Lords followed the holding in *Chorlton* in its decision of *Nairn v. the University of St. Andrews*.[49] *Nairn* was a 1908 case that involved a matter of statutory interpretation and the representation of Scottish universities in the Parliament at Westminster. Lafleur thought this decision was very much on point. A statute enacted in 1868 granted the vote to every 'person' who had graduated from a university and was not subject to any legal incapacity. Several years later, after women had been admitted to take university degrees, five female graduates claimed to be 'persons' qualified to vote. The House of Lords soundly rejected the claim. Lord Ashbourne focused on the original intentions of the legislators, and explained that when the statute extending the vote to university graduates was passed in 1868, 'the Legislature could only have had male persons in contemplation, as women could not be graduates and also because the franchise was by constitutional principle and practice confined to men.'[50] The House of Lords flatly rejected the idea that the meaning of legislative language could change over time: 'The Parliamentary franchise has always been confined to men, and the word "person" cannot by any reasonable construction be held to be prophetically used to support an argument founded on a Statute passed many years later.'[51]

Nellie McClung (right) and Emmeline Pankhurst (left), 17 June 1916

Nellie McClung, Alice Jamieson, and Emily Murphy, the day Alberta's
Women's Suffrage Bill is passed, March 1916

Emily F. Murphy. Edmonton 1929.

Emily Murphy

Henrietta Muir Edwards

Nellie McClung

Louise McKinney

Irene Parlby

Magistrate Emily Murphy in court

William Lyon Mackenzie King speaking during the federal election campaign in Coburg, Ontario, 26 July

W. Stuart Edwards

Eugene Lafleur

Justice William Nassau Ferguson

Newton Wesley Rowell

The Right Honourable Frank Anglin

The Right Honourable Lyman Poore Duff

Courtroom in the former Supreme Court of Canada building

Judicial Committee of the Privy Council courtroom

Viscount John Sankey, Lord Chancellor

Lafleur thought these decisions, interpreting the same words 'he' and 'persons,' in legislation dealing with similar issues, passed at the same time as the *BNA Act*, were fatal to Murphy's case: 'I am afraid that any Court before which the question might be raised now would consider itself bound by the decisions in the two cases referred to above.' The two English decisions were firmly rooted in the common law tradition that excluded women from holding public office. That principle was so firmly entrenched in the law in 1867, wrote Lafleur, that 'it might be cogently argued that the framers of the *British North America Act* cannot have intended without expressly so providing, (1) to modify the English Common Law; and (2) to provide that women should be eligible to sit in the Canadian Upper House, though excluded from the British.'

As if the pronouncements of the Court of Appeal and House of Lords were insufficient, Lafleur also cited the *Lady Sandhurst* case[52] where the English courts had solemnly held that a woman who had been elected to the newly constituted London County Council could not take her seat because the law creating the Council did not explicitly provide for female councillors. The common law rule excluding women from public office was so strong, Lafleur observed, that 'when you have a Statute which deals with the exercise of public functions, unless the Statute expressly gives power to women to exercise them, it is to be taken that the true construction is, that the powers given are confined to men, and that Lord Brougham's Act does not apply.'

Lafleur did not believe the more liberal view of the Alberta Court of Appeal in *R. v. Cyr*, holding that a woman could sit on the bench, would prevail in the face of these English decisions. Although Lafleur quoted Justice Charles Allan Stuart's 'more liberal and enlightened view ... that there is at Common Law no legal disqualification for holding public office in the Government of the country arising from any distinction of sex,'[53] he took a decidedly colonial view, concluding that the decision of the Alberta Court of Appeal could not displace the authority of English decisions to the contrary. 'I think that the Courts today would consider themselves bound by the decisions in the cases to which I have previously referred, and particularly by the decisions in *Chorlton v. Lings*.'

The 1921 Federal Election

Canadians went to the polls in December 1921 after a decade of Conservative rule. Prime Minister Arthur Meighen, who had assumed office upon the retirement of Robert Borden, faced the dual threat of the newly selected Liberal leader, William Lyon Mackenzie King, and a rising tide of Western Progressives.

Times were difficult for Western farmers who had expanded their production during the war to become the world's breadbasket. When buying goods and equipment they faced high tariffs to protect eastern industrial interests, and when selling their wheat they faced low post-war prices. The West became increasingly alienated from the traditional political parties that appeared to be unresponsive to the concerns of Western Canadians.

The emergence of an organized populist farmer's movement in the 1920s altered the Canadian political landscape. A United Farmers government was elected in Ontario in 1919 and, despite the relatively progressive record of the Liberals, in Alberta in 1921. In Ottawa, a group of Western Canadian MPs formed the Progressive Party under the leadership of T.A. Crerar. The farmers' movement insisted upon government intervention in the economy to regulate the grain trade and to provide government-owned transportation and utilities.

On 6 December 1921, three days before Lafleur delivered his opinion to Emily Murphy, Canadians narrowly elected William Lyon Mackenzie King as their eleventh prime minister, breaking a decade of Conservative rule. King led Canada's first minority government, and depended upon the support of the Progressives to stay in power. Under the leadership of Crerar, the Progressives won a surprising fifty-eight seats, nine more than Arthur Meighen's Conservatives. Meighen became the leader of the official opposition only because the Progressives refused to assume the role.

The 1921 election left the country sharply divided. The Liberals swept Quebec, still smarting over wartime conscription imposed by former Conservative prime minister Borden. They also swept Nova Scotia and Prince Edward Island, but won only three seats in the West. The Conservatives were shut out in six provinces, with representation from only three: Ontario, British Columbia, and New Brunswick. The dissatisfaction of the West was felt in droves; Manitoba, for example, elected J.S. Woodsworth, the future founder of the CCF, to Parliament as a Labour member. But the real story was the rise of the Progressives, who dominated Alberta, Saskatchewan, and Manitoba, and held the balance of power in the House of Commons. In addition, for the first time, all women were allowed to vote and to stand for election to Parliament. Four women ran, but only one was elected: Agnes Macphail from rural Ontario, winning as part of the Progressive wave elected to Parliament.

The election did not bode well for Murphy's appointment to the Senate. Now, she faced two hurdles. First, she needed to overcome her ties to the Conservative Party to attract Prime Minister King's attention. Second, and more problematic, was the scope of King's razor-thin plurality in Parliament. King depended on the Progressives to hold power, and the Progressives would certainly not support a constitutional amendment to reform the very institution they sought to abolish. Moreover, with a narrow parliamentary advantage, King needed to reward and reinforce political allies and alliances, especially in the West where he was weak. Patronage positions like Senate appointments would be distributed according to political need. Political survival, not the equality of women, was King's priority.

Justice William Ferguson's Second Opinion

Emily Murphy was disappointed, but neither persuaded nor deterred by Lafleur's response. Once again, she turned to her brother for help.[54] William Ferguson advised that while Lafleur's opinion 'is entitled to great weight,' he was 'not altogether satisfied that it is correct.' Putting to one side the long line of English precedent, Ferguson focused instead on the basic point that, as Lafleur himself conceded, 'the wording of the [BNA] Act itself, read along with the English Interpretation Act, permits the appointment of women to the Senate.' Ferguson developed an ingenious argument that had yet to be considered. He insisted that the words of the BNA Act, read together with a constitutional principle not mentioned by Lafleur or by the Department of Justice, should prevail in his sister's favour. Ferguson suggested that section 33 of the constitution allowed the Senate itself, not the courts, to resolve the question of who was qualified to sit: 'If any question arises respecting the Qualification of a Senator or a Vacancy in the Senate the same shall be heard and determined by the Senate.' Ferguson argued that this section was derived from a long-standing English constitutional principle that Parliament 'was considered to be a law unto itself' as to its own membership and qualifications for membership. He observed that although the BNA Act did not expressly provide that women could sit in the House of Commons, no constitutional amendment had been required to bring about that result. Instead, a simple act of the Canadian Parliament was sufficient to accomplish that feat. As he argued, the language of the BNA

Act was ambiguous on the point of gender qualification for the Senate, 'the tribunal to determine the status or qualification of a female when appointed to the Senate would be the Senate itself and not the Courts.'

Ferguson's letter provided Murphy with a solid legal foundation for efforts to secure a Senate appointment, but it also suggested that to accomplish that goal, she should pursue political rather than legal channels. But if the matter were left to politics, perhaps Ferguson was being overly optimistic about the response his sister was likely to receive. Even if Murphy could persuade the politicians to appoint her to the Senate, it was hard to believe that the men of the upper chamber would be any more likely to find her to be a 'qualified person' than the members of the judiciary.

Persuading Mr King

Murphy and her supporters realized that to secure a female appointment to the Senate they needed to muster public support if they were to persuade politicians to overcome the legal obstacles. Although she had always been a staunch Tory, in keeping with the Ferguson family tradition, Murphy's political sympathies began to shift rather pragmatically towards Mackenzie King and the Liberals. Nellie McClung, a Liberal, was enlisted to promote Murphy to the new prime minister. When McClung congratulated King on his victory in 1921, she also urged him to take action on the appointment of women to the Senate: 'I want to send you my good wishes and sincere congratulations and I also wish to respectfully draw your attention to the fact that there are no women in the Upper House and that I think it is about time that there were.' Emily Murphy, she added, had all the necessary qualifications for the position.[55] Beyond personal appeals, Murphy realized the importance of public support. In March 1922, Gertrude Budd wired Murphy to tell her that the Montreal Women's Club had passed a resolution approving Murphy's appointment to the Senate and intended to ask King to make the appointment immediately. Copies of the resolution were sent not just to King but also to Meighen and Crerar. It is unimaginable that Murphy was not actively involved in this strategy, especially in light of Budd's reassuring aside that she would 'observe strictest secrecy as requested.'[56]

There was another obstacle to Murphy's appointment. She was not the only woman being proposed for the position. In February 1923, the

Calgary Local Council of Women endorsed a resolution from the Regina Local:

> The National Council of Women urge the appointment as first woman senator of Mrs. O.C. Edwards in recognition for the splendid service she has rendered to women of Canada by her intensive study of law and by the many reforms brought about through the work of the laws committee, of which she is national convenor.[57]

As vice-president of the National Council of Women, Murphy opposed these resolutions on the ground that 'while fully approving of Mrs. Edwards' candidature, I felt that the National Council would create a dangerous precedent by lending itself to partisanship in politics.'[58] Murphy's explanation was disingenuous. Plainly, Murphy wanted to be Canada's first female senator and the candidacy of Henrietta Muir Edwards posed a threat to her ambition.

In June 1923, another Senate seat came available when Alberta Senator Amédée-Emmanuel Forget died. Again, Murphy's supporters mobilised to secure her appointment. Once more, resolutions and petitions, signed by thousands of men and women, poured into Ottawa supporting Murphy's appointment to the Senate. As one petition read:

> Whereas the women of Canada are without representation in the Senate of Canada,

> And whereas, measures affecting the welfare of women and children, together with private statutes relating to divorce are considered by the said Senate, without the advice and assistance of any representative of women,

> And whereas there is at present a vacancy in the Senate in Alberta which requires to be filled,

> And whereas Mrs. Emily Murphy is well qualified to fill such a position of trust by virtue of her training and experience acquired as a police magistrate and judge of the Juvenile Court in and for the province of Alberta, and to represent the women of Canada by virtue of her connection with various women's societies ... your petitioners pray that the said Mrs. Murphy will be appointed to the said Senate, in order that the said Senate

might be better qualified to consider matters concerning the interest of women and children of Canada.[59]

Prime Minister King said that he would be pleased to appoint a woman to the Senate, but, adopting Meighen's earlier argument, pleaded that he was powerless to act absent a constitutional amendment. Liberal Senator Archibald Blake McCoig of Ontario presented a motion to the Senate to do just that: amend the BNA Act to make women eligible for appointment. When the Liberal government refused to pursue the motion, it came as 'a sharp disappointment'[60] to Murphy. Murphy complained to King about his unwillingness to act. The response was an unconvincing note from King's private secretary, telling her that the proposed constitutional amendment was but one of a number of resolutions for which there had been 'no opportunity' to discuss.[61] Murphy could not count on the Conservatives any more than she could count on the Liberals. Gertrude Budd, Murphy's Conservative ally from Montreal, asked opposition leader Arthur Meighen to support the initiative, but to no avail.[62]

Murphy did not rely exclusively on others to do her bidding with the prime minister. Over time, she tried to bring her considerable powers of personal persuasion to bear directly upon King. Their correspondence included warm birthday and Christmas greetings and led to personal meetings,[63] including at least one dinner at Laurier House in Ottawa.[64] King himself initiated some of these contacts. He met with her to discuss her work on narcotics when she travelled to Ottawa in October 1922.[65] After all, the two may have come from different political parties, but they also shared an interest in curbing the illicit drug trade. In 1907, the Dominion government had sent Mackenzie King, then deputy minister of labour, to British Columbia to investigate claims for the property losses associated with anti-Asiatic rioting in Vancouver. Two opium merchants submitted substantial claims, which led King to look into the opium trade. King's report, The Need for the Suppression of the Opium Trade in Canada, described the ruin of white women and other moral disasters caused by the Chinese opium trade, much like Murphy did in her book The Black Candle. King's report led to the Opium Act, 1908, which prohibited the sale of opiates except for medical purposes.

At this first face-to-face meeting, Murphy told King she wanted to be a senator to have a forum for her views. King was mildly encouraging, and recorded in his diary that he had 'promised nothing, but said that

I thought if women were to have the vote they shld have any positions in prlt. which the possess'n of the vote might entitle them to.' Despite this sentiment, King did not particularly take to Murphy personally, and his assessment of her revealed his own unease and discomfort with assertive women. He found her 'very friendly and pleasant to talk with, a little too masculine, & possibly a little too sensational. I don't care for aggressive women & she possesses a little aggressiveness, – but a good purpose. I felt her to be a genuine person.'[66]

Murphy had more to overcome than King's unease with assertive women. Her pleas to King were doomed to defeat by the demands of raw politics. In mid-August 1923, King replaced the late senator Forget with another francophone, Jean Léon Coté, a Liberal member of the Alberta legislature.

King's refusal to appoint Murphy and to run into the thicket of Senate reform and possibly constitutional amendment was a matter of political pragmatism. King depended on the Progressives for the survival of his government, and the Progressives wanted to abolish the Senate, not reform or alter its composition. King admitted as much to Nellie McClung, who passed the news along to Murphy. Murphy's response to McClung was triumphant: that party politics stood in the way of her appointment, not her gender, she regarded as a moral victory. But Murphy also thought that she could turn King's political preoccupations to her advantage. She saw her appointment as a political asset, and thought King would gain more than he would lose if he appointed her to the Senate. If the appointment was unconstitutional, then King could leave it to the courts or the Privileges Committee of the Senate to say so: 'Even if I were turned down and kicked out, we would have made an enormous gain.'[67] Alas, King, one of the most politically savvy prime ministers in Canadian history, did not share Murphy's political assessment of the situation.

Undeterred, Murphy continued to press King to amend the constitution. In April 1924, she asked him once more about the prospects. Again, King reassured her that she had his support. Again, however, he failed to act. Murphy responded politely, yet firmly, when she rejected his reasoning: 'I have not been troubling you this year concerning the amendment of the *British North America Act* so as to permit women being appointed to the Upper Chamber, as it might seem as though I were questioning your sincerity in this matter,' she explained. Still, she pointed out, no adequate explanation had been offered as to why the government had made no progress on the subject. 'I am constantly in receipt of letters from different parts of Canada asking how this matter progresses, but I have stated that it was in your hands, and that I felt confident that it would be dealt with in the present session.'[68] Such criticism did not dissuade King from meeting with Murphy. When King visited Edmonton in October 1924, he called on Murphy at her courtroom.[69]

Murphy remained on good terms with King, despite the prime minister's failure to appoint her to the Senate or to try to amend the constitution. In July 1925, King gave Murphy his personal assurance that he proposed 'seeing that a resolution to the Imperial Government with respect to the rights of women for appointment to the Senate, is made one of the first matters to be considered.'[70] Murphy met privately once more with King when she travelled to Ottawa in 1925, provoking press rumours that her Senate appointment was under active consideration. She denied that the topic had been discussed and feigned lack of interest in the subject, telling reporters: 'What would a plow-pusher from the outposts of the country do among so many distinguished men of world experience?'[71]

King continued to ignore opportunities to appoint Murphy to the Senate. And there were a surprising number of opportunities to appoint a senator from the province of Alberta. Senator Coté died in September 1924, just over a year after his appointment. Senator Leverett DeVeber of Lethbridge, appointed to the Senate in 1906 by Laurier, died in July 1925. With two vacancies from Alberta alone, King stayed his hand until 5 September 1925, the same day he asked Governor General Byng to dissolve the House of Commons for a general election. Then, included in King's flood of pre-election patronage appointments were two new Alberta senators: William Buchanan from Lethbridge and Prosper-Edmond Lessard from Edmonton.

Both men were popular figures with strong ties to the Liberal Party. Buchanan was the editor and publisher of the *Lethbridge Herald*. He was elected first to the provincial legislature in 1907 and then to the House of Commons ten years later.[72] Lessard was a successful businessman who had founded the Young Men's Liberal Club in Edmonton and served in the provincial legislature as a Liberal member.[73] The Edmonton *Journal* reported that there could be 'no questioning of the claims on both public and party grounds' of both new senators.[74] Once again, the desire to reward the party faithful determined King's Senate appointments. In this context, Emily Murphy simply could not compete.

Senate Reform

King was being pulled in opposite directions on the issue of Senate reform. While women's groups pressed for a constitutional amendment to permit the appointment of women to the Senate, the Conservatives favoured the status quo and the Progressives argued for abolition or radical change.

When Mackenzie King came to power in 1921 after a decade of Conservative rule and Senate appointments, he faced a hostile majority in the upper house, one that had been willing to resist Liberal initiatives. Frustrated by the Conservative Senate's rejection of several government initiatives, King suggested in 1924 that the Senate's power to block legislation approved by the Commons be curtailed in the same way the British House of Commons had limited the powers of the House of Lords in 1911 – a bill rejected by the Lords could still become law if passed by the Commons in three successive sessions. But a year later, having appointed several Liberal senators to reduce the Tory majority, King's plans for Senate reform became decidedly more vague. The Speech from the Throne that opened the 1925 session promised Senate reform but offered no details.

From the early days of Confederation, the role and legitimacy of the Senate had been the subject of debate. On 9 March 1925, Joseph T. Shaw, an Alberta member of Parliament from the Labour Party, introduced a resolution which stated: 'That, in the opinion of this House, the Senate as at present appointed and constituted is not of the greatest advantage to Canada.'[75] Shaw skilfully presented the arguments for radical surgery to the upper house. The Dominion government's appointment of senators was inconsistent with the federal principle and the Senate's role in the protection of provincial interests. Lifetime appointments were also fundamentally undemocratic and unduly empowered the dead hand of past regimes. Furthermore, patronage appointments produced a partisan body incapable of independence. Although abolitionists argued that the Senate 'was a drag on democracy' and entrenched 'special and privileged interests,' Shaw was confident that the Senate had a legitimate role to play in the protection of provincial interests. He proposed giving the provinces the right to elect or to appoint a reduced number of senators to limited terms of eight years with one half retiring every four years. The Conservatives, who opposed Senate reform, remained in their seats. An amended motion called for a Dominion–Provincial conference 'to consider the advisability of amending the *British North America Act* with respect to the constitution and powers of the Senate.' The motion won the support of the Liberals and carried easily. There, for the time being, the matter rested.

In the general election of September 1925, King promised to reform the Senate from within by appointing a sufficient number of Liberals who could be relied on to support whatever proposals for Senate reform the government decided to put forward.[76] King's vague proposal had little impact politically, and certainly did not serve to raise the issue of Senate reform to the level of political debate during the campaign. Conservative leader Arthur Meighen, for one, labelled King's vague proposal as 'moonshine.'[77]

King's ambivalence on Senate reform was a product of the political and constitutional realities of the mid-1920s. He realized that the Dominion government could not impose Senate reform without a constitutional amendment, and a constitutional amendment would require consultation with the provinces. For the moment, then, constitutional change had to take a back seat to King's more pressing concerns: securing re-election.

The 1925 Federal Election and the King–Byng Affair

After four years of Progressive-supported Liberal rule, Canadians went to the polls on 29 October 1925. The result appeared to be disastrous for Prime Minister King. The Liberals came second, winning only ninety-nine seats to the Conservatives' one hundred sixteen. The Progressives faltered badly, reduced to twenty-four seats, but still held the balance of power. King even lost his own seat, but refused to step down as prime minister. He clung to power with support from the Progressives, and by winning a by-election in Prince Albert, Saskatchewan, he regained his place in the House of Commons.

Within days of the election, King had yet another opportunity to make good on his promise to Murphy. On 2 November 1925, Senator James Lougheed of Calgary, appointed to the Senate in 1889 by Prime Minister Sir John A. Macdonald, died. Here was yet another vacancy to which the indefatigable Murphy could aspire. Lougheed's death prompted more letters and more pressure on King from Murphy's supporters. Again, Nellie McClung tried to promote Murphy for appointment to the Senate. As she explained to the prime minister: 'Rumours are floating all about as to who shall be [Lougheed's] successor. It would be a wonderful triumph for the belief that we have held in Liberal fairness to women if Mrs. Murphy should be appointed. Forty thousand women have, thro' their Societies, asked for her. Don't ignore them.'[78]

In the spring of 1926, the vacancy remaining, Murphy also persuaded the Alberta United Farmers government to support her nomination and, as she wrote in her letter to King, 'I am emboldened to write to you personally about the matter.' She advised King that the Government of Alberta 'were not asking on the grounds of any kind of partisanship, but only because they realized that I would fairly represent the people of all classes – the agricultural classes included – that it was their earnest desire that I should be appointed.' She resorted to a familiar and teasing tone, wishing him 'a long rest this summer and some degree of freedom from all wayward and ungentle persons.' As a post script, Murphy added: 'Maybe in asking for my appointment, Alberta is trying to "swat you one" for not giving them their natural resources or, contrariwise – yes, yes, this must be the way of it – they are trying to heap the proverbial coals of fire on your head, – the Darlings!'[79]

But in the spring of 1926, King's hold on power was precarious and he was not about to use a valuable political reward to appease either Murphy or the United Farmers of Alberta, which were more closely aligned with the Progressives than the ruling Liberals. Murphy never stood a chance of filling the Lougheed vacancy. Faced with an almost certain vote of censure in the Commons over a corruption scandal involving his minister of customs, King asked Governor General Byng to dissolve the House and call an election on 28 June 1926. Immediately before tendering his resignation, King appointed Daniel Riley, a well-known rancher from High River, to fill the latest Alberta Senate vacancy.

What followed King's resignation was an unforeseen constitutional crisis. The Governor General refused to dissolve Parliament and call an election, pointing out that Arthur Meighen, who had more seats than King, should be given the opportunity to form a government. Meighen took office at the end of June, but was defeated on a non-confidence vote in September, throwing the country back into a general election campaign.

The Governor General's handling of the situation worked to King's advantage. During the campaign that followed, King directed his fire not at Meighen and the Conservatives but at Byng, the British Governor General who had refused the advice of Canada's prime minister. The customs scandal that had threatened to consume King's government and led to his earlier resignation now seemed to be a distant memory for the electorate, as the constitutionality of Byng's behaviour dominated the campaign.[80] The Liberals won 116 to the Conservatives' ninety-one, and with the support of eight Liberal-Progressives, King won his first majority, solidifying his power for another four years.

Despite her steady string of disappointments, Murphy refused to give up. She continued to press King hard for a Senate appointment, and the tone of her letters to the prime minister continued to be jocular and familiar. In a note thanking him for a letter in the midst of the 1926 campaign, Murphy offered her 'most earnest wishes for your success' and added 'I'm more than ever persuaded that you're quite a nice man – well, as men go!'[81] This was followed two weeks later with a piece of doggerel, surely an unusual communication between a provincial judge aspiring to a seat in the Senate and the man she hoped would be returned as the nation's prime minister.

> For Artie ain't the party;
> Artie's in the river
> With a skiver in his hiver
> Now isn't that a shiver
> For he aint't got any kiver
> He Ho!
> Quite so!
> Mister King is in the ring,
> With his own little sling,
> Hit Byng in the wing
> And, by jing, there's a sing
> 'Bout the whole blarsted thing,
> (But, Oh well! I can't think of anymore.)
> I can too – a real ballyhoo,
> But sure 'twould never do
> For the likes of me and you
> Such a horror to pursue,
> Achew! and Achew!
> (Please excuse me for the sneeze),
> Mr. King if you please
> You're the whole bloomin' cheese
> It's your photo that I squeeze[82]

Constitutional Reform

King's electoral victory in 1926 owed much to anti-imperialism and his criticism of the Governor General's role in Canada's political and constitutional life. Concerns about the role of the monarch's representative continued after the election. Constitutional change had become a priority, but what sort of constitutional reform did King have in mind? Within weeks of his triumph at the polls, he attended an Imperial Conference where the state of the imperial constitution was very much on display. Constitutional issues took centre stage at the meeting in London that ran from 19 October to 23 November, to such an extent that the Imperial Conference of 1926 has been considered, 'from the constitutional point of view,' to be 'perhaps the most important of all the Colonial and Imperial Conferences.'[83]

King was determined to build on Canada's growing sense of nationhood and the autonomy within the Empire that had emerged during the First World War. Three years earlier, at the 1923 Imperial Conference, King had fought against the idea of a united Commonwealth foreign policy that would have been directed by the British. Now, in 1926, King continued to promote Canada's autonomy.

King attended the conference, chaired by British prime minister Stanley Baldwin, with his powerful Quebec lieutenant and minister of justice, Ernest Lapointe.[84] King was not the only prime minister with concerns about the relationship between the United Kingdom and the Dominions. The leaders of the Irish Free State and South Africa favoured complete independence from the Empire, while the leaders of Australia and New Zealand favoured the status quo. The Canadian position was more unpredictable, though the British feared that Canada would support the South Africans and the Irish.[85] The dissatisfaction was so great among the leaders of the Dominions that the conference appointed a prime ministers' committee, led by the former British prime minister, Lord Balfour, to deal with constitutional relations within the Empire.

For King, clarification of the Governor General's role in Dominion politics was an especially pressing concern, and the conference's statement on the subject satisfied him. Found in the Report of the Inter-Imperial Relations Committee, the powers of the Governor General were explained as follows:

In our opinion it is an essential consequence of the equality of status

existing among the members of the British Commonwealth of Nations
that the Governor General of a Dominion is the representative of the
Crown, holding in all essential respects the same position in relation to
the administration of public affairs in the Dominion as is held by His Majesty the King in Great Britain, and that he is not the representative or
agent of His Majesty's Government in Great Britain or of any Department
of that Government.[86]

As a result, the Governor General would no longer serve as a means of
communication between the Dominions and Great Britain. Instead,
official communications would now take place directly between governments.

King may have been concerned about the role of the Governor General, but the real legacy of the 1926 Imperial Conference was the Balfour Report recognizing the Dominions as equal and autonomous
members of the Empire. Contained in the first two paragraphs of the
section on the status of Great Britain and the Dominions in the Report
of the Inter-Imperial Relations Committee, the Balfour Report provides:

> The Committee are of opinion that nothing would be gained by attempt-
> ing to lay down a Constitution for the British Empire. Its widely scattered
> parts have very different characteristics, very different histories, and are
> at very different stages of evolution; while, considered as a whole, it
> defies classification and bears no resemblance to any other political orga-
> nization which now exists or has ever yet been tried.
>
> There is, however, one important element in which, from a strictly consti-
> tutional point of view, has now, as regards all vital matters, reached its
> full development – we refer to the group of self-governing communities
> composed of Great Britain and the Dominions. Their position and mutual
> relation may be readily defined. They are autonomous Communities
> within the British Empire, equal in status, in no way subordinate one to
> another in any aspect of their domestic or external affairs, though united
> by a common allegiance to the Crown, and freely associated as members
> of the British Commonwealth of Nations.[87]

Lost in the constitutional shuffle was any consensus on a formula to
amend Dominion constitutions, although the Report made clear that
the Dominions were not subservient to Britain: 'Every self-governing

member of the Empire is now the master of its destiny. In fact, if not always in form, it is subject to no compulsion whatever.'[88] Furthermore, the conference agreed to establish a committee to examine the British Parliament's powers to disallow or reserve Dominion legislation, the Dominions' authority to give their legislation extra-territorial application, and the uniformity of legislation between Great Britain and the Dominions. Although the Balfour Report led to the *Statute of Westminster* in 1931, which enabled Dominions to abolish appeals to the Judicial Committee of the Privy Council and to amend their own constitutions, no statement emerged from the conference as to the formula that would be used to amend those constitutions. It was clear from discussions at the conference that the Parliament at Westminster would not legislate against the will of the Dominions. And, by extension, the British Parliament would not pass a constitutional amendment absent the consent of the Dominions. Of course, what remained to be determined was whose consent was necessary in a federated system like Canada's.

Discussions of an amending formula had to wait for the Dominion–Provincial Conference of 1927, which met in Ottawa from 3 to 10 November of that year. The chances of achieving agreement were significantly diminished when Ontario premier Ferguson responded to reports that the federal cabinet intended to put Senate reform and the amending formula on the agenda.[89] He insisted that he would not tolerate any constitutional 'tampering' that would alter the status quo or weaken Canada's ties to Britain.[90] Quebec premier Taschereau announced his opposition to constitutional change, insisting that to open the door to amendment would imperil minority rights and Quebec's position within Confederation. Premier Ferguson also did his best to torpedo any talk about the appointment of women to the Senate. Many women were 'as brainy as men and a number a good deal brainier,' he allowed, but admitting women would require a constitutional amendment. As Ferguson explained it, he did not favour 'promiscuous change of the agreements which had served well' since 1867.[91]

The *Manitoba Free Press* condemned Ferguson and Taschereau as 'hard-shell Tories, though nominally of different parties' who are 'fooling themselves if they think they are thereby preventing the amendment of the Canadian Constitution.'[92] By contrast, the Montreal *Gazette* praised the two men as 'hard-shell Canadians resolutely determined to preserve ... the constitutional fabric of a united Canada, and to maintain inviolate the rights of the provinces and of the minorities ...

according to the plan, sound, tried and proven, which the Fathers of Confederation themselves laid down.'[93]

Prime Minister King was compelled to put the question of Senate reform to the conference, even though he knew there was little prospect for agreement. The March 1925 resolution of the House of Commons called for a Dominion–Provincial Conference on the question, and King raised the issue of Senate reform in the 1925 election. However, by late 1927, King's enthusiasm for Senate reform, such as it was, had waned. Even if he wanted change, it would be next to impossible to reach an agreement with the provinces. Moreover, attrition through mortality had reduced the Conservative majority to six and was likely to produce a Liberal majority by the end of 1928.[94] King must have calculated that time would fix his problems with control of the Senate.

In the end, King had more to lose than to gain from pushing Senate reform. The issue was not a matter of concern to ordinary Canadians, and those who did have strong views were sharply divided. Editorial writers entered the fray, but were at odds over whether to preserve the status quo,[95] or to opt for significant change.[96] The appointment of women attracted little attention among the general electorate and editorial writers, despite the efforts of Murphy and the organized women's movement.

At the Dominion–Provincial Conference, King said nothing about Senate reform. Lapointe was given that job, explaining that the government had been 'virtually instructed' to bring the issue before the conference by the resolution of the House of Commons in 1925.[97] He reviewed some of the proposals – abolition, election, limited terms of office, mandatory retirement at seventy-five, a provincial role in appointments, and the curtailment of powers – but carefully refrained from stating the policy of the Canadian government.[98]

The Western provinces and Prince Edward Island favoured reform. British Columbia premier MacLean proposed a solution that was reminiscent of what the British House of Commons had done to curtail the powers of the House of Lords. If the House of Commons adopted a bill three times, the Senate would not be able to block it. Manitoba agreed, and argued for further reforms: half the senators should be appointed by the provinces, appointments should be for a ten year term, and senators should be required to retire at the age of seventy-five.[99]

Ontario and Quebec, as noted above, strongly opposed change, as did Premiers Baxter and Rhodes of New Brunswick and Nova Scotia, respectively. With the four original partners of Confederation opposed to Senate reform, consensus was plainly out of reach. The conference was unanimous on only one point: the Senate ought not to be abolished. Additionally, the official communiqué reported 'practical unanimity against the principle of an elective Senate.'[100] Whether to curtail the powers of the Senate or reform the institution in a way that would render it more effective were subjects for discussion another day.[101]

The Liberals were not disappointed by the manner in which the conference resolution resolved the debate about Senate reform. According to one newspaper report, an unnamed Liberal minister proclaimed jubilantly: 'We got through the question of Senate reform without a ripple.'[102] The composition of the Senate, particularly the appointment of women, was not discussed. The only publicly reported response was a resolution from the Ontario Women's Liberal Association urging the appointment of a woman to the Senate.[103]

With Senate reform pushed to the sidelines, discussion of the amending formula followed. Here, too, the premiers reached no agreement. Justice Minister Lapointe took the lead on the subject, arguing that an amending formula was necessary to realize the full promise of Canadian autonomy embodied in the 1926 Balfour Report. A proponent of the compact theory of confederation, Lapointe proposed that the provinces be consulted about 'ordinary amendments,' in which case majority approval would suffice. For 'vital and fundamental amendments' ('involving such questions as provincial rights, the rights of minorities, or rights generally affecting race, language, and creed'), provincial unanimity would be required.[104]

Lapointe regarded the *BNA Act* as a treaty. When the House of Commons debated the subject of constitutional amendment in February 1925, Lapointe explained: 'The conclusion is that we cannot ask for power to alter, without the consent of the provinces, the Constitution which is their own Constitution as well as it is ours. It also follows that if it is to be considered as a treaty, surely we cannot alter its provisions without at least seeking the consent of the other parties to that treaty.'[105] He reasoned: 'If confederation was a pact, an agreement, is it possible for one of the parties to the agreement, or rather for the body which resulted from the agreement, to amend, to alter the conditions of that pact without consulting and without securing the consent of the parties to the original agreement?'[106] 'I ask my Hon. friend this question,' he told the House:

Confederation was achieved and the new Parliament was opened in 1867. Does he believe that two years afterwards, in 1869, for instance, this Parliament could have fairly and reasonably amended the British North

America Act or have asked the Imperial Parliament to amend it without the consent of the four original provinces? Could he fairly say that that could have been done two years after the opening of this Parliament? If it could not be done at that time, could it be done twenty-five years afterwards, or even fifty years afterwards, without the consent of the contracting parties in the pact of confederation?[107]

Yet the compact theory of Confederation was not the settled view of Confederation in 1927,[108] and it was not inevitable that this approach would dictate the elements of an amending formula. It is thus not surprising that there was no consensus reached on how best to amend the Canadian constitution at the Dominion–Provincial Conference. The same east-west split that blocked Senate reform prevailed on the broader question of amending the constitution. Those opposed to Lapointe's proposal did so for any number of reasons. Some argued that there was no demand for an amending formula. Others pointed out that autonomy to amend the Canadian constitution would lead to all manner of inappropriate amendments. Still others argued that the British Parliament had never refused to amend the *BNA Act*, and there was simply no reason to confer that power on the Parliament of Canada. Others warned of the inevitable political conflicts that would arise if amendments were submitted to the provinces for approval. Finally, traditionalists argued that because the *BNA Act* was a creature of the Imperial Parliament, that institution alone should have the power to change it.[109]

Following the impasse on the amending formula, the premiers and prime minister turned their attention to the familiar bread-and-butter subject of federal grants and fiscal sharing with the usual result. The provinces demanded more money, the Dominion refused to concede significant revenues, and there was vague talk of further study and discussion. On another contentious issue – the development of water-power resources – the conference agreed to disagree and to refer the whole issue to the Supreme Court.

The results of the Dominion–Provincial Conference of 1927 must have emboldened Murphy and vindicated her decision to turn to the courts to secure the appointment of women to the Senate. King's feeble effort to reform the Senate and Lapointe's failed attempts to secure a constitutional amending formula both indicated that there was no possibility of finding a political solution to her problem. However charming and encouraging he might be in private, King clearly placed the appointment of women to the Senate well down on his list of priorities. Without agreement on an amending formula, it was difficult to see how King could push ahead with his promise to amend the *BNA Act* to permit the appointment of female senators, even if he wanted to do so.

5

Going to Court

Emily Murphy decided in the summer of 1927 that she had exhausted all political channels and that it was time to turn to the courts. Murphy was far from confident that she could win a court challenge, but believed she had no other option. If, as she half expected, the tradition-bound judges could not be convinced to break with the past and refused to declare women to be 'persons' in the eyes of the law, she could reactivate the political campaign by ridiculing the constitution's deplorable failure to recognize the legal personhood of women.

A significant procedural obstacle stood in the way of Murphy's court challenge. Murphy had no legally recognized claim she could advance. No one had the right to be appointed to the Senate and the Department of Justice's legal opinion that a woman could not be appointed was only the government's internal legal advice. It had no binding legal authority. As a practical matter, the opinion blocked Murphy's appointment to the Senate, but the opinion gave Murphy no right to commence legal proceedings. The opinion was legal advice, not a government decision that could be challenged by judicial review. Furthermore, restrictive legal standing requirements made it almost impossible for an ordinary citizen to challenge the interpretation of a law unless the citizen had a personal or proprietary stake in the outcome.[1] The appointment of senators, then as now, is a discretionary power; although the Governor General approves the appointments under the constitution, it is the prime minister who decides whom to appoint to sit in the Senate. Merely aspiring to a Senate appointment would not qualify as a sufficient interest to ground a legal proceeding for a declaration of the meaning of 'persons' under the constitution.

Another problem was the cost of bringing a legal challenge. The issue was highly contentious and the case was bound to work its way to the top of the judicial hierarchy. Even if Murphy found a way to start a legal proceeding against the government, she lacked the resources to fund a case that would be fought first in the courts of Alberta and then likely in Ottawa at the Supreme Court of Canada and possibly in London before the Judicial Committee of the Privy Council. The fight would be long and costly. There was no legal aid or other scheme to fund such litigation. The cost would exceed $10,000, a sum several times the average Canadian salary and well beyond Murphy's means.

With the assistance of her brother, Justice William Ferguson, Murphy developed a strategy. Ferguson suggested that Murphy petition the government to direct a reference to the Supreme Court of Canada. Such an approach would avoid several problems. If the government could be persuaded to direct a reference, the issue of standing would disappear. The government itself had every right to pose the question and the Supreme Court would likely allow Murphy to be heard as an intervener. This tactic would also involve little delay because the case would proceed directly before the Supreme Court of Canada. Another significant advantage to this approach was cost: if the government brought the reference, the government would also pay the legal costs.

The *Supreme Court Act* allowed the government to refer directly to the Supreme Court any question of law or fact concerning the interpretation of the constitution or the constitutionality or interpretation of any federal or provincial legislation.[2] References, used from the early days of Confederation to resolve contentious constitutional issues, are a distinctive feature of Canadian constitutional law.[3] The order directing the reference states the question to be answered and the case proceeds immediately before the Supreme Court of Canada. The reference power allows the government to have a legal issue resolved immediately by the Supreme Court when the government deems it to be in the public interest to do so. Technically speaking, the court's ruling is strictly advisory and does not constitute a formal judgment. In practice, however, the court's answer on a reference is almost always treated as authoritative.

Critics complain that references raise hypothetical questions that lack the necessary factual foundation to afford a proper judicial determination. However, where a question involves a pure legal issue, the reference procedure has worked well. Mackenzie King, for one, was fond of the reference power, and used it frequently over the course of his twenty-two years as prime minister. During his three terms in office, King was responsible for directing more than thirty references to the courts, involving all manner of legislation, not simply those involving politically contentious subjects. By way of contrast, R.B. Bennett, who was prime minister for five years from 7 August 1930 to 23 October 1935, referred eight cases to the courts,[4] while the leaders who occupied the prime minister's office in the twenty-two years following King, from 1949 to 1971, used the reference power only twelve times. In more recent times, the most notable references have been the 1981 *Patriation Reference*,[5] when the Supreme Court was asked whether the Parliament of Canada could request an amendment to the *BNA Act, 1867*, without substantial agreement from the provinces, and the 1998 *Quebec Secession Reference*,[6] when the court was asked to define the constitutional rules that would govern the terms on which a province could exit Confederation.

Most popular accounts of the case suggest that Murphy uncovered an obscure provision in the *Supreme Court Act* that allowed any five interested citizens to petition the Court for an interpretation of the constitution.[7] This is not accurate. As Murphy herself explained: 'It was not necessary that five persons be named as Appellants.'[8] The *Supreme Court Act* did not allow for petitions of this kind and there has never been such a procedure.[9] The Act did, however, permit the Governor General in Council (really the cabinet) to refer a question of law or fact to the Supreme Court in Ottawa for determination. It was then left to the Court to decide who should be notified and heard on the reference.

Murphy's petition was addressed to the Governor in Council, not the Supreme Court, requesting the Governor in Council to direct a reference to the Court. Mackenzie King's government could easily have rejected the petition as ill-conceived, and the very fact that it was accepted suggests that King may have been looking for a way to avoid taking responsibility for what he regarded as a thorny question. As his frequent use of the reference power demonstrates, King believed that the courts should be allowed to determine the constitutionality of legislation and, by extension, matters of constitutional interpretation. There has been speculation that Mackenzie King himself may have suggested the ploy of a reference on the question of female senators.[10] There in no evidence to support that possibility, but the decision to accept Murphy's petition and refer the matter to the Supreme Court[11] was made at the same time the cabinet was settling the agenda for the 1927 Dominion–Provincial Conference.[12] King and Lapointe must have decided that they preferred to have the question resolved by the courts rather than by the politicians. In view of the hostility the provincial premiers demonstrated at the Dominion-Provincial Conference to any constitutional change, it certainly was in Murphy's interest to have the question of women in the Senate removed from the political arena.

At first, Murphy intended to sign the petition by herself. Quickly, she came to realize that would attract attention to the ambition she had consistently shied away from publicly admitting. To be the sole litigant would only highlight her overarching objective, and a self-serving victory might open the Senate door to women but undermine Murphy's own personal chance to secure an appointment. Murphy was also pragmatic enough to realize that victory in the courts was anything but assured; if the court challenge failed, she would have to take her appeal to the masses and address the Canadian people directly. As Murphy explained a few years later:

> If our appeal had been unsuccessful, it was my intention to request that these four splendid women – 'interested' but not 'persons' – to make with me an inclusive tour of Canada urging the electors thereof to demand a revision of the *British North America Act*. For this reason, I selected appellants who were outstanding representatives of the different political parties. Two of these had been Members of the Alberta Legislature and one was a Cabinet Minister.[13]

Murphy told only Nellie McClung about her strategy; she said nothing to Edwards, McKinney, or Parlby of her intentions.[14]

'It Was a Perfect Day in Harvest Time'

Murphy drafted the petition to cabinet and, in early August 1927, she explained her strategy to McClung.[15] She reminded her friend of the various petitions to the prime minister from the National Council of Women, the Women's Institutes, the Woman's Christian Temperance Union, and other women's organizations asking 'that women be admitted to the Senate of Canada, thus permitting us to secure our full enfranchisement.' Murphy also recalled the 1923 motion in the Senate that proposed to amend the *BNA Act* to permit the appointment of women and how it had died on the vine. After four years of waiting, Murphy explained, 'It is now held by a large and important body of opinion that such proposed amendment was not, and is not necessary.' It was 'highly desirable' that the matter be put to rest, 'without further delay in order that the women of this Dominion – comprising approximately one-half of the electorate – may enjoy their full political rights on the same terms as these are, or may be, enjoyed by men.'

Disillusioned by Prime Minister Mackenzie King's broken promises to amend the constitution, Murphy had lost all confidence in the political process. 'We have now come to realize,' she wrote, 'that the matter is one which cannot with any degree of fairness be submitted for decision to a body of male persons, many of whom have expressed themselves towards it in a manner that is distinctly hostile.' An appeal to the courts by taking 'advantage of a friendly recourse to the Supreme Court,' was 'our proper procedure under these circumstances.'[16]

Murphy's description of her proposed court challenge as a 'friendly recourse to the Supreme Court' hints that she had some indication – possibly even from Mackenzie King himself – that the government would not put up a strong fight to defend the justice department's opinion before the Court.

Murphy decided not to risk reviewing her strategy with leaders in the women's movement. She explained her strategy to McClung, telling her that because the subject of the petition was 'purely a technical one,' it was not necessary 'to submit the matter to Canadian women generally, they having already endorsed the principle.'[17] Murphy may not have been surprised to learn a few months later that it had come as a 'terrible shock to the Eastern Women that 5 coal-heavers and plough-pushers from Alberta ... went over their heads to the Supreme Court without even saying, "Please ma'am can we do it?"' and she took great pride in leading the initiative. 'We know how to stir up interest in the East – just start it going ourselves.'[18] In any event, Murphy fully expected McClung's support: 'I do not feel it even remotely necessary to urge upon you the extreme desirability of your lending your much valued influence to this matter which is so clearly allied with the political, social and philanthropic interests of all Canadian Women.'[19]

Murphy invited all four women to her home in Edmonton to sign the petition in late August 1927. Nellie McClung described the day as 'a perfect day in harvest time. Blue haze lay on the horizon. Wheat fields, now dotted with stooks, were waiting for the threshing machine. Bees droned in the delphiniums and roses.' The women 'sat on her veranda and discussed many things. Then we put our names to the petition and it was sent to Ottawa.' McClung praised her friend's drafting skills: 'Mrs. Murphy was a master craftsman in the handling of words. She had no difficulty in finding the apt word.'[20]

Murphy's petition, dated 27 August 1927, posed two questions for the Supreme Court's consideration:

> As persons interested in the admission of women to the Senate of Canada, we do hereby request that you may be graciously pleased to refer to the Supreme Court of Canada for hearing, consideration and adjudication the following constitutional questions:
>
> I. Is power vested in the Governor General in Council of Canada, or the Parliament of Canada, or either of them, to appoint a female to the Senate of Canada?
> II. Is it constitutionally possible for the Parliament of Canada under the provisions of the *British North America Act*, or otherwise, to make provision for the appointment of a female person to the Senate of Canada?
>
> These questions are respectfully referred to your consideration pursuant to Section 60 of the *Supreme Court Act*, R.S.C. 1906, cap. 139.[21]

Murphy framed these questions very carefully. She deliberately avoided asking the Court to decide if a woman was a 'person' under the *BNA Act* because she feared that to pose the question in that manner would only invite the Department of Justice to oppose the initiative and inspire a negative response from the Court. To ask 'Are women persons?' would collide directly with English precedent and the opinion of the government law officers that had dogged her from the start. Instead, Murphy decided to pose the question in positive terms. She emphasized the powers of the Governor General and the Parliament of Canada rather than attack the antiquated views of women's disabilities. Murphy's second question conceded the possibility that some form of legislation might be required to permit the appointment of women to the Senate, but carefully avoided raising the need for a possible constitutional amendment. Given the difficulties that she had already encountered on this front, Murphy's caution was understandable.

Murphy was unusually reticent when asked by a reporter to explain the petition. She 'refused to make any comment whatsoever about this matter other than to say that the communication had been acknowledged and its due consideration assured.'[22] Murphy hoped that the government would not fight the case before the Supreme Court, and the minister of justice, Ernest Lapointe, King's powerful Quebec lieutenant, leaned in that direction. Deputy Minister Stuart Edwards asked Lapointe about the role counsel would play: 'I should be glad to have your instructions as to whether the Dominion desires to retain counsel to support the opinion reached by the Department upon the question of law, or whether it is considered that the Dominion should take no part on either side.' Lapointe replied: 'I would advise that the solicitor general attend and watch the case for us, whether taking part in the argument or not.'[23] In late November 1927, Stuart Edwards thought it 'unlikely that the Department will instruct counsel to argue the opposite view,' as the minister's present intention was to have the solicitor general attend with only a watching brief.[24] The minister of justice, it would seem, planned simply to leave the whole question in the Court's hands without having the government's lawyers offer arguments in support of their earlier legal opinion. Edwards informed Murphy's counsel, Newton Rowell, that he would likely be able to present his argument unopposed.[25]

The decision to neither support nor oppose Murphy's legal proceeding would have been politically attractive to the prime minister. By directing the reference, the government would arguably be seen as supporting the women's cause, but by remaining silent on the question of principle, the government could avoid responsibility for the outcome. Murphy likely had some indication that the government might be willing to take a neutral stance before the Court, and she did not want to pose the question in a way that made it difficult for the government to adhere to that approach.

In November 1927, Murphy had second thoughts about the questions she had posed in the original petition. The new amended petition Murphy asked her four colleagues to sign now included a third question:

> If any statute be necessary to qualify a female to sit in the Senate of Canada, must this statute be enacted by the Imperial Parliament, or does power lie with the Parliament of Canada or the Senate of Canada?[26]

This new question appears to have been a veiled way of asking whether a constitutional amendment was required. Upon reflection, Murphy must have been worried that her first two questions left a gap that would leave her ultimate concern unresolved. The court could answer 'no' to the first question and 'yes' to the second, but not be clear as to whether resolution of the issue required legislation from the Parliament in Ottawa or a constitutional amendment from the Parliament at Westminster. As Murphy explained to McClung, she posed the third question owing to the uncertainty regarding Canadian autonomy: 'It would be a pity if we would have to make a second appeal to decide who should do the legislating.'[27]

When they submitted the original petition to the government in the late summer of 1927, Murphy and the other four petitioners heard nothing for two weeks. In mid-September, an official acknowledged receipt of the petition and advised that it would receive due consideration. Murphy was encouraged by press reports that the government would refer the questions to the Supreme Court and that the minister of justice was willing to provide the petitioners with counsel.[28] Buoyed by this news, Murphy told McClung: 'Our procedure in submitting this to the Supreme Court was a wise one, instead of submitting it to the favor of politicians.' This remark, of course, ignored the fact that the decision to refer the matter to the Supreme Court would be made by politicians.

But after so many years of promises and disappointments, Murphy remained wary. She thought her opponents 'will likely come out now in open opposition (forced out) because we have them by the short hair.'[29] Murphy gleefully reported to McClung the favorable editorials that appeared in the *Manitoba Free Press*[30] and in *Saturday Night* magazine.[31] The National Council of Women urged the government 'to grant the right to women to be appointed members of the Senate' and if there were 'clauses of the *British North America Act*' precluding the appointment of women, the Council urged the government to request a constitutional amendment.[32] The *Family Herald* asserted that no reasonable argument could be advanced in favour of the exclusion of women from the Senate and that 'ancient pre-Victorian ideas that the female was ... the "weaker sex" or that man alone had governing or law-making ability has been swept away in late years, especially since the Great War.' The editorial writer added that whether women wanted to sit in the Senate was 'something that they ought to be left to decide for themselves' and that some 'might even regard attendance in the Red Chamber as a punishment.'[33] Murphy warned McClung, however, that she had also heard 'the gentry are advising the Government to accede because they don't have to appoint us anyway.' Murphy was quite prepared to proceed one step at a time: 'That's another question! What we want them to do is accede.' She promised to keep up the barrage of 'stirring 'em up' letters to Ottawa.[34]

By early November, Murphy decided it was time to fire off another 'stir 'em up' shot. The government had committed itself to directing the reference, and Murphy believed it was safe to ask for more. She wrote to the government again, this time referring to the provision in the *Supreme Court Act*[35] that provided for the appointment and payment of counsel: 'Your petitioners are desirous that ... the Supreme Court of Canada may be graciously pleased, in its discretion, to permit of your petitioners nominating counsel to argue their case, the expenses occasioned thereby to be paid by the Honourable the Minister of Finance.' Murphy also had a solution to avoid delay: 'Your petitioners would further venture to suggest the desirability of this matter at issue being referred to the Supreme Court of Canada at a special session, if necessary.' This, she pointed out, would allow Parliament to deal with the matter at its next session 'should the findings of the Court indicate the necessity of such a procedure.'[36]

Newton Wesley Rowell, KC: A Man of Strong Principles

Murphy already knew she wanted Newton Wesley Rowell to argue her case before the Supreme Court. At the age of sixty, Rowell was one of Canada's leading lawyers. A brilliant, straight-laced, teetotalling Methodist from Ontario, he was nationally known to be a man of strong principles. Like his political mentor, Prime Minister Wilfrid Laurier, Rowell firmly believed that the twentieth century would be Canada's. He was an enthusiastic proponent of expanding the West and developing the North, and he welcomed large-scale immigration. By 1911, when he became leader of the opposition Liberal Party of Ontario, Rowell had established a solid reputation as an outstanding lawyer with close ties to Canada's business and political elite. He served as leader of the Ontario Liberal Party from 1911 until 1917, when he joined Prime Minister Borden's Union government as a senior minister in support of conscription. After a tumultuous political career, Rowell returned to full-time private practice in 1921.

There is no suggestion that Emily Murphy gave any thought to having a female lawyer argue the case. There were very few women lawyers in Canada, even fewer who took cases to court, and certainly none who had experience before the Supreme Court. Rowell may have been the epitome of the male establishment, but he was also an ideal choice for the Famous Five. He had the legal skill and experience to take on a case of this importance and difficulty having appeared regularly before the Supreme Court of Canada and argued three cases before the Judicial Committee of the Privy Council in 1924.[37] He also had the necessary connections to handle what was potentially a very political case. When Murphy approached him to take the case, Rowell was busy handling the federal government's litigation to recover millions of dollars in unpaid taxes from breweries and distilleries. Rowell himself had helped to uncover these unpaid taxes when he served as counsel to a Royal Commission investigating customs irregularities.[38]

Rowell's political views were similar in many respects to those of the women behind the *Persons* case. His strong support for progressive social welfare measures, fuelled by Christian evangelicalism, gained him respect from people like Nellie McClung and the social gospel movement.[39] Like McClung and Louise McKinney, Rowell was an ardent prohibitionist, who firmly believed that alcohol was a menace to democratic government, dethroned reason, encouraged crime, produced poverty, illness and death, and sapped the moral fabric of the community.[40] His determined efforts to bring prohibition to Ontario and his proclamation that 'the organized liquor forces' should not be allowed to 'triumph against the forces of a common Christianity'[41] cost him many of the precious votes he needed in his unsuccessful bid to overcome the Conservatives in the 1914 provincial election. For Rowell, adherence to principle was always more important that gaining power.

When Borden's Union government repealed the wartime probibition Order in Council in 1919, Rowell protested that the action was contrary to the public interest and a blot on the government's 'splendid record' on the issue.[42] Borden responded that Rowell's record on prohibition had been 'manly, straightforward and consistent from the first,' a stance Borden was prepared to support 'so far as public opinion seemed to render it possible,'[43] a point that clearly had been passed in Borden's view. As for women's rights, Rowell declared his personal support for women's suffrage in 1912, shortly after he became Liberal leader in Ontario and before his party was prepared to adopt the policy as its own.[44] For Rowell, women's rights were a family affair; his wife, Nell, became the first president of the Toronto Women's Liberal

Association, which was established in 1913 as the first women's organization within the party. She also helped to found the Ontario
Women's Liberal Association in 1914, serving once more as its first
president.[45]

Rowell's most courageous and controversial political move was his
decision to abandon the Laurier Liberals to join Prime Minister Borden's Union government during the conscription crisis of 1917. Rowell
had little confidence in Borden and his Conservative colleagues, and
he was personally close to Laurier and future Liberal leader Mackenzie
King, both of whom opposed conscription. However, Rowell believed
passionately that Canada could not fulfill its wartime commitments
without conscription. He tried to convince Laurier that Canadian unity
could survive conscription: 'I did everything in my power individually
and in cooperation with other Liberals to induce Sir Wilfrid Laurier as
Leader of the Liberal Party, to join Sir Robert Borden in forming a Coalition Government. In this effort I wholly failed.'[46] When Laurier could
not be persuaded, Rowell felt duty-bound to abandon his friends, his
leader, and his party and to join the Union government.

Rowell resigned as Ontario Liberal leader and joined Borden's government in 1917, a move that certainly ended his chances of succeeding
Laurier as national leader and that left the Liberal Party bitterly
divided between English and French. As Ontario Liberal leader, Rowell had refused to oppose the Conservative government's notorious
Regulation 17 that eviscerated the education rights of Franco-Ontari-
ans. Now, by abandoning the Liberals in the name of conscription,
Rowell further compounded his alienation from the Liberal Party's
francophone wing. Rowell was a key figure in the Union government.
He served as president of the Privy Council and as Borden's deputy as
chair of the War Committee. It was in this capacity that he met Emily
Murphy, Nellie McClung, and Henrietta Muir Edwards at the
Women's War Conference in Ottawa in 1917.

During the war, Rowell travelled to France to see the men at the
front lines and to London to attend the Imperial War Conference. Rowell also served as Canada's delegate at the first assembly of the League
of Nations in 1920. Rowell did not stand for re-election in 1921. He was
a key figure in the formation of the United Church of Canada in 1925
and his strong interest in international relations and love of travel took
him to conferences in Europe, Africa, and Asia. Mackenzie King tried
to entice Rowell back into politics in 1925 and 1926.[47] Despite the offer
of a post in Mackenzie King's cabinet, Rowell again declined to run,

choosing instead to devote himself to his law practice, his church, and to his passionate interest in travel and international affairs.

Prime Minister King regarded Rowell as 'the ablest lawyer in Canada on Constitutional questions.'[48] When she asked Nellie McClung for her approval of Rowell's retainer, Emily Murphy remarked: 'It is hardly necessary for me to enlarge upon Mr. Rowell's qualifications.'[49] Murphy was convinced that 'we could not have better counsel' and thought that Rowell being a Liberal had the advantage of not seeming 'to make of it a political issue, which it is not, in any sense.'[50]

The Government Responds

In early November 1927, Murphy learned that cabinet had passed an Order in Council directing a reference to the Supreme Court two weeks earlier.[51] To Murphy's dismay, however, the government's lawyers had refused to adopt her carefully worded questions. Instead, they posed the very question she had hoped to avoid: 'Does the word "Persons" in section 24 of the *British North America Act, 1867*, include female persons.'

Murphy immediately protested to Stuart Edwards, the Department of Justice official who had reluctantly given the 1921 opinion that women were not eligible for the Senate. Edwards was now deputy minister of justice. Murphy complained that the question posed by the government was 'a matter of amazement and perturbation to us.' She explained that the petitioners 'were not unmindful of the fact that the officers of the Crown had already expressed the opinion publically [sic], and to various delegations, that a female is not a "person" under the *BNA Act* and, for this, and other very excellent reasons, refrained from using the word "person" in any of our questions.'

Murphy was so disturbed by the way the question had been framed that she was prepared to risk having no reference at all. She insisted that the government's reference 'is not our question, nor a correct interpretation thereof, and that accordingly it requires to be withdrawn.' Murphy went so far as to ask Edwards to ensure that the terms of the reference were altered to include the three questions she had posed to make sure the Court directed its mind to all the possibilities and 'to avoid delay and the contingency of having to again appeal this matter to the Supreme Court.'[52]

Murphy perceived the government's tactics to be high-handed and fatal to her plans for a 'friendly' reference. The deputy minister of justice had made no attempt to discuss with her the wording of the question before having the Order in Council passed by cabinet. 'They evidently think they are going to stampede us' into accepting 'their question instead of ours,' she complained to McClung. '*Well, they're not!!*' retorted Murphy.[53] Henrietta Edwards spoke to her nephew about the case and, according to the information Murphy passed on to McClung, he told his aunt that the reference procedure could not be used to short-circuit the normal procedure for amending the constitution. If women were to be admitted to the Senate, a constitutional amendment was going to be required.

Murphy thought that the question Stuart Edwards had posed was designed to produce that very answer from the Supreme Court. The government was insisting that the case came down to this: 'no one has the power to amend the *BNA Act* but the Premiers of all the Provinces' and, Murphy added, '*they never will.*' That, Murphy exclaimed, was 'how they are hoping to get out of it.' She certainly was not cowed by the government's attitude: 'Never mind, Dear,' she wrote to McClung, 'we are going to get right after them anyway.'[54]

While Murphy's reaction was understandable, the government was under no obligation to direct the reference in Murphy's terms rather than its own. Stuart Edwards refused to budge. Murphy may have suggested the reference, but it was a procedure that only the government could invoke and the government was entitled to determine the precise terms of the question to be posed to the Supreme Court without Murphy's approval. In his sharply worded response to Murphy, Edwards acknowledged that he was 'the draftsman,' but denied any attempt 'to state the question adversely to the petitioners.' Edwards insisted that he had simply tried 'to state for reference to the Court what, in my opinion, is the only real and substantial question.' He regretted not advising the petitioners of his concerns earlier, but dismissed their three proposed questions as being 'quite unacceptable.'

Edwards aptly, but unkindly, described the reference in Murphy's first question to the power of the Parliament of Canada to appoint senators as an 'obvious solecism' as the appointment power was plainly vested in the Governor General, not Parliament. The Governor General's power 'is governed by the true interpretation of the word "persons"' as used in section 24, and it followed that the meaning of the word 'persons' was the only real question. Edwards considered the petitioners' second and third proposed questions regarding the legislative powers of Parliament to be entirely misguided. It is, he observed, 'plain and free from doubt' that only the Imperial Parliament could amend the *BNA Act*, and therefore the government would not be justified in posing either question to the Court.[55]

Murphy was not mollified by Edwards' reply and she pressed him to state definitively that the government was denying her petition. Edwards responded patronizingly. Far from denying the petition, he remarked, the government had granted it by referring to the Supreme Court 'a question which presents for decision what, appeared to me, as I am sure it will appear to any lawyer with a knowledge of the Constitution, to be the only real and substantial question raised by the petitioners' questions.'

The government did, however, agree to Murphy's request that she be permitted to retain Newton Rowell to argue the case at the government's expense. Edwards also suggested to Murphy that she 'consult with Mr. Rowell in regard to the terms of the reference.' He added confidently, 'I am sure he will satisfy you that no injustice had been done the petitioners in the statement of the question referred.'[56]

For Rowell's part, before he accepted the brief, he cleared his new retainer with Deputy Minister of Justice Edwards to ensure there was no perception of conflict of interest arising from his representation of the government in the pursuit of the distilleries for unpaid duties.[57]

No Friendly Reference

Behind the scenes, lawyers at the Department of Justice ensured there would be no 'friendly' reference that would muzzle the government lawyers from defending their opinion. Murphy must have regarded this shift in strategy as duplicitous, but the department's lawyers had a point. If the government failed to defend its own opinion, it would be obvious to the judges of the Supreme Court that the government was shifting responsibility for the decision to the courts. Indeed, if the Court felt that both sides were not being presented, it might even refuse to give an answer.

As Department of Justice lawyer C.P. Plaxton explained to Stuart Edwards, Newton Rowell would be representing the petitioners 'with his usual resource and ability,' thus the Court was certain to expect 'that the opposite view should also be presented.' Such an approach 'would seem to me not to be unreasonable,' he noted. Plaxton was particularly concerned about the department's previous opinion. 'The order-in-council which sets forth the question referred recites "that the law officers of the Crown who have considered this question on more than one occasion have expressed the view that male persons only may be summoned to the Senate under the provisions of the *British North America Act* in that behalf."' For this reason, he thought 'the Court might properly ask to be informed of the grounds which may be urged in support of the official opinion, and it would surely be a reasonable course, involving no hostility to the interests of the women concerned, for us to endeavour to justify our opinion if we can.'[58]

Murphy travelled to Toronto where she discussed the case, likely with her brother and certainly with Rowell. Rowell persuaded her that she could not expect the government to change the questions, and should proceed with the case on the government's terms. After Christmas, Murphy wrote to Stuart Edwards: 'Since coming to Toronto, I have consulted Mr. N.W. Rowell who advised that we agree to refer our questions in the form submitted by the Government to the Supreme Court of Canada.'[59]

The Supreme Court knew the reference was coming. A routine motion dealing with notice to provincial Attorneys General was presented to Justice Edmund Leslie Newcombe in late October 1927.[60] Newcombe, a Nova Scotian, had been appointed to the Court in 1924 after a thirty-year career in the Department of Justice, during which time he had argued many of the important constitutional cases on behalf of the Dominion government before the Supreme Court of Canada and the Judicial Committee of the Privy Council. Justice Minister Ernest Lapointe wanted to appoint him as Chief Justice. Prime Minister King refused because of Newcombe's Tory connections, but elevated him to the Court as a puisne judge.[61] Newcombe had been the deputy minister of justice in 1921 when the department gave its opinion that women could not be appointed to the Senate absent a constitutional amendment. Yet the opinion left little impression. When the case was listed, Newcombe could not recall the details of his own involvement with the file and wrote to Stuart Edwards, requesting a copy of the department's file: 'If you could conveniently let me see the file which we had in my time upon the subject of "Women in the Senate," or copy [sic] of the opinions which I wrote on that subject, I should be much obliged.'[62]

The file arrived in Newcombe's office with a memorandum from Plaxton explaining why the opinion had been prepared and pointing out that Newcombe had reviewed it, together with William Ferguson's opinion, in order to advise the prime minister.[63] Newcombe quickly realized that he could not sit on the case because he had advised the prime minister that he supported the department's view that women were ineligible, and advised Plaxton: 'I have ... received your memorandum respecting Women in the Senate. I do not intend to sit in this case.'[64] Although he could not sit, Newcombe followed the case closely and made arrangements to have the Department of Justice send him his own copy of the Attorney General's factum as soon as it was filed.[65]

The Department of Justice devoted enormous efforts to preparing its factum for the reference, with Plaxton writing a series of memoranda to junior lawyers, libraries, and archives to gather material from all available sources. William Smith, deputy keeper of public records, was asked to certify that no female names could be found on the rolls of pre-Confederation legislative councils. Smith complied, but then alarmed Edwards when he found some evidence that women had voted and announced his intention to publish an article entitled 'Women Voted in Quebec a Century Ago.'[66]

Only two provinces took an interest in the reference: Alberta and Quebec. The Government of Alberta, which included petitioner Irene Parlby as minister without portfolio, supported the appointment of female senators, and agreed to have Rowell present on its behalf a common case with the petitioners. By contrast, the Government of Quebec decided to intervene to oppose the appointment of women to the Senate. Unlike Alberta, Quebec's interests were directly affected. If the Supreme Court permitted the appointment of female senators, then Quebec might be forced to deal with its own prohibition on female suffrage. Moreover, not only did Quebec deny women the vote, but the province also had an appointed upper house.[67] What was problematic was section 73 of the *BNA Act*, which provided: 'The Qualifications of the Legislative Councillors of Quebec shall be the same as those of the Senators for Quebec.' If Quebec wanted to keep women out of its provincial upper house, it also had to make sure women were not allowed into the Senate in Ottawa. It was no surprise, then, when Quebec decided to intervene to oppose the petitioners.

The Petitioners State Their Case

Rowell knew that the Attorney General was bound to rely on the common law exclusion of women from public office in 1867 and the theory of interpretation holding that the meaning of words in a statute could not change over time. An experienced counsel who had argued many cases before the Court, Rowell also knew that arguments based upon equality between the sexes or changing values regarding the role of women in public life would fall upon deaf ears. His job was to convince the judges that the strict letter of the law allowed for the appointment of female senators. Rowell's Supreme Court factum was unusually short; in only two and one-half pages, he clearly presented a powerful yet elegant argument that was firmly rooted in the language of the *BNA Act* and in traditional theories of statutory interpretation.[68]

Rowell's starting point was this: 'There is nothing in the word "Persons" to suggest that it is limited to male persons. The word in its natural meaning is equally applicable to female persons and it is submitted that it should be so interpreted.' The only restriction on 'persons' who could be appointed to the Senate under section 24 was that they must be 'qualified' and the qualifications were spelled out in section 23. While section 23 used the male pronoun 'he,' according to legislation in place in 1867 when the *BNA Act* was enacted, 'words importing the Masculine Gender shall be taken to include Females ... unless the contrary as to Gender ... is expressly provided.'[69] For Rowell, the conclusion was inevitable: 'By express statutory enactment, therefore, Section 23 includes females, unless the contrary is expressly provided. It is submitted there is nothing in the *British North America Act, 1867*, expressly providing the contrary.'

Rowell bolstered this conclusion by pointing out that Parliament itself had already declared that when the constitution used the word 'persons' with reference to public office, it was capable of including women. Section 41 of the *BNA Act* provided that 'until the Parliament of Canada otherwise provides ... the Qualifications and Disqualifications of Persons to be elected or to sit and vote' in the pre-Confederation legislative assemblies shall apply to elections for the House of Commons. Parliament, without amending the constitution, had given women the right to vote during the First World War and had declared them eligible to sit in the House of Commons in 1920.[70] Parliament could only have done so if the constitution, when it spoke of 'persons' in relation to public office, included women.

A basic principle of statutory interpretation, then as now, is that language should be interpreted consistently throughout. As Rowell explained: 'The word "Persons" in Sections 24 and 41 should receive the same interpretation and there is nothing in the *British North America Act, 1867*, to justify a different interpretation.' Both provisions should be read as parallel conferrals of power and be read consistently:

if Parliament had the power to allow for female members of the House of Commons, why should the Governor General not have the power to summon a woman to the Senate?

Finally, Rowell turned to section 33 of the *BNA Act*, which provided that any question respecting the qualifications of a senator 'shall be heard and determined by the Senate.' The constitution's scheme was complete: it was for the Governor General to decide whom to appoint under section 24 and for the Senate itself to decide under section 33 whether that person was qualified to sit according to the criteria set out in section 23. This final point was a delicate one for the petitioners. If section 33 empowered senators to determine for themselves whether a woman could belong to the upper chamber, the Court might well use section 33 as an excuse to refuse to answer the reference question on the ground that the issue was for the Senate to decide, not the courts. Having come this far, the last thing Rowell and Murphy wanted to give the Supreme Court was a respectable way to avoid the real issue.

Rowell finessed this possibility by casting the argument in terms of the Court's duty to decide what powers the constitution gave the Governor General and the Senate. He argued that under section 24, read in the light of section 41, the constitution gave the Governor General the power to summon a woman to the Senate. Under section 33, the constitution gave the Senate the power to determine her qualifications. Rowell contended that if 'the Senate exercising the powers given by [section 33] determined that she was qualified as a Senator, it is submitted that her position as a Senator could not be challenged. If this be so, then the question on the reference cannot be answered in the negative.'[71]

The Case for the Attorney General

Any suggestion that the government was not going to present a strong defence evaporated with the news that it had retained none other than Eugene Lafleur, the very same prominent Montreal lawyer Murphy had asked to give an opinion on the issue in 1921. A modern lawyer would refuse to take the opposite side of a brief against a former client but, in 1927, Lafleur saw no conflict. He was, after all, arguing precisely what he had told Murphy seven years earlier.

The Attorney General's factum was submitted by Solicitor General Lucien Cannon, Lafleur, and C.P. Plaxton, but drafted by Stuart Edwards and his colleagues in the Department of Justice.[72] It differed from Rowell's in tone, length, and result.[73] Thoughts entertained earlier about a 'friendly reference' had been cast aside, and the Attorney General defended in the strongest possible terms its opinion that women could not be appointed to the Senate absent a constitutional amendment.

The Attorney General appealed to the traditional rule of interpretation: 'The courts are, of course, bound to apply the same methods of construction and exposition which they apply to other statutes of a like nature.' This meant that the words 'qualified persons' had to be given the same meaning in 1928 as they had when the BNA Act was enacted in 1867. That meaning, said the Attorney General, 'has not been extended, and cannot be influenced by, recent innovations touching the political status of women, or by the more liberal conception regarding the sphere of women in politics and social life which may, perhaps, be assumed now to prevail.' What followed was an impressive, indeed overwhelming, citation of English case law demonstrating that the common law could not abide the notion of women holding public office.

The Department of Justice had plainly left no stone unturned. The factum was the product of exhaustive legal research. Page after page, the Attorney General's submission cited and quoted from a wide range of legal authorities dating from Roman times to the present, establishing in agonizing detail centuries of the legal disability of women and their exclusion from public life. If a woman were to be put on an equal footing with a man and to escape this trap of history, there had to be a statute that said so explicitly. Murphy and her four fellow petitioners could point to no enactment that gave women the right to sit in the Senate and, therefore, the traditional common law rule prevailed. Just as Rowell tried to cast his argument in strictly legal terms, based upon the text of the BNA Act that would appeal to the staid judges, the Attorney General insisted that the petitioners' case was nothing more than an invitation for the Supreme Court to rewrite the constitution based on modern views of the role of women, and to ignore centuries of common law and the intentions of the Fathers of Confederation.

The factums were exchanged on 27 February 1928,[74] only two weeks before the case was to be argued. Rowell did not have time to read the Attorney General's factum until a few days before the hearing. When he finally did, Rowell realized the government intended to fight hard and that he faced an uphill battle. After meeting with Edwards in Ottawa to discuss another case, Rowell wrote, 'When I was in Ottawa this week I had not seen your Factum or Appendix. I have been trying to read the cases cited ever since I received it. It is a most elaborate and able Factum and indicates the argument will not be a short one, as I must endeavour to answer the formidable points raised in it.'[75]

The Attorney General of Quebec's factum added little that was new, adopting in essence the position of the federal Attorney General:

> If any such fundamental change had been contemplated as the placing of women on an equal footing with men there must certainly have been much consideration devoted to it at the time when the constitution to be provided for Canada was being settled. Certainly in the conferences leading up to the passing of the Act there never was any suggestion of such a possible change from the principle to be found in the British constitution.[76]

How, asked the Attorney General of Quebec, could 'those who having entered the married state' and thereby owed 'obedience to their husbands' exercise the powers of a senator? The Attorney General of Alberta fully adopted the petitioners' argument without injecting any distinctive Western theme.

'Purely a Matter of Law'

The Supreme Court of Canada heard the case in a single day on 14 March 1928, the day Emily Murphy turned sixty years old. Until 1946, the Court sat in dilapidated and inadequate quarters on Wellington Street, originally designed as a workshop for the construction of the Parliament buildings. In the small courtroom, fans hung from the low vaulted ceiling. There were six separate desks at the front for the judges, although as Newcombe had disqualified himself, only five judges entered when the proceedings began. The judges sat on ornate leather padded chairs in front of a carved wooden screen on top of which sat a coat of arms. In front of the judges' desks, on each side of the courtroom, there were three rows, each with a continuous narrow tilted desk and armchairs for up to eighteen counsel. Any spectators sat on the pew-like benches at the back of the room.

As the government directed the reference, Solicitor General Lucien Cannon was called upon first. It was not the first time Cannon had done battle with Newton Rowell. Cannon, a faithful Laurier Liberal, bitterly resented what he regarded as Rowell's betrayal of the party in 1917, and had frequently attacked Rowell in the House of Commons.

Cannon emphasized that the question for the court was 'purely a matter of law' and not a question of legislation. 'The whole question is a question of legal interpretation and that interpretation must be made with the guidance of the well-known principles of interpretation and also the decisions of the court in similar cases.'[76] He insisted that meant the intention of the Imperial Parliament in 1867 when the *BNA Act* was passed, not the meaning the words might have in 1928. Cannon conceded that 'the word "person" does not exclude women' and he agreed with a comment from the bench that the question to be considered was really whether women were '*qualified* persons.'

One of the judges asked Cannon to respond to Rowell's contention that the question of qualification was a matter for the Senate. Cannon replied that the Senate's powers to determine a senator's qualifications were limited to matters involving age, nationality and property. The Senate had no authority to ignore the common law: 'A person must not only be qualified in respect of the Act but they must be qualified in the common law.' Repeating the argument advanced in his factum, Cannon insisted that specific legislation was required to overcome the common law disability. It was not for the courts to imply a change in the law:

> I contend that it would be impossible to reach the conclusion that the qualifications or the privileges of the Senate of Canada could have been changed since 1867, because since that time no legislation was passed expressly changing the provisions enacted in 1867, and that unless express provisions are enacted the petitioners cannot succeed in obtaining what they seek.[78]

Eugene Lafleur, always a powerful presence before the Court, followed, with an emphasis on the tradition of the common law: 'What I contend is that in this case the petitioners have only verbal possibilities, with the whole history of the common law against the supposition.' As for French law, he added, women were considered 'remote' from holding public office. The spirit of the Attorney General's formal legal argument was captured by a pilot's comment in an article that appeared the same day in the *Toronto Daily Star* about two women on board an airplane lost on a transatlantic flight: 'A woman has no business in this long distance stuff.'[79]

Charles Lanctot, Quebec's deputy minister of justice, pointed out Quebec's special interest in the case and adopted the federal argument.

The same day Lanctot was resisting the advance of women in Ottawa, the Quebec upper house did its part by defeating a private bill that would have given married women separate rights to property and the vote in Montreal municipal elections. The Hon. J.L. Perron, minister of roads and government leader in Quebec's legislative council, insisted that women did not want rights and that there were not fifteen women in the province who favoured female suffrage.[80]

'We Are Dealing with the Charter of a Nation'

Rowell took his turn after the lunch break. For the most part, he held to the strategy of arguing the case on the basis of the language of the *BNA Act* itself. He disagreed with Lafleur's assertion 'that prima facie women are excluded from sitting in the Senate.' Properly read, the *BNA Act* yielded precisely the opposite result. 'There is nothing in the word "person" in the *BNA Act* to suggest that it is limited to male persons. The word in its natural meaning is equally applicable to female persons.' Rowell invited the Court to consider the question on the basis of the powers the act conferred. 'We are dealing with the charter of a nation,' he insisted and 'there is nothing in the *BNA Act* to suggest the necessity for any limitation or any exception in the clear wording of the Act.'[81]

Rowell invited the Court to consider 'the principle comprehended in the Act,' and appealed to the two outstanding features of the British system, the supremacy of law and the supremacy of Parliament. 'No one can assume that the imperial parliament ever intended to limit the entire freedom of the Parliament of Canada.' Parliament had the right to include women as 'persons' qualified to sit in the House of Commons under section 41 and, Rowell asked:

> If "persons" in s. 41 include women, what possible argument can be given that "persons" in s. 24 respecting qualifications for the Senate do not likewise include women ... If the Governor-General summoned a female person, otherwise qualified, to the Senate, and the Senate, exercising the powers given to it, decides she was qualified as a senator, I submit that her position as a woman could not be challenged.[82]

Any doubt on the matter was for the Senate to decide under section 33. If a woman were appointed and the Senate decided she was qualified, her position as a senator could not be challenged. Rowell was pressed by the Court: 'The argument against you is that the act does not contemplate any such situation as set out by you.' He replied: 'The British Parliament conferred power to choose persons and it had not in any way restricted the power of the executive as to who shall be chosen so far as sex is concerned.'

At one point Rowell departed from the strict legal text of his factum and urged the court to consider the needs of modern public policy: 'The Court should look at this matter from the viewpoint of public policy as it is today and not as it was fifty years ago.' This drew some fire from the bench. Justice Lamont asked, 'If public policy required change, is that not a matter for the various legislatures?' Rowell's attempt to characterize the decision of the House of Lords Privileges Committee decision to deny Viscountess Rhondda her place in the British upper house[83] as 'not the judgment of the court' did not persuade Justice Duff, who replied: 'It is the determination of the highest court in the matter, it is the report of the committee, but it is really the decision of the House of Lords itself.'

In reply, Lafleur accused Rowell of advocating 'revolutionary change' and asked: 'Does our learned friend really intend to submit that if the word "person" in s. 24 of the *BNA Act* only covered males that the act would be automatically amended because public opinion had changed since the passing of the act?' The *BNA Act* could be amended only by the Imperial Parliament, not by judicial fiat.

At the conclusion of the argument, Chief Justice Anglin thanked counsel and, as expected, announced that the Court would reserve its judgment.

6

The Supreme Court of Canada Decides

The era in which the Supreme Court of Canada decided that women were not persons has been called 'The Sterile Years'[1] because the Court's strict adherence to a narrow formalist approach to legal reasoning and interpretation rested upon purely objective principles, derived exclusively from the text of statutes and precedents. This formalist tradition refused to consider that the law should be interpreted and developed with an eye towards the social, political, and economic context in which it operated. For this reason, Newton Rowell must have realized that he would have a difficult time persuading Chief Justice Anglin and his colleagues to take the bold step of proclaiming that women were eligible for appointment to the Senate. He could not have been surprised when the Court unanimously rejected his submissions.

No one can challenge the ideal that our system of law should be as free as possible from the personal beliefs, biases, and prejudices of judges. The difficulty is that the law does not operate in a vacuum. Legal texts and legal decision-making are imbued with moral, philosophical, and social values. To pretend that the law is a purely objective, morally neutral phenomenon ignores the important questions of value that actually drive and determine decisions. Judges are human beings, not morally neutral automatons. They cannot escape their own experience nor can they cast aside their own moral and philosophical outlook. They cannot decide cases entirely on the basis of morally neutral, objective principles, and the pretence that they do conceals a significant component of judicial reasoning. Such an approach also discourages judges from reflecting upon and questioning the values they apply.

The law's treatment of women provides a classic example.[2] The common law denied women property rights and the rights to vote and to hold public office. The denial of equal treatment to women was the product of social and political forces. It was a matter of moral choice. There is nothing inherent or morally neutral about the subjection of women to inferior status, yet the formalist tradition of law protected those values and choices from scrutiny. Judges were discouraged from examining those values and choices, and were encouraged to perpetuate the inequality of women in the name of legal neutrality.

Another aspect of the formalist tradition to which the Supreme Court of the 1920s strongly adhered was the doctrine of parliamentary supremacy. The central feature of Canada's 1867 constitution was a parliamentary system of government modelled upon the principles of British parliamentary democracy. As the preamble to the *BNA Act, 1867*, states, Canada is to have 'a Constitution similar in Principle to that of the United Kingdom.' The central concept of the British constitution is the supremacy of Parliament. The role of the courts is limited to deciding cases by interpreting the law as set out by Parliament or as defined by the common law.

'We Naturally Have a Distrust of Judge-Made Law'

Justice Pierre-Basile Mignault, one of the Supreme Court judges who participated in the *Persons* case, offered a glimpse at contemporary views of the role of the judiciary when he gave a speech to the Canadian Bar Association in 1926: 'Of course, trained as we have been, we are apt to be shocked by a change in the law brought about by judicial decisions rather than by the action of the Legislature,' he exclaimed. 'We naturally have a distrust of judge-made law ... The reforming department of the State is not the Courts of Justice, but Parliament.'[3] Mignault was an outstanding scholar of Quebec civil law, a legal tradition that rests upon a codified system of law that imposes inherent limitations on judicial lawmaking. In his 1926 speech, he suggested that the recent trend of the French courts to expand the scope of civil liability had perhaps benefited from the perspective 'of the philosophy of law.' It was, he suggested, a trend more to be admired than to be imitated.[4]

Despite his training as a civilian, Mignault's views also reflected those of his colleagues trained in the common law tradition. The common law judges of the period joined their civilian counterparts in retreating behind the wall of parliamentary supremacy, unaffected by the irony that the foundation of the common law was built upon judge-made law.

There is, to be sure, a legitimate debate on the extent to which judges should shape or change the law to meet changing social problems, but to pretend that judges never change or 'make' the law is untenable. Judges have always played an important role in shaping the law. Precedents, established by judicial decisions, have created the common law that forms the backbone of our laws relating to contracts, property, civil liability for personal wrongs, much of family law and administrative law, and even important parts of our criminal law. This vast area of common law is constantly shaped and moulded by the courts to suit the changing needs of society. Although courts tend to leave it to the legislatures to make complex changes to the common law, the common law tradition nevertheless recognizes that courts must adapt and develop the common law to reflect changing social circumstances and evolving social needs.

Even when courts interpret and apply statutes enacted by Parliament, judges cannot avoid shaping the law to meet the needs of contemporary society. A court has to interpret the law before it knows whether to apply it. Statutes are not and cannot be written to decide specific cases. Legislatures cannot anticipate every eventuality nor do they have the capacity to revisit and revise every one of their laws to meet changing social conditions. Statutes merely set out the applicable general rules and principles, and leave specific cases for the courts to decide.

The law-making role of the courts is more obvious when one turns to the realm of constitutional law. Notwithstanding the statement in the preamble to the *BNA Act* that Canada was to have 'a Constitution similar in Principle to that of the United Kingdom,' Canada's Parliament and the legislatures have never been supreme. Parliamentary supremacy is practically impossible to import into a country with a partially written constitution, especially a federal system that divides legislative power between two levels of government and permits the courts to adjudicate the allocation of that power.

From the early years of Confederation, Canadian courts exercised the power of judicial review and struck down as invalid laws that did not respect the limits imposed by the *BNA Act*. Prior to the introduction of the *Charter of Rights and Freedoms* in 1982, most constitutional disagreements involved jurisdictional disputes between the federal Parliament and the provincial legislatures. The courts had the power to invalidate laws enacted by one level of government that properly fell within the legislative competence of the other level.

The *Persons* case was different; it did not involve the division of powers and the Court was not being asked to strike down a law that transgressed the limits of the constitution. The case did, however, involve an important question of constitutional interpretation. Constitutional interpretation differs from the interpretation of ordinary statutes because constitutions are intended to be permanent. For that reason, most constitutions cannot be easily amended. Because of the need for permanency, constitutions are written in terms of general principles intended to cover a range of subjects, and a significant interpretive role for judicial interpretation is almost inevitable. By the time of the *Persons* case, Canada's original constitution, which had been written in 1867, had been applied for more than half a century to problems that the Fathers of Confederation could not have imagined.

Unique circumstances made the *BNA Act* more challenging to amend than most constitutions. The act did not originally contain an amending formula, and, as we have seen, Canada's political leaders had been unable to agree on a formula to request a constitutional amendment from the British Parliament. Despite numerous attempts to secure an amending formula that would allow the Canadian Parliament to amend the constitution, only Westminster could amend the *BNA Act* until 1982.

Even with an amending formula, constitutional evolution through judicial interpretation is almost inevitable. Although the constitution is written in the language of one age, it must be interpreted and applied to meet the changing needs of every succeeding era. Its general language, crafted in 1867, did not and could not provide obvious answers to every issue that might arise in the years that followed. Yet, in the 1920s, the Supreme Court of Canada adhered to the view that words of the constitution had to be interpreted more or less according to their original meaning as understood in 1867, when the act was written. As the *Persons* case illustrates, the Supreme Court of Canada was unwilling to assume responsibility for keeping Canada's constitution abreast of the times.

'Women Are Not Eligible for Appointment by the Governor General to the Senate of Canada'

The Supreme Court of Canada took less than six week to render its decision. In keeping with the practice of the time, the judges, attired in their red and ermine trimmed robes, formally announced their judgment in open court on 28 April. The large crowd that attended to hear the result included the wives of Chief Justice Frank Anglin, Minister of Justice Ernest Lapointe, and Premier Louis-Alexandre Taschereau of Quebec. The majority judgment, written by the Chief Justice, was narrow and conventional in both tone and result.

Anglin, born in New Brunswick, was the first Roman Catholic from outside Quebec to serve on the Supreme Court of Canada. Wilfrid Laurier made the appointment in 1909, when Anglin was just forty-three years old. Fifteen years later, Mackenzie King appointed Anglin Chief Justice of Canada. Anglin spoke French well and was a handsome man, well-turned out with carefully groomed hair and moustache. He had the serious but serene countenance one would expect of someone in his position. Prior to his appointment to the bench, Anglin was a well-regarded Ontario corporate lawyer and civil litigator who was active in the Liberal Party. He actively sought his appointment to the Supreme Court of Ontario, to which he was appointed in 1904.[5]

Anglin was also something of a legal scholar, having written several articles[6] and a legal text on the subject of the limitation of actions against trustees.[7] He believed in 'scientific jurisprudence,' a late-nineteenth- and early-twentieth century version of legal formalism that conceived of the law in terms of fixed, immutable rules akin to the laws of science, discoverable from the very nature of things.[8] In 1923, Anglin explained: 'Our common object is to make the administration of justice as nearly certain and scientific as it is possible that any human institution can become.'[9] The values of order, predictability, uniformity, and permanence governed his thinking. He saw these values as inherent in the nature of law and social organization, and was unreceptive to arguments inviting legal change through judicial interpretation.

Anglin remained true to these jurisprudential views when he sat down to write his judgment in the *Persons* case, emphasizing that he was 'in no wise concerned with the desirability or the undesirability of the presence of women in the Senate, nor with any political aspect of the question submitted.'[10] He adhered strictly to what he perceived to be the letter of the constitution and the English precedents. He insisted that the words 'qualified persons' had to 'bear to-day the same construction which the courts would, if then required to pass upon them, have given to them when they were first enacted.'[11] This starting point, freezing the meaning of the constitution in terms of the prevailing norms of 1867, determined the outcome.

The Chief Justice carefully reviewed and quoted the long line of cases firmly establishing the common law rule that women lacked legal capacity to hold public office. There was little doubt that, in 1867, a court would have ruled that women could not be appointed to the Senate. Anglin was simply not prepared to question the thinking of another age to bring about 'the striking constitutional departure from the common law for which the petitioners contend.'[12]

Anglin gave short shrift to Rowell's argument based upon the ambiguity of the constitutional text and the rule of statutory interpretation that words importing the masculine should be read to include the feminine. As he explained, the power to appoint women to the Senate could not be 'conferred furtively, nor is ... it to be gathered from remote conjectures deducted from a skilful piecing together of expressions in a statute which are more or less precisely accurate.'[13] The word 'persons' was ambiguous, neither masculine nor feminine, and for that reason, the rule that the masculine imported the feminine did not apply. In the opinion of the Chief Justice, any ambiguity in the language of the constitution had to be resolved not by the political and social realities of 1928, but by the understandings of 1867. Because the appointment of women to the Senate would mark a fundamental departure from the common law norm, Anglin refused to bring it about by judicial fiat. Thus, he solemnly concluded: 'We are, for these reasons, of the opinion that women are not eligible for appointment by the Governor General to the Senate of Canada under Section 24 of the *British North America Act, 1867*, because they are not "qualified persons" within the meaning of that section.'[14]

Two members of the Court, Justices John Lamont and Robert Smith, agreed with Anglin's approach. Both men were newcomers on the Court having been appointed only a year earlier, Lamont from the Saskatchewan Court of Appeal and Smith from Ontario's Court of Appeal. Rowell might have hoped for more from Smith, on whose behalf he had written to Prime Minister Mackenzie King. In urging King to appoint Smith to the Court, Rowell had explained, 'He has been a great success as a judge and his appointment would give universal satisfaction.'[15]

Justice Pierre-Basile Mignault, a member of the Court since 1918, wrote a separate concurring opinion. He was a respected scholar and a revered authority of Quebec civil law. He had held the chair in civil law at McGill University, was a Fellow of the Royal Society of Canada, and the author of a multi-volume encyclopedia on Quebec's civil law. Although Mignault was a great civilian jurist, he was also a traditionalist who adhered very much to the letter of the law. He had no tolerance for creativity in the judiciary.

Judging from the tone of his judgment in the *Persons* case, Mingault's mechanical jurisprudence had an even sharper edge than that of Anglin. Mingault stated that petitioners' arguments 'have been conclusively rejected several times' and that it was 'hopeless to contend against the authority of these decisions.'[16] The 'grave constitutional change' of appointing women to the Senate could be accomplished only by a constitutional amendment from 'the Imperial Parliament, since that Parliament alone can change the provisions of the *British North America Act* in relation to the "qualified persons" who may be summoned to the Senate.'[17]

'A Striking Demonstration of His Traditionalism'

Justice Lyman Poore Duff wrote a separate opinion concurring in the result, but resting on different reasons. Duff was the most senior member of the Court, having been appointed from British Columbia in 1906, three years before Anglin. Regarded by the contemporary legal community as the Court's most illustrious member, Duff had expected to be appointed Chief Justice instead of Anglin. Tradition favoured the senior judge, but John Idington, the Court's most senior member, was too old and too infirm to assume the office. Duff, then fifty-nine years old, was the next most senior judge, and was widely regarded by the bar as a more distinguished jurist than Anglin.[18]

Prime Minister Mackenzie King had other ideas. He had 'tried very hard to secure' Eugene Lafleur as Chief Justice, but failed. King considered Duff to be a Tory sympathizer, a suspicion that may have been fuelled by suggestions from time to time that Duff should consider running for political office.[19] King recognized that Duff 'was probably abler,' and he knew that the profession preferred him, but he had been told that Duff had a drinking problem. King decided to appoint Anglin, whom he described as 'narrow, has not a pleasant manner, is very vain, but industrious steady and honest, a true liberal at heart.'[20]

The legal community was displeased and the ensuing relationship between Duff and Anglin was described as 'frosty.'[21] Duff eventually assumed the office of Chief Justice when Anglin retired for health reasons in 1933. Duff served well beyond the age of retirement, which was fixed at seventy-five in 1927 when the number of judges increased from six to seven.[22] Thanks to special wartime legislation, Duff's tenure was extended to 1944.[23]

In his extra-judicial writings, Duff described the exercise of constitutional interpretation in grand, liberal terms. In a 1915 speech to the Canadian Bar Association, he described the law 'as a living organism, possessing like every living organism, within limits of course, the power to adapt itself to changing circumstances.'[24] There are passages in his *Persons* case opinion that echo this refrain but, in the end, Duff could not bring himself to reach a result that was any different than that of Anglin and Mignault. He explained that the word 'persons' in section 24 of the *BNA Act*, in the ordinary sense of the word, could include both male and female persons. To discern their proper legal meaning, words should be interpreted having regard to 'the context in which they are found as well as by the occasion on which they are used.' This meant interpreting 'persons' in light of other provisions in the act, as well as 'the state of the law at the time the enactment was passed, and to the history, especially the legislative history, of the subjects with which the enactment deals.'[25]

Duff also disagreed with the suggestion that the case could be resolved 'upon a general presumption against the eligibility of women for legal office,'[26] or a 'presumptive exclusion of women from participation in the institutions set up under the Act.'[27] The constitution rested on no such presumption because Parliament and the legislatures had the authority to enfranchise women and to empower women to hold public office and sit in legislatures across Canada. It would be 'incongruous,' he wrote,

> if persons fully qualified to be members of the House of Commons were by an iron rule of the constitution ... excluded from the Cabinet or the Government; if a class of persons who might reach any position of political influence, power or leadership in the House of Commons, were permanently, by an organic rule, excluded from the Government.[28]

Reading this far, the reader could be forgiven for anticipating a strong and courageous dissent, endorsing the right of women to take their place in the Senate. But Duff's judgment takes a sudden and unexpected lurch towards the 'framers' intention' approach favoured by the majority as it reaches the concluding paragraphs. Like his colleagues, Duff could not escape the historical legal subjugation of women. The Senate was modelled on the pre-Confederation colonial second chambers. As he saw it, 'the *British North America Act* contemplated a second Chamber, the constitution of which should, in all respects, be fixed and determined by the Act itself, a constitution which was to be in principle the same, though, necessarily, in detail, not identical, with that of the [pre-Confederation] second Chambers.'[29] Little if any reason was offered to justify this conclusion, but it determined the outcome. It was beyond question that women were excluded from those pre-Confederation second chambers and, in Duff's view, so too must they be excluded from the Senate. Despite the lofty language of its opening paragraphs, Duff's opinion was every bit as circumscribed as that of Anglin and Mignault by an insistence upon narrowly interpreting the words of the constitution as having a meaning that was fixed and frozen in time.

Many regard Duff as a great judge, but even his sympathetic biographer concedes that his judgment in the *Persons* case was disappointing and 'a striking demonstration of his traditionalism.'[30] Despite Duff's grand extra-judicial pronouncements about the law as a living organism, capable of adaptation and change, his 'view of the law as a "social instrument" had no application to the field of constitutional law, and limited application in other fields. His declarations from the bench somehow fell short of those uttered elsewhere.'[31]

Duff concluded his opinion by suggesting that perhaps the entire matter should have been left for the Senate to decide under section 33 of the *BNA Act*.[32] However, as there was no concrete case for the Senate to decide, and the Court's opinion on a reference was purely advisory, Duff concluded that the Court was bound to give the government its advice. In any event, he added, even if the matter were open for the Senate to decide, there was no harm in offering the Court's advice as 'we must assume that the Senate would decide in accordance with the law.'[33] Such an aside virtually compelled the Senate to agree with the Court should it ever be faced with the question.

Modern legal scholars regard the Supreme Court's decision as the 'hopelessly flawed' product of 'years of sterile, mechanical thinking,'[34] a decision that 'still has to be lived down.'[35] Yet the Supreme Court's judgment caused nary a ripple in Canada's legal community, which seemed to have regarded the result as inevitable.[36]

'Why Should a Group of Men in 1867 Govern the Actions of the Men and Women of 1928?'

While most legal experts regarded the Supreme Court's reasoning as correct in law, public opinion was mixed. Many regarded the result as absurd. Editorial writers at the *Ottawa Evening Journal* ridiculed the judgment: 'It looks as though Bumble ["the law is an Ass"] was right.'[37] The Ontario Women's Liberal Association, meeting in Toronto, was outraged by the decision and declared the Supreme Court's pronouncement to be 'manifestly unjust to a large proportion of the electorate of the Dominion.'[38] Grace Hunter, who had gone to Ottawa to hear the argument, declared: 'I knew this would happen.' Mrs Gilbert McIntyre, the widow of the late deputy speaker of the House of Commons, wanted more, exclaiming: 'We have to change that ruling and become persons. We should have women on the Supreme Court anyway.'[39] Agnes Macphail, the lone female member of the House of Commons, wondered why the views of the Fathers of Confederation should prevail: 'Why should a group of men in 1867 govern the actions of the men and women of 1928?'[40]

Others accepted the Court's decision as legally correct, if wrong in result. The *Edmonton Bulletin* argued, 'To admit women to the Commons but to bar them from the Senate would be absurd.' However, the paper accepted that the courts were bound to interpret and to apply the constitution according to the intentions of its framers: 'Women in parliament was probably one thing that the "fathers" never thought about.'[41] The Montreal *Gazette* observed that as a matter of law there was 'no doubt' as to the 'soundness' of the Supreme Court's decision because those who wrote and drafted the legislation had intended 'to provide for the appointment of men only to the Senate, and as the law was then, so it remains today.'[42] Editorial writers at the Ottawa *Citizen* cautioned: 'Nothing could be sillier than to grow sarcastic or indignant' over the Court's decision. The law was 'unjust and absurd' to exclude women from the Senate, but laws had to mean today what they meant when they were enacted in 1867, and the Court had no choice but to decide the matter as it did. Nevertheless, the editorial board thought the law should be changed, and concluded: 'The women of Canada can rest assured that their fellow citizens have no wish to debar them from the doubtful distinction of being eligible for "elevation" to the Upper Chamber.'[43]

'Means Will Be Taken to Secure an Amendment to the *British North America Act*'

The same day the Supreme Court released its judgment, A.W. Neill, an Independent member of Parliament from British Columbia, asked Ernest Lapointe, the minister of justice, how the government intended to respond to the Court's ruling. Lapointe was obviously ready for the question and explained that the Court's decision was based upon the legal proposition that the words of the *BNA Act* had to be interpreted to mean what they had meant in 1867.

> In view of this judgment, and in view of the fact that women in this country now have an equal franchise with men, and in view of the further fact that one of the seats in this house is occupied by a woman, the government have decided that they should have the equal right to sit in the other chamber, and means will be taken to secure an amendment to the *British North America Act* in that respect.[44]

Lapointe's announcement was greeted with relief and joy at the meeting of the Ontario Women's Liberal Association, where it had been noted that R.B. Bennett, the new leader of the Conservative Party, had recently promised to appoint women to the Senate. Grace Hunter, who had protested the ruling the day before, expressed satisfaction with the minister's announcement. 'In 1923 when the minister of justice decided women could not sit in the senate, we were nobody's darlings, and today we are getting bouquets from both sides.'[45]

'We Must Keep Up the Fight, You Know'

Emily Murphy was gracious in defeat, perhaps because she was confident that it was a temporary setback. She told Henrietta Muir Edwards that although the Supreme Court's decision was regrettable, 'I am sure we are agreed that their decision was a sincere one and should not be adversely criticized by any of us.'[46] But she was far from resigned. As she explained to William Deacon, 'We must keep up the fight, you know. It may not be for awhile but, ultimately, we are going to succeed.'[47] Publicly, Murphy embraced 'with deep gratification' Justice

Minister Lapointe's announcement that the government intended to amend the constitution. She explained that she thought Canadians were, for the most part, in harmony with the government's position 'irrespective of class, creed, party or sex.'[48] She noted, with a certain amount of pride, that 'the discussion of this vitally important question has been kept on the highest ground at all times and at no time has it become a matter of patronage or partisanship. Neither have recriminations nor any spirit of bitterness been permitted to cloud the issue.'[49]

Privately, however, Murphy was alarmed by the prospect of a public debate on the appointment of women to the Senate. She had lost confidence in the politicians and believed her cause would be lost if it were put to a vote in Parliament: 'It would have been calamitous to our cause in my opinion. I did not want the Government to vote on the question at all as I had excellent reasons for believing it would be defeated in the Canadian Parliament even as it was previously in the highest court in Canada.' Murphy was convinced that victory could only be secured outside the country. 'I wanted to appeal it to the Privy Council,'[50] she explained.

Murphy's fears were shared by an editorial writer at the Ottawa *Citizen*, who warned that while a resolution to amend the *BNA Act* might pass the Commons, 'it is a matter of considerable doubt whether the Senate, relishing the prospect of having women in their midst, would concur in the proposition.'[51] By the same token, as Toronto's *Globe* reminded its readers, an appeal to the Privy Council would be heard by men drawn from the House of Lords that only six years earlier had rejected Viscountess Rhondda's attempt to take up her hereditary seat in the House of Lords.[52]

Emily Murphy decided it was time to convene another meeting of the Famous Five, and the women gathered in Calgary to discuss strategy. Nellie McClung described Murphy, who was determined to appeal to the Privy Council, as 'still undaunted.'[53] Because the case 'was every woman's concern,' Murphy was confident that 'the Government would be glad to have it settled.'[54] Once again, Emily Murphy drafted the petition that all five women signed.[55] She told her colleagues that an appeal to the Privy Council should not be taken 'as in anywise expressing a lack of confidence in the determination' of the King government to seek an amendment, but only that we 'can have no certainty that the exigencies of politics or the dissent of one or more of the Provinces may not preclude the possibility of such amendment.'[56]

At the end of July 1928, Murphy sent Deputy Minister of Justice W.

Stuart Edwards her request that the government permit the appeal of the Supreme Court's judgment to the Judicial Committee of the Privy Council. She advised Edwards that 'from a close study' of the Supreme Court's judgment, it was 'apparent' that the Court had decided the reference 'upon things extraneous, or upon matters or circumstances not found within the *British North America Act* itself.' The government, she asserted, had insisted upon asking the Court whether or not the word 'person' meant a female person. Murphy reverted to the technical argument that her brother William had developed: by virtue of the *Interpretation Act*, the word 'person' must be construed to include both sexes because no contrary intent was shown. 'Any question which might arise as to the qualification of a Senator is for the Senate to deal with' as provided in the *BNA Act*. Murphy complained that the Supreme Court had answered the wrong question. The judges had gone outside the text of the act to interpret the word 'qualified.' According to Murphy, 'this is not and was not the point at issue so that, accordingly, our question remains unanswered both in fact and effect.'[57]

The government quickly agreed to have the case proceed to the Judicial Committee. Leaving the courts to resolve the issue would alleviate any political pressure that had been created by Lapointe's promise to amend the constitution. Within two weeks, Edwards advised Murphy that the Department of Justice would not oppose the appeal. The department would also 'make reasonable provision to meet the fees and expenses of counsel to argue the case on behalf of the petitioners.'[58] Because the government had won the case before the Supreme Court, it was up to the petitioners to apply for special leave to the Privy Council. However, Stuart Edwards immediately advised the government's solicitor in London that 'the Attorney General of Canada desires to facilitate the proposed appeal' and instructed him to retain counsel who would 'appear on the application and intimate to the Judicial Committee that the Dominion does not oppose the application. The question at issue obviously is one of considerable constitutional importance.'[59] Murphy forwarded Edwards' letter to Rowell, who had already told her that he was willing to carry on with the case if the government would agree to pay his fees and expenses.[60]

Once the government agreed to support the appeal, Murphy drafted another petition insisting that any steps to amend the constitution should be put on hold until after the Privy Council rendered its decision. This one was signed by Edwards, McClung, McKinney, and Murphy, but not Parlby who was travelling in England. Murphy's petition frankly disclosed her misgivings about what might happen if the matter were left to the politicians. Here, no doubt, Murphy and the Liberal government were on common ground – both preferred to let the courts decide rather than risk a messy political fight. She explained that while Lapointe's proposed constitutional amendment was 'just and favorable,' the Privy Council should be allowed to rule on the matter before the issue was discussed at the political level. If the Privy Council were to rule in favour of the admission of women to the Senate, 'your petitioners feel that much sectional, political and sex animosity must be allayed thereby in that the question would not of necessity be discussed in either the Canadian House of Commons or in the Canadian Senate.'[61]

Murphy also decided to push the Department of Justice to pay for a second counsel for the appeal. She nominated J. Boyd McBride, an Edmonton lawyer with whom she had discussed 'every aspect of our case' and who had 'been unstinting in the time and work which he has devoted to our case.'[62] McBride, a Scot who had been called to the bar in 1912 after graduating from the University of Alberta, practised in Lacombe and in Edmonton. He was later appointed to the Supreme Court of Alberta in 1944. Murphy argued that it was important 'to have a Western lawyer, who has the viewpoint of the Western Women of Canada and of the individual Appellants (the latter all being residents of Alberta).'[63] If, as Murphy suggested, McBride had worked on the case, one can understand why he would relish a trip to London and the chance to appear before the Privy Council. McBride hoped that the apparent policy of the government 'to meet all requests of the women of Canada as represented by the Petitioners, and to afford them all assistance within reason' meant that he would get the brief.[64] When Charles Stewart, the minister for the interior, visited Edmonton, Murphy 'pressed very strongly' to have McBride appointed as junior counsel. At Murphy's urging, Stewart asked Edwards to respond favourably.[65]

Not surprisingly, Edwards was completely unsympathetic. He told Murphy that while the minister was willing to do all that could be reasonably done to bring the case before the Privy Council, 'the expense of sending a Canadian junior to London with Mr. Rowell can hardly be justified.' Eugene Lafleur would be arguing the case without a junior, and Rowell had not asked for one. 'There is nothing involved in this case introducing questions of Western law as differing from Eastern law, the fact being that the case for the appellants can be as well stated by good counsel whether he happens to reside in Montreal or Vancouver,' [66] he explained.

Murphy, no doubt gratified by the government's cooperation on the application for special leave and the Privy Council's quick decision in mid-November to hear the case,[67] and aware that Rowell certainly did not require the assistance of a junior from Alberta, graciously accepted the government's refusal to pay for McBride.[68]

7

The Judicial Committee of the Privy Council and the Canadian Constitution

The Judicial Committee of the Privy Council – also known as the JCPC – was Canada's court of last resort until 1949. This august imperial institution, one of the last vestiges of Canada's colonial past, served as the final judicial arbiter for legal disputes throughout the Empire and played a pivotal role in Canada's constitutional evolution for more than eighty years. Scholars still debate the merits of the Judicial Committee's influence on Canada's constitutional arrangements.[1] In the seemingly unending string of jurisdictional disputes between Canada's Parliament and the provinces, the Judicial Committee favoured provincial autonomy at the expense of Ottawa. Provincial rights advocates, especially those from Quebec, praised the Privy Council for preserving provincial autonomy. Centralists, however, believed that the Fathers of Confederation had intended to create a powerful federal government, yet in its interpretation of the provisions of the *British North America Act*, the Privy Council had ignored the framers' intent.

By 1929, the JCPC was the source of growing frustration among most English Canadian constitutional scholars.[2] They believed that the Privy Council had ignored the intentions of Canada's centralist founders when it curtailed the federal government's powers, thereby distorting, even thwarting, Canada's constitutional arrangements. Although the issue Emily Murphy and her four colleagues raised did not involve the division of powers between Parliament and the provinces, if Newton Rowell could persuade the JCPC to ignore the original meaning of 'persons' in section 24 of the *BNA Act* as it had done so regularly when dealing with the division of powers, the Famous Five might just win their case.

The Role of the Judicial Committee (JCPC)

Although the Judicial Committee served as Canada's highest court until 1949, it was not, strictly speaking, a court of law. Rather, it was (and continues to be) an advisory body to the sovereign who, in the British legal tradition, is the fountain of all justice under the constitution. The sovereign receives petitions from all corners of the British Empire demanding the justice of the Crown, and the JCPC advises the sovereign on the proper disposition of these petitions.

Parliament created the Judicial Committee in 1833 to deal with these petitions or appeals which, until then, had actually been brought before the King in Council.[3] Viscount Richard Haldane, who had argued many cases before the Judicial Committee as a barrister and later presided over it as Lord Chancellor, grandly stated: 'This is the supreme tribunal of the Empire, and every subject of the King-Emperor is entitled to go in.'[4]

In keeping with their roles as advisors, judges of the JCPC do not issue judgments but rather report on recommendations to the Crown. That advice is tendered at a formal meeting of the entire Privy Council where it is received by the sovereign and embodied in an Order in Council. As a consequence, a sitting of the JCPC has none of the formal trappings of English courts.

The JCPC never sat with the other courts in Westminster Hall or at the Royal Courts of Justice in the Strand but rather in the Council Chamber at the corner of Downing Street and Whitehall. The Council Chamber looks more like a corporate boardroom or a university hall than the typical courtroom. It is roughly twenty-five metres in length and width, with a very high ceiling and three large windows on each side, and is panelled in wood. The judges enter at the far end of the room, between two large fireplaces and beneath the royal coat of arms that sits over the door. Sandwiched between the door and the bench is a table upon which the books and papers for the day's cases are placed. Around the room are portraits of JCPC luminaries.

The advisory nature of the JCPC stands in contrast to the austere majesty of the room and the solemnity of the argument of an appeal before the Empire's highest tribunal. Underscoring its role is the placement of the judges and counsel in close proximity, seated in the centre of the room within an area enclosed by a wooden railing. Litigants are seated at the side and there is seating for the public at the rear, though no more than about a dozen places. The judges, at least three but usually five, are dressed in suits, not gowns or wigs, and sit at a horseshoe-shaped table of oak facing the lawyers and clients. By tradition, one chair is left vacant; as Viscount Haldane explained, the empty chair exists 'for a very highly constitutional reason – the Sovereign is supposed to come and sit there, and dispense justice to the whole Empire.'[5] The judges are not seated on an elevated dais but at the same level as counsel, who address the JCPC from a lectern in the centre.

Despite the absence of the usual judicial trappings, the proceedings are conducted as any other judicial proceeding with one important exception. As the purpose of the proceedings is to provide advice to the sovereign, the Judicial Committee speaks with one voice. 'If any Judge were to say that he had not agreed with his colleagues, the sword of the Constitution would descend upon him,'[6] Viscount Haldane told an audience in 1923. If JCPC members disagree, those differences remain hidden from public view because their advice is given unanimously.

Almost from the moment of its creation in 1833, the role and function of the Judicial Committee of the Privy Council was the subject of vigorous debate. Some thought the imperial ambitions for the JCPC could best be fulfilled if it assumed general appellate jurisdiction for the United Kingdom as well as the colonies. Others argued that role should be assumed by the House of Lords and that the JCPC was not required.[7]

Just as the original four colonies of British North America came together in 1867 to form Canada, the United Kingdom entered a period of significant constitutional reform. The 1867 *Reform Act* expanded suffrage to bring the vote to the working classes. Calls for legal reform became louder. The archaic and disfunctional dual court structure that divided law from equity was the product of inefficiency and unfairness, brilliantly depicted to the lay public in the 1850s by Charles Dickens' *Bleak House* and its portrait of endless litigation in the case of *Jarndyce v. Jarndyce*.

In 1869, a Royal Commission on the Judicature recommended the fusion of law and equity, and with it, the creation of a new Court of Appeal.[8] The appellate jurisdiction of the Privy Council and the House of Lords was outside this commission's mandate, but in 1872, another committee proposed to transfer the Judicial Committee's jurisdiction to the House of Lords, where the Lord Chancellor and four salaried judges, known as 'Lords of Appeal,' would hear appeals.[9] In late 1872, Lord Selborne, the new Liberal Lord Chancellor and long-time advocate of appellate reform, introduced the Judicature Bill to abolish the appellate jurisdiction of the House of Lords and to create a Supreme Court, composed of a High Court and a Court of Appeal. The proposed Court of Appeal, from which there would be no further appeal, would have nine permanent members and would eventually assume the appellate jurisdiction of both the House of Lords and the Judicial Committee. The bill received Royal Assent in August 1873, and was scheduled to come into force in November 1874.[10] Reform efforts then hit a snag.

In February 1874, the Liberal government of William Gladstone fell. Prime Minister Disraeli opposed reforming the House of Lords, but his new Lord Chancellor, Lord Cairns, enthusiastically supported the reforms of the previous government.[11] In late 1876, Lord Cairns proposed a compromise. The appellate jurisdiction of the House of Lords would be restored and the Judicial Committee of the Privy Council would sit as a separate judicial body throughout the year in its own courtroom. Law Lords would be salaried and chosen from either the superior courts or professional bars in England, Scotland and Ireland. They could sit in either the House of Lords or the JCPC and would serve as peers for the duration of their appointment. Others eligible for service in the House of Lords or Judicial Committee included past and present holders of high judicial office.[12] The resulting legislation, the *Appellate Jurisdiction Act*, included most of Lord Cairns' proposals and passed with little difficulty in 1876.[13] It is this act that governed the appellate jurisdiction of the House of Lords and, by extension, the Judicial Committee of the Privy Council in 1929 when the *Persons* case was argued.

The JCPC was, first and foremost, an imperial institution. As the British Empire grew, so did the JCPC's workload, and as the backlog of cases mounted, so too did requests for more judges. By 1870, the JCPC had developed a significant build-up of cases, and the Parliament at Westminster responded with various efforts to alleviate the burden. By 1887, the number of people eligible to sit on the JCPC increased to include four Lords of Appeal, six judges of the Court of Appeal, numerous English privy counsellors who held or had held judicial offices, two judges from former colonies, one judge from India, and one judge from another of the Dominions.[14] Later, Westminster allowed the Chief Justice or any Justice from the High Courts of Australia and Newfoundland to participate in Judicial Committee adjudication.[15]

With the dawn of the twentieth century came renewed interest in the idea of a single, unified Imperial Court of Appeal. The Court would have jurisdiction over all appeals within Britain and the Empire, eliminating the need for the Judicial Committee and the judicial role of the House of Lords.[16] A conference to discuss such a court was held in 1901, but the meeting was mired in such logistical concerns that the creation of an Imperial Court of Appeal proved impossible.[17] Ten years later, during the Imperial Conference of 1911, the British government pledged to improve appeals to the JCPC, adding two more Lords of Appeal.[18] Two years later, the new Lord Chancellor, Richard Haldane, increased the number of colonial judges from five to seven and the number of Lords of Appeal from four to six.[19]

These increased judicial resources and additional representation did not satisfy all the Dominions, including Canada. Appeals to the Privy Council were expensive and, even with additional colonial representation, few of the judges who heard Canadian cases had any familiarity with Canada.[20] Although there was little enthusiasm within the Empire for a unified Imperial Court of Appeal, Viscount Haldane remained a strong proponent, and in July 1917, he chaired a committee on the machinery of government that recommended such a court. This proposal, like so many before, came to nothing.[21] Prime Minister Borden and Justice Minister Doherty opposed the idea on the ground that the conditions in Canada and other parts of the Empire were so diverse as to preclude the 'uniformity of jurisprudence throughout the Empire' as a desirable goal.[22] Despite Haldane's efforts, the Judicial Committee that heard the *Persons* case was an institution with declining support in Canada and in other parts of the British Empire.[23]

Discomfort and dissatisfaction aside, business was booming for the Judicial Committee. In 1913, it heard 92 cases over a period of 124 days. During the same period, the House of Lords heard 64 appeals in 115 days.[24] By 1917, the House of Lords heard 47 cases over 110 days and the JCPC heard 116 appeals over 164 days. Three years later, the war now over, the Privy Council heard 142 appeals over the course of 175 days.[25] Through the 1920s, appeals before the JCPC became more time-consuming, just like those in the House of Lords. Parliament introduced changes to help the courts cope with the workload, increasing the number of Lords of Appeal from six to seven in 1929.[26]

When the Judicial Committee heard the *Persons* case in the summer of 1929, it heard eleven appeals over twenty-four days from four Dominions and colonies. All but two of these appeals took more than a day of argument and all but three came from Canada. Most were heard in panels of five, though a few – including one patent case from Canada – were heard by panels of three.

Few Canadian judges had enjoyed the distinction of an appointment to the Judicial Committee. In 1897, the practice developed of appointing the Chief Justice of Canada, then the Right Honourable Sir Samuel Henry Strong. However, in 1919, Justice Lyman Poore Duff, the long-serving member of Canada's Supreme Court, was appointed to the Judicial Committee as the only puisne judge of the Supreme Court to sit on the British Empire's highest tribunal. During the 1920s, Duff shared this honour with then Chief Justice of Canada, Frank Anglin. The two took turns sitting on the JCPC in alternate years, and in the summer of 1929, it was Duff who travelled to London to hear appeals to the Judicial Committee. Having sat on the case in the Supreme Court of Canada, Duff obviously could not hear the *Persons* case. Instead, the appeal was heard by a panel of five: the newly appointed Lord Chancellor John Sankey, a retired English trial judge, two sitting English judges, and a retired Indian colonial judge.

The Judicial Committee and Canada's Constitution

By the time the *Persons* case came before the JCPC, many Canadian lawyers and legal scholars not only expressed concern about its interpretation of the division of powers under the *BNA Act* but also asked more fundamental questions about the basic role of the Privy Council. Chief Justice Anglin, the author of the Supreme Court's majority opinion in the *Persons* case, had been openly critical of the Privy Council and its decisions. In 1923, before he became Chief Justice, Anglin took the unusual step of adding the weight of his Supreme Court office to urge the abolition of appeals to the Privy Council, stating that if his court 'was the Supreme Court in name,' then 'it should be the Supreme Court in fact.'[27]

Anglin was not alone in his disapproval of the Privy Council and its interpretation of Canada's 1867 constitution. In a series of post-war constitutional decisions, the JCPC with Viscount Haldane at its helm gave restricted meaning to federal powers in favour of provincial autonomy.[28] In 1921, the Judicial Committee narrowly interpreted the federal power to legislate in relation to 'trade and commerce' and 'peace, order and good government.' Centralists argued that the Fathers of Confederation gave Parliament the 'trade and commerce' power so that the Dominion would have broad power to regulate the national economy and the 'peace, order and good government power' to deal with matters of national concern. The Privy Council thought otherwise. Fearing that a generous interpretation of 'trade and commerce' and the residual 'peace, order and good government' clauses would swallow areas of responsibility that it thought fell more properly to the provinces under 'property and civil rights' and 'matters of a merely local or private nature in the province,' the Privy Council insisted on curtailing federal jurisdiction. The argument that the Fathers of Confederation had intended the opposite result fell on deaf ears.

In the 1921 *Board of Commerce* case,[29] two closely related federal statutes were at issue: the *Combines and Fair Prices Act*[30] and the *Board of Commerce Act*.[31] The former regulated the investigation and prohibition of combines – monopolies – while the latter established a board of commissioners to administer the act.[32] The Supreme Court of Canada had been evenly divided over whether the legislation was constitutional, but the Judicial Committee did not share the Court's hesitation. Viscount Haldane[33] decided in November 1921 that Parliament had overreached its constitutional grasp when it tried to justify this antitrust regime as the regulation of trade and commerce or the exercise of residual power to legislate for the peace, order, and good government of Canada, the 'POGG' power. Parliament might be able to legislate in areas of provincial jurisdiction in 'highly exceptional circumstances,' for example to meet special conditions of war, but this was not such an occasion.[34] The legislation had been passed 'after peace had been declared' and had no geographic or temporal limit.[35] Viscount Haldane insisted that it was only in times 'of war or famine, when the peace, order and good government of the Dominion might be imperiled under conditions so exceptional that they require legislation of a character in reality beyond anything provided for by the enumerated heads in either sec. 92 or sec. 91 itself' that Parliament could rely on POGG. Haldane stressed the narrowness of the residual power, which, in his words, had 'always been applied with reluctance, and its recognition as relevant can be justified only after scrutiny sufficient to render it clear that the circumstances are abnormal.'[36]

Two years later, in *Fort Frances Pulp and Paper Co. v. Manitoba Free Press Co.*[37] the Judicial Committee continued to limit the residual power of POGG to emergency situations. The JCPC upheld the Dominion's authority to regulate the prices and distribution of paper, but only for so long as the effects of the war remained. According to Viscount Haldane, the Dominion could not enact this type of legislation 'in normal circumstances,' but war was a threat to national survival and, as such, called for a certain amount of constitutional latitude:

> In the event of war, when the national life may require for its preservation the employment of very exceptional means, the provision of peace, order and good government for the country as a whole may involve effort on behalf of the whole nation, in which the interests of individuals may have to be subordinated to that of the community in a fashion which requires sec. 91 to be interpreted as providing for such an emergency.[38]

By the mid-1920s, with Viscount Haldane still leading the charge, any chance for an expansive approach to the Dominion's authority under the division of powers appeared to be lost. The coup de grace came in 1925 when the Judicial Committee rejected an attempt to justify federal labour legislation under POGG in *Toronto Electric Commissioners v. Snider*.[39] The *Industrial Disputes Investigation Act*[40] required that labour disputes relating to public utilities be referred to a three-person board of conciliation before a strike or lockout could be declared. The issue was whether a federal statute could regulate employment in this manner. In the Ontario Appellate Division, Justice William Ferguson – Emily Murphy's brother – wrote the majority opinion. Ferguson took an expansive approach to the Dominion's authority in relation to trade and commerce, criminal law and peace, order and good government, arguing that the industrial age had transformed labour relations and labour disputes from mere local matters to issues of national import with interconnections between trade and public order requiring the attention of the national government.[41]

In January 1925, the Privy Council reversed Ferguson's opinion. Again, Viscount Haldane wrote the decision. Once more he insisted that the Dominion's residual power had to be strictly limited. The provinces had the authority to regulate industrial relations, and many provinces had already done so. Viscount Haldane rejected the Dominion's claim that issues of local importance could become matters of national significance and thus evolve into an issue properly within federal jurisdiction. He also dismissed the intentions of the Fathers of Confederation with a dash of his pen, marking the final transformation of a broad residual power into a narrow slip of authority to be used only in emergencies. Viscount Haldane warned, 'The circumstance that the dispute might spread to other Provinces was not enough in itself to justify Dominion interference, if such interference affected property and civil rights.'[42]

Richard Haldane faced a significant obstacle when it came to restricting POGG to emergency situations. *Russell v. The Queen*,[43] a nineteenth-century judgment of the Privy Council, upheld federal temperance legislation under the residual power. Having restricted POGG to situations of 'extraordinary peril to the national life of Canada as a whole,'[44] Haldane explained away *Russell* on the basis 'that the evil of intemperance at that time amounted in Canada to one so great and so general that at least for the period it was a menace to the national life of Canada so serious and pressing that the National Parliament was called on to intervene to protect the nation from disaster.'[45]

No doubt staunch proponents of temperance such as Lousie McKinney and Nellie McClung agreed with Haldane's assessment of the perils of drink, but for many, including Anglin, the Lord Chancellor's portrayal of colonial drunkenness as a national emergency was risible. While some authors praised Viscount Haldane's judgment for clarifying the constitutional status of liquor, and others hoped the decision would stabilise relations between the Dominion and the provinces more generally in matters of constitutional affairs, most constitutional experts were critical.[46]

In 1925, Anglin took the unusual step of ridiculing Viscount Haldane's reasoning in a judgment he wrote that sought to regain some of the Dominion's lost ground. In *Canada v. Eastern Terminal Elevator Co.*,[47] Anglin asserted Canadian national pride to refute the argument that drunkenness could ever have reached the state of emergency: 'I should be surprised if a body so well-informed as their Lordships had countenanced such an aspersion on the fair fame of Canada even though some hard-driven advocate had ventured to insinuate it in argument.'[48] A Canadian Bar Association editorial congratulated the Chief Justice 'on his moderate and courteously worded but withal intrepid defence of the character of the Canadian people at the time in question.'[49]

The Chief Justice of Canada was not the only one to criticize the Privy Council's ruling in *Snider*. In 1926, Professor Herbert Smith of McGill University published an article in the *Canadian Bar Review* attacking the decision.[50] Smith's complaint was simple: because the

Privy Council refused to consider parliamentary debates to determine the meaning of the *BNA Act* – 'the courts are forbidden to adopt historical methods in solving a historical problem'[51] – the JCPC had fundamentally misinterpreted the meaning of the residuary power provision of the Canadian constitution. He argued that

> an arbitrary and unreasonable rule of interpretation has produced the very serious result of giving Canada a constitution substantially different from that which her founders intended that she should have ... A study of the available historical evidence gives us a clear and definite idea of what the fathers of Canadian confederation sought to achieve.[52]

For Smith, the Judicial Committee's interpretation of the *BNA Act* had undermined the framers' intentions: 'By excluding this historical evidence and considering the *British North America Act* without any regard to its historical setting the courts have recently imposed upon us a constitution which is different, not only in detail but also in principle, from that designed at Charlottetown and Quebec.'[53] *Snider* was merely one example in which the Judicial Committee 'definitely relegated the words "peace, order and good government" to the position of a reserve power to be used only in cases of war or similar national emergencies.' He reasoned that the provinces, not the Dominion, now held the true residuary power. 'The real residuary power of legislation in normal times is now held to be contained in the words "property and civil rights," with regard to which the legislative power of the provinces is exclusive,' Smith explained. 'The specific powers enunciated in section 91 are to be treated as exceptions to the general jurisdiction of the provinces to legislate upon property and civil rights.'[54] Haldane's approach to constitutional interpretation, according to Smith, was simply wrong headed. 'I do not think that it is going too far to say,' he concluded, 'that this result is the precise opposite of that which our fathers hoped and endeavoured to attain.'[55]

In early 1926, the Judicial Committee struck yet another blow to federal authority that also implicated Canadian autonomy. In February of that year, the Privy Council rejected a provision of the Canadian *Criminal Code* that abolished appeals to the JCPC. *Nadan v. The King*[56] was the last significant constitutional decision by the imperial court before the *Persons* case was heard in the summer of 1929. Originating in Alberta, the case involved prosecution under federal and provincial liquor legislation. The issue was whether Parliament had the power to enact section 1025 of the *Criminal Code*, which purported to remove the right of appeal to the Privy Council in criminal cases.[57] Lord Chancellor Cave, on behalf of the JCPC, determined that the section was *ultra vires* because it contravened both the *Judicial Committee Acts* of 1833[58] and 1844,[59] as well as the *Colonial Laws Validity Act* of 1865.[60] The Parliament in Ottawa could limit criminal appeals within Canada, but had no authority to interfere with the powers of the imperial tribunal or His Majesty's prerogative rights.

The Lord Chancellor emphasized the important protections provided by the royal prerogative, including appellate jurisdiction: 'The practice of invoking the exercise of the royal prerogative by way of appeal from any Court in His Majesty's Dominions has long obtained throughout the British Empire,' and, he wrote, had 'ripened into a privilege belonging to every subject of the King.'[61] Acknowledging the breadth of authority conferred upon Parliament in relation to criminal law and peace, order and good government, Lord Cave explained that 'however widely these powers are construed they are confined to action to be taken in the Dominion; and they do not appear to their Lordships to authorize the Dominion Parliament to annul the prerogative right of the King in Council to grant special leave to appeal.'[62]

The *Nadan* decision, like *Snider*, provoked an uproar in Canada. Chief Justice Anglin appealed to national pride when he urged Prime Minister Mackenzie King to abolish Privy Council appeals in *all* cases, not just criminal ones: 'My Canadianism leads me to the opinion that we should finally settle our litigation in this country. If we are competent to make our own laws, we are, or should be, capable of interpreting and administering them.'[63] Newton Rowell also wrote to the prime minister, describing the Privy Council's ruling as 'startling and reactionary,'[64] and to Justice Minister Ernest Lapointe complaining that the ruling 'ignores the constitutional developments of the past twenty-five years.'[65]

When the Imperial Conference convened in the autumn of 1926, Canada and the other Dominions discussed precisely what Anglin had suggested: whether to abolish all appeals to the Judicial Committee of the Privy Council. There was no consensus, but the groundwork was laid for those Dominions that wished to do so. British authorities made clear that they had no wish to shackle the Dominions to the Privy Council. As the report of the Conference recounted: 'It became clear that it was no part of the policy of His Majesty's Government in Great Britain that questions affecting judicial appeals should be determined otherwise than in accordance with the wishes of the part of the Empire primarily affected.'[66]

With imperial legal ties unravelling, the future of the Judicial Committee of the Privy Council as Canada's final court of appeal was in doubt as it prepared to hear the *Persons* case. Those, especially Quebeckers, who favoured a decentralized confederation of autonomous provinces were sympathetic to the Judicial Committee's approach. Those who supported a strong central government resented its efforts to curtail federal power and believed the imperial court had betrayed the historical record. The Privy Council's ruling that Canada could not free itself from the JCPC's jurisdiction seemed to make matters even worse.

From Emily Murphy's perspective, the Privy Council's repeated rejection of the framers' intentions augured well. At the very least, it gave her reason for hope, however modest. If Newton Rowell could persuade the JCPC to ignore the original meaning of 'persons,' he would overcome the decisive point in the Supreme Court's decision. But this was only the first step. To win, Rowell would also have to get past the long line of English jurisprudence denying women the right to assume public office. Unless he could overcome that significant hurdle, women would remain non-persons according to Canada's constitution, and Prime Minister King would be able to continue to avoid appointing a woman to the Senate of Canada.

8

Waiting to Be Heard

Whatever misgivings Canadian lawyers may have had about the role of the Judicial Committee of the Privy Council, those who were able to argue their cases in London relished the experience. They enjoyed the luxury, then relatively rare, of travelling to London and, although many Canadian lawyers resented the colonialism, they still revered British judges. To argue a case before the Privy Council was the pinnacle of an advocate's career. Newton Rowell had enjoyed the experience in 1924, when he had argued three cases before the JCPC,[1] and he welcomed the opportunity to appear before the British Empire's highest tribunal in 1929.

Rowell arrived in London with his adult daughter Mary in late June 1929 and quickly settled into a comfortably furnished apartment in Queen Anne's Mansions, St James's Park. The weather was unusually warm and much attention was focused on summer sports. The Wimbledon draw, including American W.T. Tilden and Frenchman H. Cochet, but not defending champion R. Lacoste, was announced on 20 June. Two weeks later, Cochet emerged as the men's champion having beaten Tilden in the semi-final. American H.N. Wills won her third successive women's title. Throughout the summer, England's cricket team was engaged in a test series with the visiting side from South Africa. On 4 July, the annual Henley Royal Regatta got underway. The Royal Academy of Arts offered its annual Summer Exhibition, and at the Warren Gallery, one could view recent paintings by D.H. Lawrence.

Although it was summer, politics was prominently in the news. A month earlier, in May 1929, Ramsay MacDonald's Labour Party had narrowly defeated Prime Minister Stanley Baldwin's Conservatives. MacDonald had failed to win a majority, but with the support of David Lloyd George's Liberals, he formed a Labour government. The newly elected government held its first cabinet meeting at 10 Downing Street on 21 June, which, for the first time, included a woman.[2] The next day, Buckingham Palace announced that the King would return from Windsor at the beginning of July, to be followed by a thanksgiving service at Westminster Abbey on 7 July.[3] Signalling the King's recovery from an illness, the announcement was met with extraordinary enthusiasm: the King's return, said the *Times* editorial writer, would be 'a scene that will rank above any in the memory of modern Londoners.'[4] Reports on the King's medical condition were prominent in the weeks to follow. At one point, his X-ray was given front page coverage.[5]

The new Parliament met for the first time on 25 June to elect the speaker. A week later, the House of Commons got down to serious business with the King's speech and debate on the government's program. Internationally, the news was grim, and included ominous reports of the Sino–Soviet crisis over Manchuria,[6] continuing debates about wartime reparations and status of the Rhineland,[7] and a war in Afghanistan.[8] From fascist Italy, where 'no aspect of Italian society is free from State control, least of all education,'[9] came an article written by Benito Mussolini that condemned beauty contests and proclaimed that the greatest mission for women was to be in the home. There was no place for women as lawyers in the legal profession, nor as teachers in higher education, because they brought about 'a sort of effete atmosphere.'[10] Reports from the courts included an extended inquiry into a sensational poisoning case in Croydon,[11] and, by today's standards, an unusual focus on the details of divorce cases, some of which were tried by jury.[12]

When Rowell went to the Privy Council in Downing Street to find out when the case would be heard, he was given disappointing news. The JCPC was 'making slow progress,' he reported in a letter to his wife,[13] and the hearing had not yet been formally scheduled. The delay was the result of both political changes afoot in Great Britain and the more general backlog of work before the Judicial Committee.

The change in government meant a new Lord Chancellor. Sitting at the apex of the English judicial structure, the Lord Chancellor also presided over the Judicial Committee of the Privy Council. Rowell was disappointed to learn that 'the elections and change in Lord Chancellor has ... upset the arrangements' for the Privy Council's sittings, and discussed the turn of events with Justice Lyman Duff, who had unexpectedly been asked to sit on one case to provide the requisite quorum.[14]

Rowell had hoped the *Persons* case would be heard on 11 July, but he soon realized that was unlikely because the case had been pushed to the bottom of the list. Rowell waited a full month while the Judicial Committee, most days sitting in two panels, worked its way through a heavy list of cases set down for hearing that summer, several of which were from Canada. A patent case was heard for several days in mid-June,[15] followed by a matrimonial case from Quebec.[16] In early July, the JCPC spent four days hearing another Quebec appeal, this one involving a disgruntled Montreal resident who sued the city of Montreal for dumping sewage on his land.[17] Next came a case involving the intricacies of proceedings against the Crown,[18] and then several days were spent on an important appeal dealing with the Dominion's powers to regulate the fishery in British Columbia.[19] In mid-July, a case from Ontario involving succession duties took up two days.[20] Finally, on 22 July, the JCPC reached the *Persons* case, the same day it wrapped up a two-day appeal on another case, this one dealing with succession duties from Alberta.[21]

Although the Privy Council heard the appeal only a little more than a year after the Supreme Court released its judgment, Emily Murphy was frustrated by what she regarded as a delay. She complained to Stuart Edwards about the lack of progress.[22] Murphy had wanted the case heard in February, but the appeal was bumped by another Canadian case. The next sitting was in April, but Edwards refused to have the case listed then. Government lawyers were already booked to argue several cases at the summer sittings, but had no cases on the April list. Edwards did not want to have them make a special trip to London just for the *Persons* case.[23]

Murphy complained to Rowell, who spoke to Edwards, telling him that his clients expected him 'to get this appeal on for hearing in April.'[24] Edwards refused, explaining, 'we would not feel justified in incurring the additional expense of sending counsel to England twice, even if it is otherwise convenient for them to go ... I am not aware of any interests of the petitioners which will suffer by reason of the hearing of the case being postponed until the summer sittings.'[25] Murphy and Rowell were fortunate that Edwards refused to push to have the case heard in April. Had Edwards gone along with their request, Lord Chancellor

Hailsham, a much more conservative judge than John Sankey, would have presided and the result might well have been different.

This lengthy list of appeals attracted the very best of the Canadian bar, and Rowell enjoyed some familiar company as he waited in London. In addition to Duff, W.N. Tilley, the leader of the Ontario bar who appeared frequently before the Judicial Committee, also had a case on the list.[26] Eugene Lafleur, another regular before the JCPC and the lawyer Emily Murphy had contacted for an opinion on the appointment of women to the Senate, had two cases in addition to the *Persons* case.[27] Aimé Geoffrion, Lafleur's highly regarded colleague from Quebec, argued three appeals.[28] Lucien Cannon, Canada's solicitor general, argued the Crown liability appeal,[29] and C.P. Plaxton appeared on the fisheries case.[30] Cannon had argued the *Persons* case before the Supreme Court of Canada, but took no formal part in the presentation of the federal government's argument before the Privy Council.

The English Bar was also well represented as the Judicial Committee worked its way through the Canadian list: Geoffrey Lawrence, QC, later president of the Nuremberg War Crimes Tribunal and member of the House of Lords, had no fewer than six briefs on the Canadian list, including the *Persons* case where he assisted Lafleur.[31]

Although he was mildly impatient with the delay, Rowell enjoyed a busy month of social events, theatre, and political talk. It was accepted practice for counsel to charge a regular fee while waiting in London to be reached on the list, so Rowell could enjoy himself and, at the same time, expect to be paid for his time.

A regular churchgoer, Rowell sometimes attended two services on Sundays and did the same on his first Sunday in London. The morning service he attended was not to his liking. 'There was a great congregation and an old-fashioned sermon on the meaning of salvation,' he wrote to his wife, Nell. 'I am afraid many did not enjoy it much nor did it appeal to me.' He then attended the evening service at Westminster Abbey with no sermon to complain of.[32]

· The next week, Rowell attended the funeral of General William Booth, the founder of the Salvation Army. The funeral procession attracted thousands of onlookers and it halted business in the City as it passed through.[33] Rowell described it as 'one of the most impressive sights I have seen in years.'[34] That evening, Rowell and his daughter attended the theatre where they saw *By Candlelight*, a German play adapted for London's West End and billed as having had 'London's Longest Run.' The play offended their traditional tastes. Rowell described it to Nell as 'brilliant but ultra-modern ... Sex, sex and suggestive beyond words ... I am afraid I am not up to date in my tastes.'[35]

There were also plenty of dinners to attend. A few days after Booth's funeral, Rowell attended a dinner where he 'had a great chat with Neville Chamberlain,' the former minister of health, Chancellor of the Exchequer, and future prime minister of England.[36] At another dinner, this one in late June, he was paired with Lord Reading, the formidable Rufus Issacs, a leading English counsel, former Lord Chief Justice, ambassador to Washington, and Viceroy of India.[37]

By late June, Rowell realized that he would have to change his travel arrangements. At the time, he must have been encouraged to read an editorial in the *Daily Telegraph* that strongly endorsed the view that women were persons and that urged the Privy Council to rule accordingly.[38] As he waited in London, Rowell continued to see the sights. In early July, he attended the House of Commons to hear Winston Churchill in debate. He was not disappointed by Churchill's spirited attack on the government, reported in the *Daily Telegraph* as 'good hard hitting from the Front Opposition Bench' that 'hugely tickled' the House.[39] By 6 July, however, it was clear that the JCPC would not hear the *Persons* case for at least another ten days, and Rowell had to change his travel plans once more.

This change of plans gave Rowell time for a trip to Oxford and to Rhodes House as the guest of Philip Kerr, who was the secretary of the trust.[40] On Sunday, 7 July, Rowell attended the thanksgiving service for the King at Wesminster Abbey. Broadcast live on BBC Radio, the service was described by the press in rapturous terms as 'a notable service' and a 'public tribute of loyalty.'[41] Rowell sat close to no fewer than four past, present, and future prime ministers – David Lloyd George, Stanley Baldwin, Ramsay MacDonald, and Winston Churchill. John Sankey, the newly appointed Lord Chancellor, who also attended the service, was less impressed and described it as 'very uninspiring.'[42]

Rowell's daughter left England by 11 July, while he continued his busy swirl of social and political activity – lunch at the Travellers' Club with Sir Frederick Whyte, a former Liberal MP who was now a political advisor to the national government of China to discuss affairs in that country, followed by lunch with deputy Liberal leader Sir Herbert Samuel at the House of Commons to discuss the plight of the British Liberal Party and the situation in Palestine. Then, Rowell was off to have tea at the Home Office with an old friend, Geoffrey Dawson, the editor of the *Times*, to discuss Labour Party affairs. Rowell also dined with the Labour government's foreign secretary, Arthur Henderson, and enjoyed 'a very interesting evening on politics.'[43] He also had time to visit Cambridge as a guest of Professor J. Holland Rose, the editor of the *Cambridge History of the British Empire* for which Rowell had just written a chapter on the development of the Canadian constitution.[44] The day finished with dinner in the Hall and a visit to King's College Chapel, described by Rowell as 'the most stately and beautiful of all the buildings.'[45]

Rowell decided to keep the next week free to ready himself at long last for his argument before the JCPC. Then, unexpectedly, the *Persons* case was bumped once more by the hearing of another case.[46] The delay left Rowell with time for lunch with the Duchess of Devonshire in the City, where he learned that 'London Bankers are not entirely at ease over the present financial situation and the withdrawals of gold both to the US and France.'[47] He also found time for another evening at the theatre, seeing *One Little Kiss*. The play was billed as a 'new farce' and, despite its suggestive title, Rowell found nothing objectionable about the storyline.[48] Rowell, it would seem, preferred light entertainment to the possibility of seeing the Russian Ballet's *Swan Lake* at the Royal Opera House in Covent Garden, John Galsworthy's new play *Exiled* or Edgar Wallace's murder mystery, *Persons Unknown*.[49]

John Sankey: A Reforming Lord Chancellor

The Office of Lord Chancellor has no Canadian counterpart. The Lord Chancellor plays three significant and different roles: judicial, legislative and executive. Judicially, the Lord Chancellor oversees the United Kingdom's appellate courts, both the House of Lords and the Judicial Committee of the Privy Council. At the time of the *Persons* case, both bodies required the Lord Chancellor's active involvement. Legislatively, the Lord Chancellor is the presiding member of the House of Lords. He – there has never been a 'she' – also plays an executive function as a member of the cabinet, serving as the government's chief legal advisor on everything from judicial appointments to general law reform. These activities have been subject to great scrutiny and repeated reform efforts, often in conjunction with debates about the appellate jurisdiction of the House of Lords and, by extension, the role of the JCPC.

In the early twentieth century, the Lord Chancellor was almost inevitably a barrister with previous political experience in the House of

Commons. Most had not held full-time judicial office before their elevation. Indeed, only three men since 1800 had served as lower-court
judges before their appointment as Lord Chancellor.[50] John Sankey,
who had never served in the House of Commons and was appointed
directly from the Court of Appeal, was a clear exception in this regard.[51]

In his two most famous decisions, *Woolmington v. D.P.P.*[52] and the
Persons case, Sankey elegantly captured a fundamental legal principle
with striking and memorable phrases that still reverberate decades
later. Both decisions have stood the test of time as great judgments. In
Woolmington, a case about the onus of proof in a criminal proceeding,
Sankey famously stated,

> Throughout the web of the English criminal law one golden thread is
> always to be seen, that is the duty of the prosecution to prove the pris-
> oner's guilt [subject to a special rule for insanity and any statutory excep-
> tions] ... No matter what the charge or where the trial, the principle that
> the prosecution must prove the guilt of the prisoner is part of the
> common law of England and no attempt to whittle it down can be
> entertained.[53]

However, perhaps because of his preoccupation with non-legal
issues as Lord Chancellor and his reluctance to sit in the House of
Lords as an ex-Lord Chancellor, Viscount Sankey did not leave a significant body of jurisprudence. The author of his entry in *Lives of the
Lord Chancellors* credits Sankey with only modest success as a jurist:
'Sankey's judgments are clear, careful, and correct, but they do not
entitle him to a place among the great English judges.'[54] Canadian
women might beg to differ, and recent evaluations of Sankey's tenure
as Lord Chancellor have been more positive. About the Lord Chancellor who pronounced women to be persons, Robert Stevens writes, 'he
achieved remarkable distinction, being one of the most important and
innovative lord chancellors of the twentieth century.'[55]

The summer sitting of 1929 was the first time Sankey presided in the
Judicial Committee of the Privy Council, and the *Persons* case was one
of the first he heard in his new role as head of the English judiciary.[56]
The judgment was also the first decision Sankey wrote as Lord Chancellor.

John Sankey was a man of humble origins despite his Oxford education. He was called to the bar in 1892 and had a varied practice on the
South Wales circuit, with a concentration on workers' compensation

cases. Like Rowell, Sankey was a keen churchman, becoming the Chancellor of the Diocese of Llandaff in 1909, the same year he was appointed QC. Even after his appointment to the bench in 1914, Sankey remained deeply involved in the affairs of the Welsh church.

Sankey's initial political instincts were conservative. Elected to London County Council under the Conservative banner in 1910, he was appointed to the High Court Bench in 1914 by Richard Haldane, Lord Chancellor in Asquith's Liberal government. His entry in *Lives of the Lord Chancellors* describes him as a solid judge who performed his duties 'without fuss or notoriety.'[57] During the First World War, Sankey served as chair of the Alien's Advisory Committee where he spent most of his time reviewing the cases of Irishmen interned after the 1916 uprising. He described the task as 'very hard work – you want the patience of Job and the temper of an Archangel.'[58] He said it was 'one of the hardest and certainly the most disagreeable job [he had] ever done.'[59]

In 1919, Prime Minister Lloyd George appointed Sankey as the chairman of a commission to investigate the coal-mining industry. The industry, plagued by low production, squalid working conditions, and bitter relations between the owners and the miners, was in crisis because of the social and political upheaval of the war, the rise of the Labour movement, and the demands of workers for a greater share of the nation's wealth. This appointment transformed Sankey's political outlook and changed the direction of his career.

The commission was established amid the threat of a national strike that would have crippled the British economy just as it was emerging from the devastation of the war. The commission comprised three owners' representatives and three miners' representatives, with Sankey as the chair. Sidney Webb, a social reformer and the founder of the Fabian Society, and R.H. Tawney, a prominent economic historian and an activist in the Workers' Educational Association, were among the miners' representatives.

The hearings were difficult and acrimonious, and they 'soon turned into a bruising adversarial contest.'[60] Tawney described the owners and steelmakers who testified as 'extraordinarily incompetent, not to say stupid.' Sankey thought they were 'hopeless.'[61] Even the staid *Times* said that the owners 'cut a sorry figure' and that the miners' 'case was better presented, but it was also a better case.'[62] Presiding over the hearings was 'like sitting on a barrel of gunpowder,'[63] Sankey explained. He held the miners in only slightly higher esteem than he held the owners: 'It would be possible to say without exaggeration of the miners' leaders that they were the stupidest men in England if we had not frequent occasion to meet the owners.'[64]

Sankey's work on the commission had a profound and lasting effect upon him. As Professor Heuston explained, the future Lord Chancellor's 'sense of justice, always strong, was outraged by the descriptions of the living conditions of the miners; and his sense of decency was shocked by the cynical and selfish attitude of the owners.'[65] The commissioners could not reach a consensus, and ultimately had to produce three separate reports: one from the owners, one from the miners, and one from Sankey himself. There was 'great unpleasantness and bitterness'[66] among the members of the commission, and, at the end, Sankey was disturbed when one of the owners refused to shake his hand.[67]

Sankey was entirely persuaded by the miners' cause, and his recommendation – that the industry be nationalized – shocked his conservative judicial colleagues. 'Coal mining,' he wrote, 'is our national key industry upon which nearly all other industries depend. A cheap and adequate supply of coal is essential ... 'Half a century of education has produced in the workers ... far more than a desire for the material advantages of higher wages and shorter hours,' he reasoned. 'They now have ... a higher ambition to taking their due share and interest in the direction of the industry to the success of which they, too, are contributing.' State ownership, he concluded, was necessary to ensure satisfactory conditions for the workers. As he explained, 'the relationship between labour and the community will be an improvement upon the relationship between labour and capital in the coalfields.' To the argument that state control would fail through lack of initiative, Sankey disagreed. The experience of the war had shown 'the existence of a new class of men ... who are just as keen to serve the State as they are to serve a private employer and who have been shown to possess the qualities of courage in taking initiative [sic] necessary for the running of an industry.'[68]

To Sankey's great disappointment, Prime Minister Lloyd George shelved the report in the face of stiff opposition from the Conservatives. But Sankey was a changed man, drifting steadily away from an innate conservatism towards an increasingly pro-Labour outlook. His social and intellectual circle now included many who were sympathetic to the cause of Labour. Among this group were the Fabian socialists Sydney and Beatrice Webb, who often included Sankey in their dinner parties with another famous Fabian, George Bernard

Shaw.[69] Others included the left-leaning political scientist Harold Laski, who described Sankey in a letter to U.S. Supreme Court Justice Felix Frankfurter as 'our best judge, with insight, scholarship and exquisite taste. His one defect is keen churchmanship.'[70] In turn, Sankey complimented Laski's *The Grammar of Politics* as 'indeed a magnum opus,'[71] having read the book carefully. Although he never cited it in his judgments, he praised it in his extra-judicial legal writing and the book had a strong influence on Sankey's jurisprudential outlook.[72] He reported to Laski: 'I saw so many of my own views so admirably put ... it has supplied me with many a useful argument.'[73]

Sankey was also close to Richard Haldane, who had appointed him to the bench in 1914. Haldane had also moved to the ideological left following the First World War and now supported the Labour Party. When the first Labour Party government was formed in January 1924, Sankey, although still a trial judge, was high on the list of candidates for the office of Lord Chancellor because of his work on the Coal Commission. However, as Sankey himself predicted, Prime Minister Ramsay MacDonald passed him over in favour of the more experienced Haldane. Haldane, a former Lord Chancellor, had persuaded MacDonald that his fledgling Labour government needed the respectability of his reputation and peerage.[74] As MacDonald apologetically told Sankey, Haldane had 'held a pistol to his head and threatened to give no help, unless he is made Chancellor.'[75]

Sankey was extremely disappointed, and was certain that his career was over: 'I shall never get anything now. All my chances are gone.'[76] Amid this funk, he resolved to retire on 23 April 1929, the day he would be eligible for his judicial pension.[77] Gradually, however, Sankey overcame his disappointment, encouraged no doubt by Haldane himself who remained a friend. In fact, Haldane reassured Sankey by urging him to 'be prepared to be Lord Chancellor in the next Labour Govt,' even if, he also warned, 'it is a disagreeable job.'[78] Laski was also encouraging: 'To waste your time on assize is really wicked.'[79]

When Stanley Baldwin's Conservatives came to power in November 1924 following the short-lived Labour government, Sankey's opportunities for judicial advancement seemed to dwindle. However, in 1928, Baldwin's government appointed Sankey to the Court of Appeal. The appointment came as a surprise to Sankey in light of his well-known Labour sympathies. As Sankey explained to Laski: 'I did not expect to get it from the present regime & tho' I am glad to get it, I have many regrets at leaving the King's Bench, where my work, especially on Circuit, gave me extra time for extra judicial duties.'[80] A few weeks later, Sankey invited Laski to dinner to celebrate the appointment, and confessed: 'I leave the realities of the King's Bench for the abstractions of the Court of Appeal with regret. I still say I should have preferred politics to the law, M[ember of] P[arliament] to L[ord] J[ustice] & still hope.'[81]

Sankey's hope was soon fulfilled. The Baldwin Conservatives were defeated in May 1929, and Haldane, Sankey's rival for the office of Lord Chancellor in 1924, had died almost a year earlier. On 5 June, Ramsay MacDonald, returned to the office of prime minister, told Sankey that he wanted to make amends for 1924 and offered him the post. Sankey accepted without hesitation. It was, as he explained, 'the ambition of a lifetime realized.'[82] On 8 June 1929, Sankey received the Great Seal. Two days later, he was sworn in at the Law Courts and was created a peer. Within the month, Sankey was hearing appeals in the Privy Council.

As Lord Chancellor, Sankey had an eye for reform. The *Times* applauded the spirit of his speech at the annual Lord Mayor's Judge's Dinner at Mansion House in early July 1929 when he announced his intention to investigate the position of individuals in disputes with the Crown, as well as the increase in powers of administrative tribunals.[83] By the time Sankey had decided the *Persons* case in October, he had appointed a Committee on Ministers' Powers (the Scott-Donoughmore Committee) to investigate subordinate legislation and the exercise of quasi-judicial powers by government departments. Later, he created a permanent Law Revision Committee, and encouraged reforms in legal education, appointing his old friend Harold Laski as the chair.[84]

Shortly before his appointment as Lord Chancellor, Sankey delivered a lecture entitled 'The Principles and Practice of the Law Today,'[85] in which he talked about the growth of the post-war administrative state. He outlined how this new administrative state featured sweeping regulatory powers, specialized administrative tribunals, and the removal of the common law court's jurisdiction, developments which he regarded with considerable misgiving. Recognizing that the courts could be criticized for delay and excessive expense, he argued that these shortcomings could not justify unchecked bureaucratic power.

Sankey's views, however, were considerably more nuanced than those of most judges.[86] He challenged the assumptions underlying A.V. Dicey's rejection of the European model that featured a separate body of administrative law in his common law classic, *The Law of the*

Constitution. Dicey's views had dominated judicial and scholarly thinking for more than half a century. In view of the growth of the administrative state, Sankey argued, the time had come to take a fresh look at a specialized body of administrative law to ensure fairness and transparency in decision-making. A reviewer described Sankey 'as a great master of the common law, which he rightly regards as a living organism adaptable to all the changing needs of modern civilization.'[87]

There is nothing in Sankey's judicial writing as a trial judge and later as a member of the Court of Appeal that reveals a philosophy to distinguish him from the traditional English mould. However, just as he had moved to the left politically, he gradually formed a more liberal view on the task of judging. A year before his appointment as Lord Chancellor, Sankey invited Laski, Tawney, and Haldane to dinner where they discussed the role of judges in lawmaking 'for hours.' In a letter to Justice Oliver Wendell Holmes of the U.S. Supreme Court, Laski recalled that 'Sankey took the obvious and sensible view that judges inevitably legislate, even if it is what you have called "interstitial legislation,"' while Haldane insisted upon the traditional view that judges merely declare that which is already the law. Sankey and Haldane also disagreed in their assessments of various judges, Laski wrote. 'Haldane seemed to look for what I may call a "man of the world" quality in their decisions; Sankey was more interested in the endeavour to make the case emit a big, working principle.'[88]

Lord Sankey and the *Persons* Case

John Sankey had little time to prepare for the *Persons* case, which he heard six weeks to the day after his appointment as Lord Chancellor. He was still unfamiliar with the details of his new post at the pinnacle of the English legal hierarchy and preoccupied with the political issues that confronted the new Labour government. He described his schedule as 'desperately busy' and himself as 'overworked,' as he dashed each day from presiding at the House of Lords at Westminster to the Judicial Committee in Downing Street and then back to the House of Lords in the late afternoon.[89] Sankey was so busy with his new duties that he even missed the Oxford–Cambridge cricket match, which ended in 'an inevitable draw.'[90] 'I had good tickets but was so busy with work as Lord Chancellor,' he wrote with a certain sense of frustration, 'that for the first time for years I was unable to go.'[91]

Sankey may well have discussed the *Persons* case with Harold Laski when the two met for lunch on 17 July, though Laski would undoubtedly have been more interested in any information he could pry from the Lord Chancellor about the cabinet meeting held earlier that morning. The following day, Sankey took the train to Cardiff where he received an honorary degree at the University of Wales. The next week, he continued to rush from the Privy Council to the House of Lords to cabinet on business, all the while complaining about visits to the dentist for relief from chronic problems with his teeth.

As Lord Chancellor, Sankey did not deem it necessary to keep his distance from the counsel who appeared before him. On 23 July, the second day of the *Persons* case appeal, he hosted a dinner for Rowell and the other members of the Canadian bar in London. Sankey recorded the event in his diary with his usual attention to the cost: 'Gave dinner to a number of Canadian K.C.'s and Law Lords at the House of Lords. Went off well at cost £37.1.5.'[92]

Though Sankey's role in the *Persons* case was pivotal, there were four other members of the panel. Unless at least two of them agreed with his approach to Canadian constitutional interpretation and his willingness to recognize that women were persons under the *BNA Act*, the Supreme Court of Canada's decision would stand. About those men, far less is known in modern Canadian legal circles.

Charles Darling: Poet, Wit, and Trial Judge

Charles John Darling, the second judge on the panel that heard the *Persons* case, was a popular figure in the legal community with a mixed reputation as a judge. Darling had no formal education, having been privately tutored as a child because of his delicate health. He entered the legal profession first as an articling student in a solicitor's office and then as a pupil in a barrister's chambers. He was not a prominent member of the bar – his *Times* obituary notice described his practice as 'microscopic'[93] – and in the early years of his practice, he devoted considerable time to journalism and politics.

Despite his lack of formal education, Darling was a well-read man and a published poet, who took great pleasure in displaying his literary knowledge.[94] Elected as a Conservative member of Parliament in 1888 after two defeats at the polls, Darling made no mark as an MP; during more than ten years in Parliament, he said next to nothing on social or economic issues.[95]

Rumours of his possible appointment to the bench in 1897 provoked an unusual public reaction. Without mentioning Darling by name, a leader in the *Times* described him as a man of 'acute intellect and considerable literary power,' but asserted that he had 'given no sign of legal eminence' and argued that his appointment was based solely on his political affiliation.[96] The Conservative Lord Chancellor, Lord Halsbury, Darling's personal friend, appointed him to the King's Bench two days later. The *Times* editorial writer acknowledged that Lord Halsbury had elevated a few lesser-known barristers who had turned out to be fine judges, but added 'these instances scarcely excuse some recent appointments. Mr. Justice Darling has a pretty wit, and his sense of irony will enable him to appreciate the irony of fate which places him where others might have expected to be.'[97] The Liberal *Daily Chronicle* was even more scathing: 'Mr. Darling has only two conceivable qualifications for a judgeship – that he is an extreme partisan of the Government now in office, and that his seat is supposed to be safe ... He has no serious knowledge of the law and has never handled any important practice at the Bar. The whole transaction is grossly scandalous.'[98]

In the next twenty-six years, Darling proved himself to be a competent – though occasionally erratic – trial judge. He presided over a number of difficult and sensational murder cases with considerable skill. His best-known trials are legendary.[99] In 1911, he presided at the trial of Steinie Morrison for the brutal murder of a Russian immigrant on Clapham Common. The jury convicted, but Morrison maintained his innocence. Darling's conduct of the trial was upheld on appeal but Winston Churchill, then the Home Secretary, commuted the death sentence to life imprisonment. The sensational 1922 trial of Herbert Armstrong, a Welsh solicitor, for poisoning his wife attracted wide publicity, as did the trial of the notorious 'Chicago May' for attempted murder in 1907.

On occasion, Darling was prone to behave with 'a levity quite unsuited to the trial of a criminal case,'[100] or to make highly inappropriate remarks. Darling was not a profound legal thinker nor was he a great judge. But he did have a certain literary flair and, for the most part, displayed common sense, sound judgment, and a good understanding of human nature. Although profoundly conservative in his personal views, Darling proved himself capable of putting those views to one side and applying the law as he saw it. To this end, he rendered significant judgments in support of trade unions[101] and abortionists.[102]

Lord Darling's approach to women's political rights was mixed. In 1913, he tried a jury case involving several prominent suffragettes, including Emmeline Pankhurst, the woman who so influenced Emily Murphy and Nellie McClung when she visited Canada in 1911. Several shop owners had sued Pankhurst and the Women's Social and Political Union for conspiracy, alleging that an article in *Votes for Women*, a union journal, had incited militant suffragettes to go on a rampage of general violence and window-breaking. Darling's interventions demonstrated that he was no supporter of female suffrage. He asked one witness why she had adopted suffragist opinions and was told that her friends had been sent to prison for standing at the corner of a square. 'I see,' Darling replied, 'because your friends were sent to prison you thought women ought to have votes.'[103] Darling's jury instruction favoured the plaintiffs, and the jury found the defendant suffragettes liable.

After Darling's retirement from the bench, he was elevated to the peerage where he confronted the question of whether women could be admitted to sit in the House of Lords. It is unknown if Emily Murphy or Newton Rowell knew of Darling's stand in the debate, but it certainly looked promising for their case. By 1924, the man who had been so opposed to giving women the vote in 1913 had come to realize that admitting women to the Lords was 'the logical outcome of the increasing tendency to equality between the sexes.' The next year, in 1925, Darling applied the same logic in support of making women liable for their own civil wrongs, though his reasoning on this point would hardly appeal to any feminist:

> The Law having taken away the power of the husband to see that his wife does not commit torts by administering to her that castigation which he was accustomed to administer till the politer age ... it seems to me perfectly logical ... [that] he ought not to be responsible for the mischief she does, now that he is no longer allowed to beat her.[104]

As a retired trial judge and member of the House of Lords, Darling was entitled to sit on appeals to the Privy Council. His temperament made him ill-suited to the task. As Darling's *Times* obituary noted: 'For dealing with the problems that come before that tribunal, he was not well suited, and the jests that had been well received in the Strand seemed somewhat out of place in Downing Street.'[105] Darling's sympathetic biographer offered a kinder explanation: 'These cases are appeals, and have neither perhaps the same degree of human interest nor equivalent opportunity for epigrammatic intervention as cases in the King's Bench. Darling missed the gallery.'[106] Nevertheless, Darling enjoyed his encounters with lawyers from the Dominions. Three years before the *Persons* case, he toured Canada as a guest of the Canadian Bar Association, entertaining Canadian lawyers who revelled in the amusing after-dinner speeches of a visiting English judge. During this visit, Darling was also entertained to dinner at the home of retired prime minister Robert Borden.[107]

Darling and Sankey were not just judicial colleagues, but long-time friends. They sat together as judges of the Criminal Court of Appeal. As bachelors, they often dined together, and did so the week before the *Persons* case was argued.[108] Undoubtedly, they discussed the new challenges Sankey faced as Lord Chancellor. It is possible they also discussed the important case from Canada they were about to hear.

Lord Merrivale (Henry Edward Duke): Matrimonial Judge

The third judge on the panel to hear the *Persons* case was Lord Merrivale (Henry Edward Duke), who came to the case with ten years of experience as a matrimonial judge. Appointed to the Court of Appeal in 1918, Lord Merrivale became president of the Probate, Divorce, and Admiralty Division the following year, a post he filled until his retirement in 1933. Lord Merrivale, like Sankey, was a man of humble origins. However, unlike Sankey, Merrivale had not gone to a public school nor had he even attended university. Instead, he studied for the bar while working as a journalist in the House of Commons press gallery. Sankey described Merrivale as an effective advocate, although more at ease persuading the ordinary juryman of the rightness of his client's case than arguing a rarefied point of law.[109]

Lord Merrivale came to the bench after mixed success in politics. He was first elected to the House of Commons in 1900 as a Unionist from Plymouth in his native Devon, lost the next election in 1906, but returned to Parliament in 1910. Six years later, Lord Merrivale rose to prominence when Prime Minister Asquith appointed him chief secretary for Ireland, a position aptly described by Sankey as 'the graveyard of many reputations.'[110] In that position, Merrivale was confronted with the impossible task of brokering a settlement just as Sinn Fein and the Irish Republican Army were gathering strength. He lasted two years as Irish secretary, resigning in 1918, and his performance attracted negative reviews. As the *Times* recalled in Merrivale's obituary, 'it cannot be said that he showed imagination or breadth of view, and he had no appreciation of the Irish psychology.'[111]

Rowell would have known that as England's senior family law judge Lord Merrivale was fully aware of the claims for women's rights. After all, Lord Merrivale's workload had increased significantly in 1923, when Parliament reformed the divorce laws to allow the wife to divorce the husband for adultery.[112] Lord Merrivale was a competent, efficient, and dignified judge, traits vital to the successful conduct of matrimonial litigation, but he was not a legal scholar and his jurisprudential contribution was modest.

Thomas Tomlin: A Commercial Judge

Thomas Tomlin was the only judge to hear the *Persons* case who had a regular seat among the Law Lords of the House of Lords, an office to which he had been appointed only five months earlier. Tomlin had been a highly regarded barrister who specialized in wills, trusts, and commercial law and had argued many cases before the House of Lords and the Judicial Committee. Appointed as a trial judge in 1923, Tomlin sat in the Chancery Division where he heard a large number of patent cases. Known to interrupt counsel frequently with tough, probing questions, Tomlin earned a reputation as an active judge. He certainly never hesitated to tell counsel when he disagreed with an argument. Six years after his appointment to the bench, in 1929, Tomlin was appointed directly to the House of Lords, one of the few trial judges to have bypassed the Court of Appeal on his way to a seat on England's highest court.

Tomlin was Sankey's contemporary at Oxford, and when he died in 1935, readers of the *Times* obituary columns were reminded that he had earned a first in jurisprudence and a second-class BCL degree to better Sankey's undistinguished third.[113] However, despite his stronger academic record, Tomlin had a less inquiring mind and was known as a down-to-earth, common-sense judge who had 'little ... speculative interest in the history and philosophy of the law.'[114]

Lancelot Sanderson: A Colonial Judge

The fifth judge to serve on the panel hearing the *Persons* case, Sir Lancelot Sanderson, was not a well-known legal figure. He was a keen sportsman who had studied at Harrow and Cambridge before practising as a barrister on the Northern Circuit. Elected to the House of Commons in 1910 as a Unionist MP, Sanderson was appointed Chief Justice of Bengal in 1915, a post he filled for eleven years. As Chief Justice, Sanderson restricted himself to appeals involving points of English commercial law, and 'his tenure of office left no permanent landmark in Indian legal history.'[115] Sanderson returned to England following his retirement from the Indian bench in 1926, and often sat in the Privy Council on appeals from India and occasionally from the Dominions. Sankey and Sanderson had been friendly while in practice[116] and the two men socialized frequently after Sanderson's return from India.[117]

A Favourable Bench?

Rowell knew that to win the case, he had to convince the Privy Council to overrule the Supreme Court of Canada and to abandon the centuries-old rule excluding women from public office. Only seven years earlier, that rule of gender exclusion had barred a woman peer from entering the House of Lords.[118] That was a weighty precedent, bolstered by the long line of other 'persons' cases that had denied women the vote and entry into universities and the professions.[119]

Rowell was probably pleased with the panel he had drawn. He hardly wanted a bench composed of technical lawyers, and of the five, only Tomlin fit that description. The others may have been more difficult to read. Sankey's progressive political outlook would have marked him as one likely to be sympathetic to Murphy's cause, although it would have been difficult to identify Sankey's views on women's political rights. A life-long bachelor who lived with his sister and mother, Sankey had limited contact with women in his day-to-day life as a barrister and judge. He revealed his rather austere views on marriage in an interview given a month after rendering his decision in the *Persons* case: 'I am a bachelor, but I am not at all sure that marriage is not one of the best careers of the lot – always provided that you can get the right partner.'[120] His diary is also replete with entries expressing devotion to his mother, even long after her death in 1921. He described her as 'my only love and friend,' and was devastated by her death: 'Now I have nothing left, love, hope, ambition gone.'[121] Even eight years later, in 1929, the year he reached the pinnacle of his career as Lord Chancellor, Sankey complained that he had 'had no happiness' since her death, that he was 'nervous and seedy from time to time ... [and] very depressed. I long to see my darling mother again and to be with her. May God grant it to me.'[122] He continued for more than twenty years after her death to use black-edged notepaper, describing himself as being in perpetual mourning.[123]

Despite his conservative veneer, Lord Darling had supported the admission of women to the House of Lords four years earlier when he had proclaimed in debate: 'I should be glad to know upon what grounds of logic or convenience a lady should be excluded from this House while admitted to the other ... if they may sit on the Throne, why may they not sit on these benches?'[124] Lord Merrivale, on the other hand, was more problematic. He was familiar with women's issues through his work as a family law judge, and, like Sankey and Darling, had a political background and political instincts that might make him less likely to take a narrow legal approach to the case. However, Merrivale had opposed the initiative that Darling had supported to admit women to the House of Lords, labelling the proposal the work of 'feminist agitators.'[125] The views of Tomlin and Sanderson were anyone's to guess.

9

The Judicial Committee of the Privy Council Decides

The Judicial Committee of the Privy Council finally reached the *Persons* case on 22 July 1929. Although the Supreme Court of Canada heard the case in a single day, the Judicial Committee allowed four days for oral argument.

'The Constitution of a New Nation'

In his written argument, filed well before the hearing,[1] Newton Rowell pointed out that the word 'person' appeared in no fewer than thirteen other sections of the constitution[2] and that, in several sections, 'person' almost certainly included women. For instance, women had been given the vote and the right to sit in Parliament and in all provincial legislatures except in Quebec. The right conferred on 'any person' by section 133 to use either English or French in Parliament, the Quebec legislature, and certain courts could hardly be restricted to men. Furthermore, Canada was a new nation, and, in Rowell's view, it should not be constrained by antiquated English decisions that denied women the right to hold public office. These decisions, he argued, 'are not applicable to the construction of such a statute as the *British North America Act*, creating the constitution of a new nation with legislative bodies having plenary powers. The question is not one of the granting or withholding of the franchise but of granting or withholding of executive and legislative powers.'

Rowell focused on the opening paragraphs of Justice Duff's reasons, which rejected the idea that the constitution could permanently entrench the common law disability of women, and urged the Privy Council to take an expansive view 'that the Constitution in its executive branch was intended to be capable of adaptation to whatever changes in the law and practice relating to the election branch [*sic*] might be progressively required by changes in public opinion.' He argued that when the Imperial Parliament had enacted the *British North America Act* in 1867, it 'did not withdraw from the control of the Executives, the Parliament and the Legislatures ... the right to determine whether women should or should not be eligible for any or all public offices.' The better view, Rowell argued, was that the constitution 'conferred upon the Executives, the Parliament and the Legislatures so created, full power and authority to deal with such matters.'

'A Constitutional Change so Fundamental and Momentous'

The Attorney General of Canada's written argument consisted almost entirely of quotations from the judgment of the Supreme Court of Canada with particular emphasis on the judgment of Chief Justice Anglin.[3] The Attorney General insisted upon strict adherence to the doctrine of original intent, arguing that the *British North America Act* 'ought to be construed to-day according to the intent of the Parliament which passed the Act, i.e., by reference to the natural and ordinary meaning of the words used at the date the statute was passed.' The disability preventing women from holding public office was so clearly the law in 1867 that had the framers of the constitution 'intended to remove that disability ... and effect a constitutional change so fundamental and momentous, they would have declared that intention in apt and explicit language and not by the furtive process of general words or on an indirect implication.' To this the Attorney General added that 'the fact that from 1867 to the present time men only have been considered eligible for appointment' established 'as unbroken and continuous usage showing that the contemporaneous interpretation of the enactment by persons of authority has been uniformly consistent with what is now claimed on behalf of the Attorney-General of Canada to be its true legal interpretation.'

Quebec filed a written case,[4] signed by Charles Lanctot and Aimé Geoffrion, stressing the province's special interest in the question. Section 73 of the *British North America Act* provided that the qualifications for membership in Quebec's upper house, the Legislative Council, were the same as those of the senators appointed from the province of Quebec. The Attorney General of Quebec tied this argument to Justice Duff's concern about the pre-Confederation exclusion of women from second legislative chambers. If women were to be allowed to sit in the Senate, 'a different provision from Section 73 would have been made for the Legislative Council of the Province of Quebec.' The province was 'deeply concerned with any changes which might be made in the composition' of the Senate, a body 'established for the safeguard of the rights of the Provinces.' Yet after this brief was filed and before the case was heard, under pressure from prominent Quebec feminist Idola Saint Jean,[5] Premier Taschereau withdrew Quebec's opposition to the appeal and took no part in the oral argument. The only other province to intervene – Alberta – filed a brief argument adopting the arguments of the women, signed by J.F. Lymburn and Rowell.[6]

'Words May Change Over the Course of a Century'

Argument before the Judicial Committee of the Privy Council began on 22 July 1929, and continued for three more days.[7] In addition to the lawyers, the audience consisted of about a dozen observers, mostly women, along with Rev. Canon H.J. Cody, a staunch conservative clergyman from Toronto.

The judges asked Rowell questions during his argument, indicating 'that they believe themselves concerned entirely with the meaning of the word "persons" used in the BNA Act 62 years ago, and the meaning then attached to the word by the imperial Parliament.'[8]

Rowell emphasised Canada's autonomy. He insisted that the BNA Act conferred complete self-government in domestic matters, thus freeing Canada from the original intentions of the framers. Lord Darling tested the proposition by asking whether the Canadian Parliament could rule that no male person should be appointed to the Senate. Rowell paused and then answered cautiously: if Parliament's ruling did not alter the terms of the BNA Act, it could do so, but not if the decision altered the constitution.[9]

Rowell argued that as women could now sit and vote in the provincial legislatures and in Parliament, they must be capable of serving in the cabinet as members of the Privy Council under section 11 of the BNA Act, which speaks of 'the Persons who are to be Members of that Council.' Rowell explained: 'If women could not be members of the

Privy Council and therefore members of the Dominion Cabinet, it was introducing an anomaly which was entirely unknown.' Sankey appeared to agree with this point: 'Then a woman may become a Prime Minister of Canada, and, although she is Prime Minister, she may not sit on the Privy Council.' Lord Merrivale added: 'She could not be Prime Minister without being a Privy Councillor.' Rowell pointed out that Irene Parlby had been a cabinet minister for seven years in Alberta under an interpretation of 'person' that included women. As Lord Darling observed wryly: 'If it does not include women then she has been sitting illegally for seven years.'[10]

It was Rowell's submission that the appointment of women to the Senate would not change the *BNA Act*. The disability of women from public office, he argued, was based on public policy not legal doctrine, and Canada should be free to break with the past. Lord Darling challenged Rowell: 'Is there any interpretation of public policy?' to which Rowell responded, 'No, my Lord.' This prompted a further intervention from Darling that drew a laugh: 'I suppose it is what the judges think is expedient at the time.' Rowell tried to give the same thought a more legal spin. 'Words may change over the course of a century,' he noted, to which Lord Tomlin countered, 'We must interpret the words in their meaning at the time the Act was passed.' As he frequently did at such moments, Lord Darling turned to literature and poetry for inspiration: 'When Pope wrote "Essay on Man" or when Darwin wrote his "Descent of Man" he did not exclude one sex.'[11]

'Is Any Woman Capable of That?'

Lafleur, at the age of seventy-two, made what turned out to be his final appearance before the Privy Council.[12] He insisted on a strict interpretation of the constitution; all that mattered was the natural meaning of the words at the time of Confederation. It was, he stated, 'obviously the intention of the legislature to use the term [persons] to exclude women from participating in high judicial functions.'[13] Appealing directly to English precedent, Lafleur argued: 'There was no room for an inference that the framers of the statute intended to render women eligible for membership in the upper chamber of the Canadian Parliament while they remained excluded from the British Parliament on which the Canadian Parliament was expressly modelled.'[14]

Counsel for the Dominion faced a number of questions that indicated the JCPC members had carefully prepared for the hearing. Geoffrey

Lawrence, the English barrister retained to assist the government of Canada, suggested that prior to 1919, there had never been a female member of the Privy Council. Lord Merrivale, relying on his knowledge of legal history, observed that centuries ago, Anne, Countess of Pembroke, had sat on the bench of His Majesty's justices. Then, Lord Darling asked two questions that suggested he was not prepared to view women as the full equals of men. The oath of a privy councillor was to advise the King 'without regard to love and affection,' he noted. 'Is any woman capable of that?' Lawrence responded succinctly in the negative. A privy councillor, Lord Darling observed, has 'to keep the King's counsel secret.' Was any woman capable of that? To this, Lawrence gave a more cautious reply: 'I leave that to your lordships,'[15] he responded.

Had Lord Darling asked these questions in a Canadian court seventy years later, he would have faced censure, if not removal from office. In 1929, however, his comments attracted a headline in the Canadian press, but no public suggestion that he had spoken out of turn.

In his reply, Rowell urged the judges not to refuse the appeal on the ground that the proper procedure was to amend the constitution. That, he pointed out, was very difficult to do. Rowell then made an overtly political point. No one, he observed, seemed to be opposed in principle to the admission of women to the Senate. Indeed, Rowell contended that the minister of justice had announced that the government would take legislative steps if the case failed before the courts. This submission prompted Lafleur to interrupt with a clarification: 'No,' he argued, 'he said he will consider it.' Lord Merrivale responded, 'It will probably depend on whether the pressure applied is strong enough.'[16]

At the conclusion of the argument, Lord Sankey politely announced that we 'could not possibly give judgment this term' and that, as expected, the case would be reserved.[17] 'We will take time to consider what advice we should humbly tender His Majesty. We cannot decide at this term, which is just closing. We thank you, gentlemen, for the great assistance you have rendered us, and we wish you a pleasant journey to Canada.'[18]

Lord Sankey dined with Prime Minister MacDonald that evening as the Canadian counsel prepared to leave London. Although he had undertaken the task of writing the opinion to decide the *Persons* case, Sankey had no intention of letting it get in the way of his well-deserved holiday. He recorded in his diary simply: 'End of term. I hope I have done my work as Lord Chancellor well.'[19] Upon arriving in Wales, Sankey wrote: 'It is a great relief to get a rest and change after all my hard work.'[20]

'I Believe We Have a Very Good Chance of Winning the Appeal'

The English solicitors representing the government reported tersely their impressions of the hearing: 'The indications are that the Appellants will succeed and that the [JCPC] will advise that the word "Persons" in section 24 of the *British North America Act* includes female persons.'[21] Rowell reported to Emily Murphy that she should not expect to learn the result of the appeal until mid-October, but he was cautiously optimistic about the result:

> As far as one could judge from the judges' observations during argument, they appeared to favour the Appellants' contentions rather than those of the Respondent, and I believe we have a very good chance of winning the appeal, although one should not count on it because we had a very uphill fight with the unanimous judgment of the Supreme Court against us.[22]

J.F. Lymburn, Alberta's Attorney General who had travelled to London to represent the province, confirmed Rowell's view when he met Murphy in early August upon his return to Edmonton. He reported that Rowell had 'presented a wonderful case – that nothing was omitted and that the facts were marshaled in a masterly and logical way.' The members of the JCPC had displayed 'marked and courteous attention' to counsel, and 'their remarks on the different points augur well for a victory.'[23]

'A Living Tree Capable of Growth and Expansion within Its Natural Limits'

The debate before the JCPC in the summer of 1929 involved more than just the appointment of women to the Senate of Canada. What was at stake was the meaning of the *British North America Act*. Was it little more than a statute, a legislative enactment of the Parliament at Westminster the meaning of which was frozen in time? Or was it a document designed to be the enduring 'charter of a nation,' one that was adaptable to meet the changing needs of an evolving and maturing nation?

This should not have been a difficult question for the Judicial Committee of Privy Council to answer in light of its past rejection of the centralised vision of Confederation offered by many of Canada's Founding Fathers. Having ignored the framers' intent with respect to the division of powers, why would it be any more difficult to do so in order to permit the appointment of women to the Senate? And yet the obviousness of this point was not apparent to the litigants, nor to their counsel. Although Rowell implied that the interpretation of a constitution was a different exercise than the construction of a statute, this was not the focus of his submissions to the Judicial Committee. What Rowell failed to enunciate, Sankey clarified in his opinion.

Two themes pervade the judgment Lord Sankey delivered on 18 October 1929. The first is the recognition that legal rules or customs are the products of a particular social and historical context. Laws may outlive the customs and traditions that gave rise to them, and courts should take this into account when interpreting the law in a different historical context. Sankey carefully reviewed the legal authorities that Lafleur had cited to demonstrate the long tradition of excluding women from public office, and acknowledged the centuries of legal discrimination against women, but refused to view the law in static terms or to be bound by the past. 'The exclusion of women from all public offices,' he wrote, 'is a relic of days more barbarous than ours' when 'the necessity of the times often forced on man customs which in later years were not necessary.'[24] Sankey recognized the influence of both social customs and traditions, 'which are stronger than law and remain unchanged long after the reason for them has disappeared.' The traditional exclusion of women from public office 'is not of great weight when it is remembered that custom would have prevented the claim from being made or the point being contested.'[25]

Lord Sankey explained that the word 'persons' was 'ambiguous, and in its original meaning would undoubtedly embrace members of either sex.' If the 'original meaning' of the word could include women, it would be social tradition and custom, not the law, that excluded women. In an approach that was consistent with the Judicial Committee's routine rejection of history and historical purpose, Sankey concluded: 'The appeal to history therefore in this particular matter is not conclusive.'[26] In Sankey's view, it was wrong 'to apply rigidly to Canada of today the decisions and the reasons therefor which commended themselves, probably rightly, to those who had to apply the law in different circumstances, in different centuries, to countries in different stages of development.' Referring to the judgment of the Supreme

Court in language that no doubt rankled Chief Justice Anglin and his colleagues, Sankey dismissed their 'appeal to Roman law and to early English decisions' as an insecure foundation 'on which to build the interpretation of the *British North America Act* of 1867.'[27] As the word 'persons' could include both genders, Sankey wrote, 'to those who ask why the word should include females the obvious answer is why should it not?'[28]

Sankey's second theme was the difference between statutory interpretation and constitutional interpretation. He characterized the evolution of the *British North America Act, 1867* as an affirmation of Canadian unity and self-determination. Again, Sankey emphasized the importance of social tradition and custom in legal development. As the final court of appeal for 'the Britannic system,' which includes 'countries and peoples in every stage of social, political and economic development and undergoing a continuous process of evolution,' the Privy Council 'must take great care therefore not to interpret legislation meant to apply to one community by a rigid adherence to the customs and traditions of another.'[29] Ironically, this voice of supreme colonial power was insisting upon the very independence and legal maturity that Canada's own judges had refused to claim for themselves.

It is within this context that Lord Sankey presented what has come to be the most memorable phrase in modern Canadian constitutional law, the very essence of constitutional interpretation in the post-*Charter* era: 'The *British North America Act* planted in Canada a living tree capable of growth and expansion within its natural limits.' The living tree metaphor described the constitution in the organic terms of growth and evolution. It was, wrote Sankey, neither the duty nor the desire of the Privy Council 'to cut down the provisions of the Act by a narrow and technical construction, but rather to give it a large and liberal interpretation' to allow the Dominion to be 'mistress in her own house.'[30]

Reading the *British North America Act* as a living document designed 'to provide a constitution for Canada, a responsible and developing state,' Sankey concluded that the word 'persons' in section 24 must include women. He found 'that there are some sections in the Act ... which show that in some cases the word 'person' must include females.' Section 133, giving 'any person' the right to use English or French in Parliament, the federal courts, and the Quebec legislature and courts, could hardly be restricted to men.[31] As Rowell had argued, Parliament and all the provincial legislatures except Quebec had acted on the power conferred by sections 41 and 84 to extend the franchise to qualified 'persons' to enfranchise women.

The 'living tree' metaphor was Sankey's invention. Counsel did not mention it in their arguments and the phrase was previously unknown to Canadian constitutional law. However, the concept of an organic constitution had deep roots in English legal thinking and resonated with the Fathers of Confederation in 1867.[32] Sankey may have been aware of similar language used by American scholars and judges to describe constitutional interpretation. In language strikingly similar to Sankey's 'living tree' metaphor, Oliver Wendell Holmes described the provisions of the American constitution as 'organic living institutions transplanted from English soil' and stated that their meaning could not be determined by using a dictionary 'but by considering their origin and the line of their growth.'[33] A Civil War–era lawyer in defending President Lincoln's expansive use of the war's power, described the constitution as resembling a tree 'native to the soil that bore it, - waxing strong in sunshine and in storm, putting forth branches, leaves, and roots, according to the laws of its own growth ...'[34]

Sankey concluded his first judgment as Lord Chancellor in the simple yet time honoured tradition:

> Their Lordships have come to the conclusion that the word 'persons' in s. 24 includes members of both the male and female sex, and that, therefore, the question propounded by the Governor General should be answered in the affirmative, and that women are eligible to be summoned to and become members of the Senate of Canada, and they will humbly advise His Majesty accordingly.[35]

He was proud of his judgment and immediately recognized its historical significance, taking the unusual step of reading it formally in court rather than simply releasing written copies.[36] Furthermore, although Sankey rarely mentioned specific cases in his personal diary, the *Persons* case was an exception, garnering a simple notation in his journal.[37]

'A Matter of Much Gratification'

The Canadian press applauded the decision, which it reported with mixed coverage. The *Toronto Daily Star* gave it a front-page headline: 'Canadian Women Win Right to Senate Seats.'[38] The *Edmonton Journal* welcomed the decision, observing that women could sit in the House of Commons, so their exclusion from the Senate was 'illogical.' It was, the paper recorded, good to have the 'anomaly removed.'[39]

Other newspapers featured the decision in less prominent places in their publications. For instance, the Toronto *Globe* relegated the story to page six,[40] while the *Manitoba Free Press* gave the front page to Ramsay MacDonald's visit to Canada and buried the *Persons* case on the back pages. London's *Daily Express* followed the same pattern and reported the *Persons* case decision on page seven while giving front page coverage to another Canadian constitutional story: 'Dominion Status: King's Speech Changes.'[41] Prime Minister Ramsay MacDonald, on the last day of his Canadian visit, had agreed with his Canadian counterpart Mackenzie King that the phrase 'the governments of our dominions' would replace 'our dominions' in the King's speeches.

For the most part, however, the British press accorded the decision significant coverage. The English dailies fastened on the phrase 'a relic of days more barbarous than ours'[42] and warmly applauded the judgment. The *Evening Standard* proclaimed that the judgment 'will have an indirect bearing on the political activities of women throughout the Empire.'[43] The *Daily Telegraph*, which had given the case the most extensive coverage of any English newspaper, called the decision 'a significant advance towards the equality of political rights for both sexes which is sometimes, quite erroneously, supposed to be already the rule of the civilized world.'[44] Yet, as if to disprove the very point that a new age for women's rights had dawned, in the days that followed, several dailies printed stories and editorials that had a decidedly sexist tilt.[45]

During this period, reform of the House of Lords was a topic of lively discussion in England.[46] The imbalance created by the dead hand of the past and hereditary peerages had even led some to say that the House of Lords must be either 'mended or ended.'[47] The *Manchester Guardian* observed that the Judicial Committee's decision 'can hardly fail to affect the claim of women here to admission to the House of Lords in their own right, whether by creation or inheritance.'[48] The *Daily Telegraph* suggested: 'Perhaps Second Chambers may remain the last male preserve. But not, we suspect, for many more years.'[49]

The decision also attracted international coverage. The *New York Times* published several stories on the decision's impact and influence on the role of women in public life.[50] It also reported that the British press was filled with speculation about what it meant for the venerable House of Lords, which still excluded women.[51]

Emily Murphy offered a gracious response to the Privy Council's judgment:

> It is a matter of much gratification to myself and my co-appellants in Alberta. The same is applicable to all the women of Canada. We are not considering the pronouncement of the privy council as a sex victory but rather as one which will now permit of our saying 'we' instead of 'you' in all affairs of state.[52]

She mentioned Quebec's last-minute withdrawal of its opposition as making for 'a fuller national unity.' Asked what qualifications a woman should have for the Senate, Murphy said she could do no better than to quote the constitution of the Irish Free State. Individuals suitable for such a position were 'citizens who have done honor or useful public service to the nation or who because of special qualifications or attainments represent important aspects of the national life.'[53]

The other women involved in the litigation also offered their observations. Nellie McClung praised Murphy for her hard work and diligence:

> We are naturally elated, though I must say we never despaired of ultimate victory. I am particularly pleased for Mrs. Murphy's sake. It was she who discovered that any five subjects could ask the government for an interpretation of any point of law. It was she who wrote all the letters and arranged every detail of the controversy. Her handling of the whole matter has been a masterpiece of diplomacy.[54]

Two of the Famous Five were pleased with the result, but had reservations about the Senate as an institution. Henrietta Muir Edwards applauded the principle of women's equality but distanced herself from the goal of having a woman appointed to the Senate:

> I care not whether or not women sit in the Senate. We have striven to gain recognition for the personal individuality of women; we have sought the right to a place in the Senate because of the principles involved. Now that the principle has been established, it is immaterial whether or not the right is used. This decision marks the abolition of sex in politics. It had been a long uphill fight.[55]

Irene Parlby reacted similarly:

I am sure that every woman in Canada will be very pleased to hear of the decision of the Privy Council in favor of women. We always felt that we had a very just appeal. Women in Canada are not particularly desirous of entering the Senate, but they felt that if they desired to do so the privilege should be theirs.[56]

Agnes Macphail, the only woman then sitting in the House of Commons, praised the decision as a moral victory, but also ridiculed the Senate as an institution:

I think the Senate, as it is presently constituted, is a menace to good government. I am not interested in the appointment of women to the Senate, but if women would like to serve there, they are equally capable of doing so, as the few hours of the few weeks spent by the senators in session would not be at all difficult. The divorce committee of the Senate is the only part at all over-worked.[57]

One of Macphail's opponents in the House of Commons quipped: 'I am sure Miss Agnes Macphail would make a fine senator.'[58]

Prime Minister Mackenzie King, cautious as always and aware that there were now five vacancies in the Senate, with a long list of aspiring candidates, said that he was pleased by the decision,[59] making it sound as though the government had won the case. For good measure, King added that if the decision had gone the other way, it had been his intention to seek a constitutional amendment.[60] Retired prime minister Sir Robert Laird Borden, likely surprised to learn that his book had been cited by Lord Sankey to justify the organic 'living tree' approach to constitutional interpretation[61] declined any comment.[62] Quebec Premier Taschereau's comment, no doubt gracious in intention, was glaring in its sexism: '"Miss Canada" had now emerged from her girlhood and had taken her seat as a full partner at the hearth of the nations of the world "as all good girls do."'[63]

Even some of the newspapers that supported the decision nevertheless expressed concern about the Senate as an institution. For example, the editorial board of the Ottawa *Citizen* praised the decision, but concluded: 'It is hard to believe that now that [women] have gained the privilege of being made senators, they will be particularly eager to take advantage of it.'[64]

Several commentators greeted the decision with remarks that were intended to be amusing, but do not appear that way to the modern reader. As one *Toronto Daily Star* writer asserted:

The only important immediate effect of the privy council ruling looked for is a liberal sprinkling of feminine letters subtly perfumed among the personal mail addressed to the Rt. Hon. W.L. Mackenzie King. The prime minister is in for a hard time. It was bad enough sorting out the claims of the men willing to sacrifice their ambitions and enter the Upper Chamber at their chief's command. If feminine wiles enter in, the task will be hopeless.[65]

Another observer noted: 'The only difficulty I foresee may arise from the impression that Senators must be persons of advanced years. Where are we going to get women willing to declare that they are old enough to qualify for this service.'[66]

Even some women expressed the kind of attitude that drove Murphy and McClung to despair. For instance, Miss Frances Carrie, a Conservative Party worker, asserted: 'I have always thought that men were much more qualified for such positions, but we have to keep up with the times.'[67] McClung was not amused by such comments, but she did her best to use irony in her ongoing quest for gender equality. Referring to a newspaper interview given by several prominent women and the 'indulgent laughter, mock congratulations and ironic expressions of gratitude' that greeted the news of the Privy Council's decision, McClung quipped: 'It does sound humorous. But there had to be a ruling on it ... And now, with the Senate doors open, there are only two great institutions, that will not accept women on equal terms, the church and beer parlours.'[68]

On a more serious note, McClung told a meeting of the Women's Club of Calgary, gathered to celebrate the victory: 'The findings of the Privy Council that we are "persons," once and for all, will do so much to merge us into the human family. I want to be a peaceful, happy, normal human being, pursuing my unimpeded way through life, never having to stop, to explain, defend or apologize for my sex.'[69]

'The Account Is Made Out on the Basis of My Regular Charge for Important Cases'

Newton Rowell was well compensated for his victory before the Judicial Committee on behalf of Murphy and her supporters, and from government coffers no less. He charged the government a fee of $10,000 to argue the case in the Privy Council, a healthy increase from the $2,000 fee he had charged to argue the case before the Supreme Court of Canada. The difference was explained by the month and a half taken up by transatlantic travel and waiting in London for the case to be reached by the Privy Council, all time that was charged out at Rowell's full rate.

Rowell's fee represented a substantial sum, but as he told Mackenzie King when negotiating his fee as counsel to the Customs Enquiry Commission in 1926, 'he was an expensive man.'[70] For the sake of comparison, in terms of 2006 dollars, Rowell's fee converts to more than $120,000.[71] Furthermore, Rowell's $10,000 fee for the *Persons* case was the same amount as the annual salary he was paid in 1936, when Lapointe and King appointed him Chief Justice of Ontario at the age of sixty-nine. Few Canadian families earned $10,000 a year and those who did lived in relative luxury. Rowell lived comfortably but he was not an ostentatious man, and he usually donated a significant portion of his income to his church, its overseas mission work, and to the Toronto Hospital for Sick Children.[72] He likely gave a substantial portion of his handsome *Persons* case fee to charity.

Rowell explained his account in a letter to Emily Murphy who, as his client, had to approve it before it was submitted to the Department of Justice for payment.

> The account is made out on the basis of my regular charge for important cases, viz: $250.00 per day, save that although I was absent from my office fifty days, or forty-five days apart from Sundays, attending the Privy Council, I have fixed a fee of $10,000 for the argument.'[73]

Rowell added $1,750 for seven days of his own time in Canada, $975 for thirteen days of his assistant's time spent on legal research, and $1,480.77 for travel expenses and other disbursements, for a total of $14,205.77. A lawyer from the Department of Justice advised Stuart Edwards that the account was too high, suggesting that Rowell's fee be reduced to $8,000 or $8,500 because Lafleur had only charged the government $5,517.73 in fees and disbursements for his services before the Privy Council.[74] The Department of Justice took its time and considered the suggestion, but when Rowell pressed Edwards for payment, the deputy minister relented and paid the account in full.

'Matters of Political Expediency'

Some senior members of the Canadian legal community regarded Sankey's decision as both radical and politically motivated.[75] Irked by some of the public praise heaped upon the Privy Council for rescuing the constitution from the narrow legalism of the Supreme Court, George F. Henderson, KC, a prominent Ottawa lawyer, published an unusually stinging attack on the Privy Council's judgment in the *Canadian Bar Review*. A bencher of the Law Society of Upper Canada and convenor of the editorial committee for the Canadian Bar Association publication, Henderson acknowledged that 'under ordinary circumstances, a criticism of a judgment of the Judicial Committee of the Privy Council is inadvisable,' but the *Persons* case judgment 'has led to so much press criticism of the Supreme Court of Canada ... proper respect for the administration of justice in Canada demands examination and comment.'[76]

The fundamental difference between the approach of the Supreme Court and that of the Privy Council, according to Henderson, was that the Supreme Court was 'a court of law' while the Privy Council was not bound by precedent and did not decide cases on legal grounds alone. The Privy Council was 'entitled, if not obliged to advise on grounds of public policy, and to take into account matters of political expediency.'[77]

Henderson's observation was surely ironic. No one claimed that the Judicial Committee of the Privy Council could legitimately decide cases on grounds of political expediency. Henderson argued that the Supreme Court had applied the settled rules of statutory interpretation that Lord Sankey and his colleagues had 'simply ... brushed aside,' ignoring in the process points that were 'obvious ... to a legal mind.'[78] Henderson also accused the Privy Council of being the willing tool of Mackenzie King, whom he claimed had secretly invited the JCPC to amend the constitution by judicial fiat:

> It has been rather plainly suggested that those now in authority in Canada wished the judgment to be as it is, and it is not impossible that, if this is the fact, the Learned Law Lords had knowledge of that fact; but one wonders if the average Canadian would care to think that judicial legislation has altered the constitution of the Senate of Canada.[79]

Henderson was not alone in regarding Sankey's judgment as completely out of line. A. Berridale Keith, a noted British constitutional scholar, described it as 'an unfortunate' decision 'which even its admirers have found difficult to reconcile with the judicial function.' In his view, the judgment was so problematic that 'no decision of the Privy Council is probably harder to defend as sound in law.'[80] However, the highly esteemed W. Ivor Jennings, another British constitutionalist, took a more charitable view. Jennings agreed that the decision was 'most remarkable' in that it 'departed from the traditional methods,' but added many welcomed the innovation as 'the strictly legal or historical method of interpretation leads often to nonsense.'[81]

There is no evidence to support Henderson's suggestion that the Privy Council was party to a constitutional subterfuge. If speculation is in order, it is more likely that Frank Anglin encouraged Henderson to write his scathing attack on the Privy Council. Anglin, who had harshly criticized the JCPC before it decided the *Persons* case, was unrepentant about his judgment in the case, and felt vindicated by Henderson's article. A year after the JCPC's judgment, when faced with the argument that the Supreme Court should modify a legal rule it considered to be out of touch with social values,[82] Anglin adopted Henderson's attack on the JCPC to justify adherence to his mechanical jurisprudence. The court had to decide whether the mother of an illegitimate child could maintain an action for damages occasioned by the child's death under a Quebec *Civil Code* provision allowing a 'parent' to sue. The mother relied on the *Persons* case, arguing that an interpretation of the *Civil Code* that excluded her from recovering damages 'savours of barbarism and would shock the sensibilities of persons holding enlightened views.' She urged the court to interpret the *Civil Code* in a manner 'more consistent with humane and liberal ideas.'[83]

Anglin insisted that the question was one for the legislature to answer: 'The short answer to this contention is that the courts must await the action of the legislature, whose exclusive province it is to determine what should be the law.' Referring to Henderson's article in the *Canadian Bar Review*, the Chief Justice continued: 'Whatever may occur elsewhere it would seem to be the plan of this 'Court of Law and Equity' [citing the *Supreme Court Act*] to give effect to the intention of the legislature as expressed, not to make the law as they think it should be. *Judicis est jus dicere, non dare* [It is a judge's duty to declare existing law, not to make new law].'[84]

Anglin unapologetically took issue with Lord Sankey on the role of the courts. For the Chief Justice, his role was to apply the literal meaning of the words contained in legislation or the constitution. Any changes should be left to the politicians. By contrast, Lord Sankey thought it was appropriate to decide cases in terms of broad organic principles that were adaptable to the times, particularly when, as Rowell had put it, the court was dealing with 'the charter of a nation.'

10

The Political, Cultural, and Legal
Legacy of the Persons Case

Reminding the prime minister of Sir Walter Scott's dictum, 'Who leaps the wide gulf should prevail in his suit,' Emily Murphy wrote to Mackenzie King within a day of the Privy Council's decision, urging him once more to appoint her to the Senate. She portrayed herself as the ideal non-partisan candidate; from a family of Conservatives, Murphy had become a Liberal and she now enjoyed the confidence of both the UFA and the labour movement. As she explained to the prime minister, he would have the chance to appoint other women to the Senate on partisan grounds, but 'the first appointment will be given on high grounds – that is to say as representing the women of Canada generally ... Canadians,' Murphy claimed, 'are expecting my appointment.' In doing so, she wrote, '[you would] demonstrate that your sympathies were with the claims of the Appellants, and that you were in accord with the decision of the Privy Council.'[1]

Although there was no vacancy from Alberta, Murphy told King that she had been 'informed by Alberta Liberals that this is not an insurmountable difficulty.' This was a dubious suggestion. It is hard to see how Murphy and her supporters could get around section 23 (5) of the *BNA Act*, which requires a senator to be 'resident in the province for which he is appointed.' Perhaps Murphy was referring to section 26 of the constitution, which allows the Governor in Council to add four to eight senators representing equally the four divisions of Canada.

King's response was not encouraging. He may have been sympathetic to the fight of the Famous Five, but he was non-committal about Murphy's appointment to the Senate. He promised to bring her 'representations ... to the attention of [his] colleagues at such time as we may have under consideration the filling of existing vacancies in the Senate,' but viewed as 'insurmountable' the difficulties associated with Murphy's appointment to represent any province other than Alberta.[2]

King remained true to his word and appointed a woman to the Senate of Canada on 15 February 1930, but the appointment went to Cairine Wilson from Ontario, not to Emily Murphy. Indeed, it is virtually impossible to see how King could have managed to appoint Murphy to fill the Ontario vacancy, yet she was bitterly disappointed. In a letter to Ontario premier Howard Ferguson, a close friend of her brother William, Murphy wrote that she had made 'no unfavourable comment' about the appointment, but was 'too ruffled in spirit to forward any congratulations to Ottawa.' Reiterating her appeal as a non-partisan candidate, Murphy claimed that 'nearly all the women, whether Conservatives, Liberals, or Progressives, felt that Mr. King would be taking high ground in making the first appointment in a non-partisan basis.' Still, she refused to give up hope, musing that the proverb 'God rights those who keep silence' might hold true.'[3]

In truth, Wilson possessed many of the political qualities that Murphy lacked, so much so that the only thing unusual about the appointment was her gender. Although her biography on today's parliamentary website describes her as a 'homemaker' and 'social worker,'[4] Wilson was also an active Liberal organizer with strong ties to the party establishment. In 1928, she helped to organize the first meeting of the National Federation of Liberal Women of Canada (NFLW), a national federation of local women's clubs, which met in Ottawa in April of that year. Wilson went on to serve as president of the organization from 1938 to 1948.[5] Furthermore, both Wilson's father, Robert Mackay, and her husband, Norman Wilson, had served in Parliament under Wilfrid Laurier; Mackay had been a Liberal senator from Quebec and her husband an MP from Ontario. In addition to her wealth and high social standing in Ottawa, Wilson was the mother of eight children.

Editorial writers praised Wilson's appointment in terms that stood in striking contrast to descriptions of the Famous Five. The *Ottawa Evening Journal* described Wilson as 'the very antithesis of the short-haired reformer' who 'talks of Freud' and the 'latest novel.' Instead, she was 'of the much more appealing and competent kind who makes a success of ... taking care of a home and ... family before meddling with and trying to make a success of everything else.'[6] Another editorial writer described Wilson as 'a lady of retiring disposition, of refinement and culture,' whose 'interest in public affairs has never been tinged with the desire for personal recognition or advancement,' noting that 'she took no part in the agitation for the recognition of women's right to sit in the Senate.' Wilson, the writer remarked, was preferable to 'one of the very industrious women politicians, spinsters, and others, who have talked incessantly of their rights as women without discharging any of their responsibilities as such.'[7]

Murphy was incensed by what she regarded as this 'odious talk' arising from 'spleen, hurt pride, jealousy and – worse than all – the loss of seats in the Senate which the gentry thought they had proscribed for all time.' The suggestion that she had failed to discharge her responsibilities was particularly galling. As she grumbled to Nellie McClung, 'Lord! I think we ought to ask now for an interpretation of the word "responsibilities."'[8] Nor did Murphy like what she read of Wilson's inauguration. A sword got caught in Senator Wilson's gown 'much ... to the amusement of the onlookers.' 'Isn't it time,' Murphy asked, 'that both the swords and trailing gowns be put out of the Senate?' She also regarded as humiliating the suggestion that Wilson's arm had been 'supported' as she went up to be sworn in: 'She went there as an equal, and not as a supported or protected person.'[9] Murphy was further riled by the suggestion contained in the Toronto *Mail and Empire* that there should be no more than five female senators, one from each region. The proposition that women should be 'satisfied' with five representatives, she complained to McClung, was 'nothing but unmitigated impertinence. We are not being elected as "women" or "men" but as "Persons."'[10]

Cairine Wilson proved to be an effective senator. In her first speech, she used the traditional language of maternal feminism to assure the nation that her duties in the Senate would not lead her to ignore her responsibilities at home. She explained that 'while engaged in public affairs' a woman 'by reason of her maternal instinct will remain the guardian of the home.'[11] This, no doubt, set her anxious male colleagues at ease. Wilson also acknowledged those who had struggled for women's rights, including the 'famous five women from Alberta' who had made her appointment possible.[12]

King was publicly proud to have appointed the first female senator, but privately he remained wary of the role of women in public life. The attendance of Agnes Macphail and Senator Wilson at a parliamentary restaurant luncheon to which the members of both house were invited perturbed King. 'I confess the presence of Miss McPhail [sic] & of (Senator) Wilson, at gatherings of the kind seems to me to lend a discordant note, or rather an incongruous one. Men do not like women at gatherings of the kind & the finer nature in women ought to cause them to remain away.' King lunched between the speaker of the Senate and the speaker of the House of Commons and recorded in his diary that both 'were of the same point of view.'[13]

Wilson served in the Senate of Canada for more than thirty years, dying in office at the age of seventy-seven. Steeped in the traditions of evangelical Christian teaching and Gladstonian liberalism, Wilson devoted her energies to feminist causes, the peace movement, and humanitarianism.[14] Between 1938 and 1948, she served as president of the National Federation of Liberal Women of Canada. During the Second World War, as the chair of the Canadian National Committee on Refugees, she struggled with limited success to convince King's government to admit Jewish refugees fleeing Nazi Germany. She also argued for liberalized divorce laws, equal pay, equal employment opportunities, and better welfare for working mothers. She was active with the National Council of Women, the Young Women's Christian Association, the Red Cross, and the Victorian Order of Nurses.[15] Cairine Wilson may have been selected as a safe alternative to the likes of Emily Murphy, but she nonetheless represented many of Murphy's ideals.

Another Chance for Emily Murphy?

Emily Murphy retired from the bench on 11 November 1931, but she never gave up her desire for a seat in the Senate. In April 1931, the death of Senator Prosper Lessard of Alberta created just such an opportunity. However, Mackenzie King's Liberals had been defeated in the 1930 general election, and Conservative leader R.B. Bennett was now Canada's prime minister. Murphy knew Bennett from his days as member of the Alberta legislature when he had been her ally in the promotion of improved property rights for women. Having spent the past decade trying to curry favour with Mackenzie King and the Liberals, Murphy now set out to renew her ties to the Conservative Party. As with previous Senate vacancies, supporters wrote to the prime minister to urge Murphy's appointment. Two of the organizations in which Murphy was a prominent member, the Montreal Women's Club and the Edmonton Press Club, were particularly outspoken in their support, writing to Bennett to encourage her appointment.[16]

Bennett was willing to disregard political affiliation when he chose Lessard's replacement, but he could not ignore the importance of religion. Deciding that tradition dictated Lessard would be replaced by a Catholic 'as the sole representative of the Catholic minority in our province,'[17] Bennett appointed Pat Burns, a well-known Liberal from Calgary. Burns was a wealthy, philanthropic rancher who had built a fortune on cattle as well as on the marketing of dairy and food products. His appointment was announced in spectacular fashion at a banquet marking his seventy-fifth birthday and the opening of the Calgary Stampede. *The Albertan* described Burns as 'the greatest single captain of industry in the West.'[18] Murphy was not given any serious consideration for the appointment.[19] She never stood a chance.

'There the Matter Stopped'

Two of the Famous Five died within a few months of each other in 1931. Louise McKinney died in June, and Henrietta Muir Edwards, still mentioned as Murphy's rival for the Senate, died in November. Two years later, in October 1933, Emily Murphy died of diabetes at the age of sixty-five. Almost to her dying day, she maintained her correspondence with Mackenzie King, gently chiding him in September for not making a speech when he visited Edmonton in September: 'We decided you were afraid of Agnes and the C.C.F.'s ... You should have me chasing her on ... the hustings. You would be surprised with all the nasty words I picked up in the Police Court.'[20]

In 1935, Prime Minister Bennett appointed Canada's second female senator, Iva Campbell Fallis, to represent Ontario. The Murphy family aspiration for a place in the upper chamber survived Emily's death. Kathleen Kenwood, Emily Murphy's daughter, revealed to Nellie McClung in 1939 her wish to fill a vacancy from Alberta so that she could 'carry on the work' Emily Murphy 'wanted to see done there.' [21] It was, however, almost fifty years after Viscount Sankey declared women persons under the *BNA Act* before a female senator was appointed from Alberta. In 1979, Prime Minister Joe Clark appointed Martha Palamarek Bielish, a Progressive Conservative.

In contrast to McKinney, Edwards, and Murphy, both Nellie McClung and Irene Parlby lived for many years after the decision in

the *Persons* case. Though they would have been superb senators, neither aspired to the office. Parlby blamed the complacency of women
for the government's repeated failure to reward the women of Alberta
for their struggle to gain full personhood: 'Mr. King appointed one
woman and later Mr. Bennett appointed another. There the matter
stopped. I fancy women appeared to take so little interest in the matter
that the powers that be thought it was safe to let the matter slide and
be forgotten.'[22]

Nellie McClung resisted overtures to return to politics. King tried to
entice her to run in Calgary West against R.B. Bennett in the 1930 general election because he could not stand the prospect of the Conservative leader winning his seat without a fight. 'I believe that you can beat
Bennett,' King wrote. So strong was his desire to see McClung run
against Bennett that King told her he 'would rather see you enter the
lists against Mr. Bennett than I would see myself secure in the next parliament, by an acclamation arranged for the two leaders.'[23] Despite
King's flattery, McClung would not budge and Bennett easily won re-
election in Calgary West.[24]

Despite her unwillingness to return to a career in electoral politics,
McClung remained keenly interested in public affairs. She wrote regular newspaper and magazine columns that gave her an effective platform for her views. When King was returned to the prime minister's
office in 1935, he appointed McClung to be a governor of the newly
formed CBC. In 1938, she accepted King's invitation to serve as a Canadian delegate at the assembly of the League of Nations in Geneva.

McClung was the only member of the Famous Five to witness Prime
Minister Mackenzie King's commemoration of the *Persons* case in June
of 1938. At the entrance of the Senate chamber, King unveiled a com-
memorative bronze tablet donated by the Canadian Federation of
Business and Professional Women. In front of three hundred senators,
members of Parliament, cabinet ministers, and representatives of
women's groups, King praised the Famous Five for raising 'the whole
question of women's rights and responsibilities with respect to the
conduct of public affairs.'[25]

As the threat of war loomed in 1938, Nellie McClung reminisced
about the battle for suffrage and pondered the place of women in public life. She was wistful about the promise of suffrage. She and other
advocates of women's voting rights had thought the vote meant liberty: 'We believed that enfranchisement meant emancipation. We
spoke glibly of freedom. We were obsessed with the belief that we

could cleanse and purify the world by law. We said women were naturally lovers of peace and purity, temperance and justice.' The fight to
win the vote for women was like nothing before. 'There never has been
a campaign like the Suffrage campaign,' she explained. 'You were
either with us or against us. We had all the arguments, and mixed with
our zeal for public righteousness, there was a definite contest of animosity for those who opposed us.' Taking stock, she believed that the
feminine voice in politics had accomplished little; it had failed to quell
the evils of discontent, materialism and war:

> We rejoiced over their discomfiture when victory came to us. But when
> all was over, and the smoke of battle cleared away, something happened
> to us. Our forces, so well organized for the campaign began to dwindle ...
> We had no constructive program for making a new world ... So the
> enfranchised women drifted. Many are still drifting.[26]

McClung retired to Victoria and continued to write her weekly columns on public affairs. In 1945, she published *The Stream Runs Fast: My
Own Story*, the second volume of an autobiography she had started a
decade earlier.[27] Six years later, in September 1951, Nellie McClung
died at the age of seventy-eight.

Like McClung, Irene Parlby had grown tired of electoral politics by
the time the *Persons* case was released. Parlby had decided in 1929 that
she did not want to run for re-election in the provincial election of June
1930. However, Henry Wise Wood, the president of the United Farmers of Alberta, pressured her to continue by warning that her departure from politics would cause 'irreparable loss to the organization.'
'No one else could have made the contribution you have,' he argued,
'no one else can fill your place.'[28] Responding to Parlby's obvious hesitation, Nellie McClung observed, 'the hostility to women in public life
is not lessening.' Having achieved a position of some influence, she
warned that Parlby's exit from political life 'will be a great loss to our
forces.'[29] Emily Murphy joined in the appeal to keep Parlby in provincial politics. 'Dear, dear Lady,' Murphy wrote, 'We cannot possibly
spare you so please do agree to stand once more. There will be a multi-
tude of disappointed women if you don't.'[30] Parlby reluctantly agreed
to run again and was returned once more as a member of the victori-
ous United Farmers of Alberta.

On the eve of the election, Parlby's career took an unexpected turn.
Prime Minister Bennett asked her to serve as one of Canada's three del-

egates to the League of Nations Assembly in Geneva. Parbly agreed, though her health suffered from the strain of the trip and her duties in Geneva. She eventually returned to the provincial legislature and spoke frequently of the lessons she had learned about international relations and collective security. As the time for the next election drew near, she decided firmly to end her political career. In November 1934, Parlby announced her retirement from politics.[31]

In retirement Parlby remained a strong and respected voice on public affairs. She actively opposed William Aberhart's Social Credit party that swept the UFA from office in 1935 after the scandal that erupted when Premier Brownlee was sued for the seduction of a young clerk.[32] Aberhart acknowledged the contribution of the Famous Five when he accepted portraits of the women that were donated to hang in the provincial legislature in March 1939,[33] but so far as Parlby was concerned Aberhart and his Social Credit colleagues were no better than fascist thugs. During the 1940 provincial election, Parlby returned to the political stage to blast Social Credit for 'whacking lies' and its repression of any criticism of its policies. She even accused Aberhart of adopting Hitler-style tactics to ignore the rights of Parliament and free speech.[34] Parlby's efforts were to no avail; Aberhart and the Social Credit Party were re-elected, albeit with a reduced majority. Irene Parlby died in 1965 at the age of ninety-seven.

John Sankey

Sankey remained a loyal supporter of Prime Minister Ramsay MacDonald, though the prime minister's tenure was tumultuous, especially after 1931 during the period of coalition government. MacDonald repaid Sankey by refusing to bow to Conservative pressure to replace him as Lord Chancellor with Lord Hailsham. As MacDonald explained to a friend, he needed a 'gentle feminine hand to look after me and wagging finger to admonish me, and so I stick to Sankey, wise, devoted and never troublesome. If he pours a bottle of boiling water over me now and again – well, don't all old ladies do that when their hands tremble with affection.'[35]

When Ramsay MacDonald resigned as prime minister in 1935, Sankey's term as Lord Chancellor came to an end. MacDonald was succeeded by Stanley Baldwin and Sankey was replaced by the man he himself had replaced in 1929, the Conservative Lord Hailsham.

During his time as Lord Chancellor, Sankey was preoccupied with some of the non-legal duties that came with his office and this limited the time he had available to sit as a judge. In particular, he chaired two important Imperial Conferences, one dealing with Ireland and the other with Indian independence, always with the same steady hand that he had demonstrated as chair of the Coal Commission. Similarly, in 1932 and 1933, Sankey quelled a revolt by some judges furious over proposals to cut judicial salaries.

Although Sankey rarely spoke in the House of Lords, he had the satisfaction of introducing the government's bill to reform working conditions in the coal mines. The bill was a less drastic measure than what he had proposed in 1919, but it was also the best the minority Labour government could do. Sankey's speech earned praise from far and wide. Future United States Supreme Court Justice Felix Frankfurter, still at Harvard Law School, who followed Sankey's career closely through their mutual friend Harold Laski, wrote: 'Will you permit me to say with what enlightenment I have read the full text of your speech in Hansard moving the Coal Bill.'[36]

Traditionalists may regard Sankey's legacy as less than memorable,[37] but his contribution to Canadian constitutional development beyond the *Persons* case is noteworthy.[38] Following his bold judgment in the *Persons* case, Lord Sankey continued to offer an expansive constitutional vision of the role of the Dominion Parliament in Canadian federalism. This approach stood in marked contrast to that of his well-known predecessor and friend, Viscount Richard Haldane. Haldane favoured expanded provincial powers at the expense of the Dominion, but Sankey was not so inclined. He recognized the power of the central government and Canadian autonomy, even independence, within the Empire.

In the *Aeronautics Reference*,[39] the JCPC with Sankey at its helm was asked to determine which level of government had the constitutional authority to control and regulate the new field of aeronautics. Sankey wrote a strong judgment in favour of the Dominion's powers, reversing the decision of the Supreme Court of Canada.[40] He upheld the *Aeronautics Act*,[41] a statute enacted pursuant to an international aeronautics convention, and relied on the Dominion's power to ensure the performance of Canada's obligations arising under foreign treaties.[42]

As in the *Persons* case, Sankey's judgment was premised on an overarching approach to constitutional interpretation. The *BNA Act*, he explained, was 'a great constitutional charter' and its interpretation should not 'allow general phrases to obscure the underlying object of the Act, which was to establish a system of government upon essentially federal principles.' To distance himself from the Privy Council's expansive approach to provincial rights, Sankey stated that while past cases were 'useful' guides they were not determinative: 'It is always advisable to get back to the words of the Act itself and to remember the object with which it was passed.' In Sankey's view, the purpose of the *BNA Act* was to create a strong central government. As he explained,

> While the Courts should be jealous in upholding the charter of the Provinces as enacted in s. 92 it must no less be borne in mind that the real object of the Act was to give the central Government those high functions and almost sovereign powers by which uniformity of legislation might be secured on all questions which were of common concern to all the Provinces as members of a constituent whole.[43]

Sankey took a similar approach to Canadian autonomy in *British Coal Corporation v. The King*.[44] Effectively reversing the Privy Council's judgement in *R. v. Nadan*, which prohibited the Dominion government from abolishing criminal appeals to the JCPC, Lord Sankey relied on the *Statute of Westminster* of 1931 to permit the abolition of criminal appeals, upholding a federal law to that effect passed in 1933. In 1949, following a lengthy reference that took seven years to resolve,[45] the Parliament of Canada took the final step and abolished appeals in civil cases, thereby severing the link with British justice that had allowed Emily Murphy and the Famous Five to achieve personhood for Canadian women.

Newton Rowell

Newton Rowell remained active in his church and international affairs for the rest of his life, serving as the president of the Canadian Institute of International Affairs. He also remained a dedicated and active member of the bar. He was elected an honorary bencher of Lincoln's Inn in England, a rare achievement for a lawyer outside Britain, and served as president of the Canadian Bar Association from 1932 to 1934.

Rowell also continued to litigate constitutional cases (and others) before the Supreme Court of Canada, often representing the Government of Canada. In addition, he appeared several more times before the Judicial Committee in London.[46] Particularly noteworthy was

Rowell's involvement in the case of the *Proprietary Articles Trade Associ-*
ation case,[47] when he fended off another challenge to Canada's anti-
combines legislation. Rowell also represented the federal government
in the Bennett New Deal cases,[48] defending legislation that sought to
introduce a national minimum wage, maximum hours of work, an
unemployment insurance scheme, and help for insolvent farmers. The
legislation, introduced by R.B. Bennett in the dying days of his government in 1935, was the Conservative government's rather late response
to the ills of the Great Depression. It was left to Mackenzie King, who
had been returned to office in 1935, to deal with the constitutional
validity of the package.

It has been suggested that King was hostile to the legislation and
that he referred the issue of its constitutionality to the courts as a matter of political expediency.[49] However, King consistently respected the
role of the courts in making constitutional determinations and there
may well have been nothing sinister in his move.

Bennett was pleased that Rowell was chosen to defend his legislation before the courts,[50] and Rowell did so with great zeal. For Rowell,
defending the legislation, much like his fight for the Famous Five to
secure the recognition of women as persons, was more than a mere
retainer. He believed fervently in the legislation and its objectives.
Before the Supreme Court, the cases met with divided success, but
most of the legislation was declared unconstitutional. The Privy Council granted special leave to appeal, but Rowell was too ill to travel to
London. Louis St Laurent, a future minister of justice and prime minister, argued the appeals in the fall of 1936 when the Privy Council
upheld most of the decisions of the Supreme Court of Canada, declaring much of the legislation unconstitutional. The decisions in these
cases helped to promote the idea that Canada ought to abolish outright
all appeals to the Privy Council.[51]

In September 1936, Ernest Lapointe, once again King's minister of
justice, offered Rowell, now seventy years old, the post of Chief Justice
of Ontario. After some thought and consideration about his ill health,
Rowell agreed.[52] Within a year, in August 1937, King turned to Rowell
again, this time to lead a Royal Commission on the division of powers
between the Dominion and provincial governments. Rowell accepted
and served as the chair of the Royal Commission on Dominion–Provincial Relations, also known as the Rowell-Sirois Commission, until
the autumn of 1938. He suffered a heart attack in the spring of that year
followed by a stroke that affected his speech, and resigned as chair of

the commission and as Chief Justice of Ontario in October 1938.[53] Rowell died in November 1941 at the age of seventy-four.

Mackenzie King and the Political Legacy of the *Persons* Case

Prime Minister King maintained his fondness for references to the courts to determine the constitutionality of legislation and his respect for the role of the judiciary as the final authority on constitutional issues. King's high esteem for the judiciary was demonstrated in the 1930s when the government decided to find a new home for the Supreme Court of Canada. The Court sat in a hopelessly inadequate building, originally constructed to house workshops for the Parliament building. It was finally condemned as injurious to health and a fire hazard in 1936.[54] King rejected a proposal to move the Supreme Court to Sussex Drive in favour of a plan to house the court in a new building on Wellington Street adjacent to Parliament. He insisted that the Court's building and location should reflect its importance as a central national institution. Placing the Court beside Parliament was his way of 'presenting a fine symbolic picture of the different branches of the Government – the Executive & the Judiciary – paralleling the Legislature on Parliament Hill – also a symbolic picture of Confederation itself.'[55]

Mackenzie King had ample opportunity to appoint more women to the Red Chamber. Between the time of Cairine Wilson's appointment in February 1930 and his retirement in November of 1948, Mackenzie King appointed sixty-seven more senators. Despite King's praise for the Famous Five and Murphy's belief that he supported the appointment of women to the Senate, not one of King's new senators was a woman. King's successors did not do much better. Together, R.B. Bennett, Louis St Laurent, John Diefenbaker, and Lester B. Pearson, over a twenty-five-year period, appointed one hundred thirty-four senators. Only eight of them were women.[56]

It was only with the arrival of Pierre Trudeau in 1968 that the number of women appointed to the Senate began to increase, although still not significantly. Of the eighty-one senators appointed by Trudeau during his fifteen years in office, twelve were women, more than the combined total of his predecessors. Joe Clark, with a minority government and nine months as prime minister, managed to appoint one woman among his eleven Senate appointments, while John Turner, prime minister for mere months, appointed three senators, not one of whom was a woman. Brian Mulroney, in office from 1984 to 1993, with the greatest majority in Canadian history, appointed fifty-seven senators, thirteen of whom were women. Kim Campbell, Canada's only female prime minister, made no senate appointments at all. Most impressive is the record of Jean Chrétien, who appointed thirty-three women in the seventy-five appointments he made to the Senate in just over a decade. Six of Paul Martin's seventeen appointments were women. The result is that in 2006 only thirty-three of Canada's one hundred and five senators are women.

The Cultural Legacy of the *Persons* Case and the Famous Five

Over the years, Canadians have come to honour the *Persons* case as a symbol of equality and the legal recognition of the full personhood of all citizens. That recognition, like the appointment of women to the Senate, was not soon in coming. It was not until the revival of the feminist movement in the 1970s and the approach of the fiftieth anniversary of Viscount Sankey's judgment that Canadians renewed their interest in the case and its legacy. In 1979, Edward Schreyer created the Governor General's Awards in Commemoration of the *Persons* case to recognize the legal and political fight of the Famous Five, rewarding individuals who have made a long-standing and substantial contribution to the equality of women in Canada. As well, *Persons* Day celebrations sponsored by the Women's Legal Education and Action Fund commemorated the case as a focal point in the struggle for gender equality. The Famous Five Foundation promotes education about the women behind it.[57] Twenty years after the creation of the Governor General's Awards, in honour of the seventieth anniversary of Sankey's judgment, a statue of the Famous Five, promoted by the Famous Five Foundation and sculpted by Barbara Patterson of Edmonton, was unveiled at Calgary's Olympic Plaza. The same statue sits on Parliament Hill amid the various political dignitaries of Canadian history and was unveiled in Ottawa on 18 October 2000. That year, the Bank of Canada issued a new $50 bill with the Famous Five statue on the reverse.

Along with celebrations of the *Persons* case have come attacks on the racism and xenophobia of Murphy and her fellow petitioners.[58] Others have defended the women as products of their age. Nancy Millar, the author of a popular account of the *Persons* case,[59] explained in 1999, 'Every age has its language and understanding. Who among us is so wise that we can be right for all seasons and all reasons?'[60] Liberal member of Parliament Jean Augustine, who spoke on behalf of the National Liberal Women's caucus to promote placing the Famous Five on the $50 bill, stated: 'Members of the women's caucus are very well aware that the Famous Five held some views that would be unacceptable today. Nevertheless, members believe that people must be viewed in the context of their times and that this should not detract from the enormous impact of their accomplishments.'[61]

The Legal Legacy of the *Persons* Case: The Living Tree

The *Persons* case ranks among the most significant in Canadian constitutional history. Yet, as we have seen, Lord Sankey's constitutional permission to appoint women to the Senate did not open the floodgates, even to the present day. The broader constitutional legal legacy of the *Persons* case, like its cultural legacy, is of relatively recent origin. Although more than fifty years passed between the Privy Council's decision and the enactment of the *Charter of Rights and Freedoms* in 1982, it is Lord Sankey's approach to constitutional interpretation that has dominated the Supreme Court of Canada's approach to *Charter* interpretation.

The idea that the constitution was a timeless document capable of adapting over time to meet the changing needs of Canadian society did not have an immediate resonance in the Canadian legal community. Most constitutional scholars and judges had been hostile to the manner in which the Privy Council ignored the original meaning of the *BNA Act* for the purposes of granting greater powers to provincial governments. Even those who accepted that the courts had to be free to allocate legislative powers for problems that could not have been predicted in 1867 resisted the proposition advanced in the *Persons* case that the courts were now free, on the basis of changed social circumstances, to permit what had plainly been forbidden when the constitution was written. Unrepentant to the end, Chief Justice Frank Anglin typified this attitude by distancing himself from the living tree principle and insisting on a limited role for judicial interpretation.[62]

One finds only passing references to the living tree principle in the decisions of the Supreme Court well into the 1970s.[63] In June 1979, almost exactly fifty years after Lord Sankey's judgment, Canadian courts rediscovered the living tree. The Supreme Court of Canada struck down a Quebec law that restricted the use of English in tribunals that did not exist in 1867 and were not mentioned in the language rights guarantees of the *BNA Act*. The court referred to Lord Sankey's determination to 'give the *British North America Act* a broad interpretation attuned to changing circumstances,' and quoted the living tree passage with approval. The Court held that 'it would be overly-technical to ignore the modern development' of new government agencies 'which play so important a role in our society, and to refuse to extend to proceedings before them the guarantee of the right to use either French or English by those subject to their jurisdiction.'[64]

Several more cases followed through the early 1980s in which Justice Brian Dickson endorsed the living tree metaphor. As he explained in a 1980 decision:

> There is nothing static or frozen, narrow or technical, about the Constitution of Canada ... If the Canadian Constitution is to be regarding as a 'living tree' and legislative competence as 'essentially dynamic' then the determination of categories existing in 1867 becomes of little, other than historic, concern.[65]

Despite these references to the living tree, the *Persons* case did not come into its own until the dawn of the *Charter* era. In 1984, the landmark decision *Hunter v. Southam Inc.*[66] introduced the purposive approach to constitutional interpretation, requiring the courts to go beyond literal meaning and to delve into the fundamental and underlying reason for the law or guarantee at issue. In that case, Justice Dickson invoked the living tree to describe his vision of a constitution: 'Drafted with an eye to the future ... to provide a continuing framework for the legitimate exercise of governmental power and ... for the unremitting protection of individual rights and liberties.' A constitution, so difficult to amend, must 'be capable of growth and development over time to meet new social, political and historical realities often unimagined by its framers.'[67]

The Supreme Court's adoption of the living tree approach to *Charter* interpretation stood in stark contrast to an alternative approach to constitutional interpretation then gaining in influence in the United States: original intent, based on a particular conservative vision attributed to the framers of the American constitution.[68] In *Reference re Motor Vehicle Act (British Columbia) s. 94(2)*,[69] the Canadian Supreme Court was asked to interpret the section 7 guarantee of 'life, liberty and security of the person and the right not to be deprived thereof except in accordance with fundamental justice.' The federal Department of Justice submitted evidence that the officials responsible for the wording of section 7 had assured the joint parliamentary committee responsible for the final draft of the *Charter* that the phrase 'principles of fundamental justice' was entirely procedural in nature. Yet the Supreme Court refused to be bound by this narrow, albeit original, interpretation, and ruled that section 7 allowed the courts in some cases to review and strike down laws that were substantively unjust. As Justice Antonio Lamer wrote, 'If the newly planted "living tree" which is the *Charter* is to have the possibility of growth and adjustment over time, care must be taken to ensure that historical materials, such as the Minutes of Proceedings and Evidence of the Special Joint Committee, do not stunt its growth.'[70] In 1991, Justice Beverley McLachlin echoed the sentiments of Justice Lamer in a decision upholding Canada's election boundaries law. 'The past,' she wrote, 'plays a critical but non-exclusive role in determining the content of the rights and freedoms granted by the Charter. The tree is rooted in past and present institutions, but must be capable of growth to meet the future.'[71]

Lord Sankey's approach to constitutional interpretation, although contested by some scholars,[72] now seems to be just as firmly entrenched as the *Charter of Rights and Freedoms* itself. The Supreme Court considers the living tree a foundational constitutional principle listing it as such in the *Quebec Secession Reference*,[73] and invoking it in the *Reference re Same-Sex Marriage*. As the Court explained in the *Same-Sex Marriage* reference, 'one of the most fundamental principles of Canadian constitutional interpretation' is to ensure that the constitution 'by way of progressive interpretation, accommodates and addresses the realities of modern life.'[74]

Although it is most often associated with so-called liberal or progressive causes, some litigants and judges have invoked the living tree principle to promote more traditional constitutional values.[75] In *Reference re Same-Sex Marriage*, both sides invoked Lord Sankey's approach to constitutional interpretation to deal with Parliament's power over marriage and divorce.[76] Proponents argued that the definition of this legislative power had to evolve to reflect changing social mores, and opponents argued that such an interpretation would exceed the living tree's 'natural limits.' The Court declined to find that same sex marriage exceeded the natural limits of the living tree, and held that 'a progressive interpretation of the head of power must be adopted.'[77] An argument based on the natural limits approach could only succeed 'if its proponents can identify an objective core of meaning which defines what is "natural" in relation to marriage.' Instead, there were 'competing opinions on what the natural limits of marriage may be.' The Court determined, the 'only objective core which ... is "natural" to marriage is that it is the voluntary union of two people to the exclusion of all others.'[78]

The living tree metaphor has a timeless quality because it infuses constitutional interpretation with life at the same time that it imposes discipline through limits; the living tree is capable of growth and expansion, but only within its *natural limits*. The Supreme Court has respected this symmetry and limited the doctrine's reach where appropriate. Justice Dickson, arguably the leading modern exponent of the living tree metaphor, insisted that interpretation, whether statutory or constitutional, was a disciplined exercise that did not confer unfettered discretion upon the judiciary.[79] In *R. v. Big M Drug Mart Ltd.*, he warned that the court must be careful 'not to overshoot the actual purpose of the right or freedom in question, but to recall that the *Charter* was not enacted in a vacuum, and must therefore ... be placed in its proper linguistic, philosophic and historical contexts.'[80] Later cases have respected what the court perceived to be the limits of natural growth.[81] Chief Justice Beverly McLachlin has embraced the living tree on several occasions, but in a 2002 decision, writing for the majority of the Court, she rejected an attempt based on the living tree principle to recognize a constitutional right to basic welfare.[82]

Universal Personhood and the Living Tree

By the time the *Persons* case was decided in 1929, Emily Murphy, Henrietta Muir Edwards, Nellie McClung, Louise McKinney, and Irene Parlby had each reached the height of their respective political and public lives. In many respects, however, they had lost touch with the concerns of younger women and they failed in their attempt to rekindle the passions of the suffrage movement in their fight to secure the appointment of women to the Senate. Although they won their case before the Privy Council, their legal victory did not produce significant political results in their own time. The recognition of women as legal persons was a momentous legal achievement, but full personhood required more than an edict from the Judicial Committee of the Privy Council in London at a time when that institution's authority was being questioned and in an era not yet ready to embrace women as true equals.

All five women involved in the *Persons* case were crucial to the effort, but the case never would have happened without Emily Murphy. And though Murphy fought for an important principle, she was motivated by her personal ambition to be appointed Canada's first female senator. An examination of the beliefs and attitudes of Emily Murphy and her four colleagues reveals a serious discontinuity to the modern reader. The Famous Five fought for the legal recognition of the equality of women, but their philosophy of maternal feminism was a spent force and many of their views about race and the disabled are repugnant to modern eyes. They were the product of a bygone era when social and cultural difference was shunned rather than embraced and when the vigorous legal protection of equality rights for all was not yet a reality. When assessing the contributions of these women, we must remember that equality is an evolving concept. It takes different shape and form in different times, and it may be that the champions of equality in one era will fail to live up to the ideals that emerge in another. Despite what modern readers may regard as their serious flaws, it cannot be denied that the Famous Five ultimately played a major role in the evolution of the Canadian approach to equality. With the courage and determination to fight the *Persons* case to the bitter end and to secure a victory few could have predicted, Emily Murphy and her colleagues created a legacy that transcends their own shortcomings.

The legacy of the *Persons* case – the ideal of universal personhood and the living tree approach to constitutional interpretation – embodies the very purpose of the *Charter of Rights and Freedoms*. Rediscovered by the judiciary almost fifty years after Lord Sankey's decision, the living tree approach to constitutional interpretation renders the *Charter* capable of responding to the changing needs of society while at the same time balancing the rights of individuals with the demands of democratic accountability.

Notes

Introduction

1 *Edwards v. Attorney General of Canada*, [1930] A.C. 124 at 128.
2 *Re Board of Commerce*, [1922] A.C. 191; *Fort Frances Pulp and Paper Co. v. Manitoba Free Press Co.*, [1923] A.C. 695; *Nadan v. The King*, [1926] A.C. 482. See John Saywell, *The Lawmakers: Judicial Power and the Shaping of Canadian Federalism* (Toronto: University of Toronto Press, 2002), 150–86.
3 *Toronto Electric Commissioners v. Snider*, [1925] A.C. 396.
4 Viscount Haldane, 'The Judicial Committee of the Privy Council' (1923) 1 *Cambridge L.J.* 143 at 150.
5 H.A. Smith, 'Residue of Power in Canada' (1926) 4 *Can. Bar Rev.* 432; V.C. MacDonald, 'The Canadian Constitution Seventy Years After' (1937) 15 *Can. Bar Rev.* 401 at 426; W.P.M. Kennedy, 'The British North America Act: Past and Future' (1937) 15 *Can. Bar Rev.* 393 at 398–9; F.R. Scott, 'The Consequences of the Privy Council's Decisions' (1937) 15 *Can. Bar Rev.* 485 at 493–4; Richard Risk, *A History of Canadian Legal Thought* (Toronto: University of Toronto Press, 2006), 241.
6 [1930] A.C. 124 at 135.
7 Ibid., 136.
8 Ibid., 128.
9 Ibid., 126.
10 J. McLaren, 'Maternal Feminism in Action – Emily Murphy, Police Magistrate' (1988) 8 *Windsor Yearbook of Access to Justice* 234; A. Acorn, 'Snapshots

Then and Now: Feminism and Law in Alberta' (1996) 35 *Alta. L.R.* 140;
Linda Kealey, ed., *A Not Unreasonable Claim: Women and Reform in Canada
1880s–1920s* (Toronto: Women's Press, 1979), 7; Veronica Strong-Boag,
Introduction to Nellie McClung, *In Times Like These* (1915; reprint Toronto:
University of Toronto Press, 1972); Marlene LeGates, *In Their Time: A His-
tory of Feminism in Western Society* (London: Routledge, 2001), 243; Sarah
Carter, Lesley Erickson, Patricia Roome, and Char Smith, eds., *Unsettled
Pasts: Reconceiving the West through Women's History* (Calgary: University of
Calgary Press, 2005).

11 McClung, *In Times Like These*, 22.

12 Henrietta Muir Edwards, 'Motherhood, God's Greatest Gift,' *Canadian
Home Journal*, May 1931.

13 'Hon. Irene Parlby Visiting Scotland Tells of Women's Political Status in
Canada,' *Edmonton Journal*, 9 October 1928.

14 'The Political Position of Canadian Women,' in *Women of Canada: Their Life
and Work* (National Council of Women 1902), 51.

15 'The New Chivalry,' *Red Deer Advocate*, 26 February 1915, Glenbow
Archives, Clippings File for Nellie McClung.

16 *The Stream Runs Fast* (Toronto: T. Allen, 1945), 27.

17 Undated clipping, Parlby Papers, File 1.

18 'Support of Red Cross and Food Problem Main Work of Farm Women,' *Calgary Herald*, 22 January 1918.

19 See Carol Hancock, *Nellie McClung: No Small Legacy* (Kelowna, BC: North-
stone, 1996), especially chap. 5; Russell Allen, ed., *The Social Gospel in Canada* (Ottawa: National Museums of Canada, 1975); Mary Kinnear, 'Religion
and the Shaping of "Public Woman": A Post-Suffrage Case Study,' in Margaret Van Die, ed., *Religion and Public Life in Canada* (Toronto: University of
Toronto Press, 2001).

20 McClung, *In Times Like These*, 22

21 Acorn, 'Snapshots Then and Now,' 141. See also Jennifer Henderson, *Settler
Feminism and Race Making in Canada* (Toronto: University of Toronto Press,
2003), chap. 3.

22 Acorn, 'Snapshots Then and Now,' 141–2; Mariana Valverde, '"When the
Mother of the Race is Free": Race, Reproduction, and Sexuality in First
Wave Feminism,' in F. Iacovetta and M. Valderde, eds., *Gender Conflicts:
New Essays in Women's History* (Toronto: University of Toronto Press, 1992),
chap. 1.

23 McClung, *In Times Like These*, 97.

24 McKinney, 'The Farmers Opportunity,' Speech at the U.F.A. Convention,
22 January 1919, McKinney Papers.

25 King appointed Cairine Wilson, a loyal Liberal, to the Senate on 15 February 1930, several months after the Privy Council declared women to be persons and shortly before he was defeated by R.B. Bennett in August 1930. See chapter 10 in this volume.

1: First of the Five

1 Lorna Sage, *The Cambridge Guide to Women's Writing in English* (Cambridge: Cambridge University Press, 1999), 456.
2 For a critical feminist perspective on Murphy's writing, see Jennifer Henderson, *Settler Feminism and Race Making in Canada* (Toronto: University of Toronto Press, 2003), chap. 3.
3 Emily Murphy, *Open Trails* (Toronto: J.M. Dent, 1920), 186
4 Byrne Hope Sanders, *Emily Murphy: Crusader* (Toronto: Macmillan, 1945), 125–6.
5 Catherine Cavanaugh, 'The Women's Movement in Alberta as Seen through the Campaign for Dower Rights, 1909–1928' (MA thesis, University of Alberta, 1986), traces the history of the struggle for improved property rights.
6 Undated, unsigned letter from 'A Western Canadian Wife,' Murphy Papers Edmonton, Correspondence, Folder 1.
7 See Margaret McCallum, *Prairie Women and the Struggle for Dower Law, 1905–1920* (Winnipeg: Canadian Legal History Project, Faculty of Law, University of Manitoba, 1992).
8 *Overland v. Himelford*, [1920] 2 W.W.R. 490.
9 *Married Woman's Home Protection Act*, S.A. 1915, c. 4, s. 7.
10 *Dower Act*, S.A. 1917, c. 14.
11 Emily Murphy to Hon C.W. Cross A.G., 23 March 1916, Murphy Papers Edmonton, Box 1, File 24.
12 Emily Murphy to Hon. C.W. Cross, 24 June 1916, Murphy Papers Edmonton, Box 1, File 24, referring to Cross's letter, not in the file.
13 Mrs Snider to Emily Murphy, 15 June 1916, Murphy Papers Edmonton, Box 1, File 28.
14 *Edmonton Morning Bulletin*, 14 June 1916.
15 'Woman Magistrate in Edmonton,' *Edmonton Journal*, 14 June 1916.
16 Amanda Glasbeek, 'Maternalism Meets the Criminal Law: The Case of the Toronto Women's Court' (1998) 10 *Can. J. of Women and Law* 480.
17 Lawson-Tancred, 'Women as Magistrates' (1923) 25 *Home and Politics*.
18 *Star Weekly*, 24 December 1920, Murphy Papers Edmonton, Box 1, File 30.
19 Interview, *Toronto Daily Star*, 21 September 1929, Murphy Papers Edmonton, Scrapbook 1.

20 William Arthur Deacon, Emily Murphy Obituary, *Mail and Empire* (Toronto), 4 November 1933, Murphy Papers Edmonton, Box 1, File 31.

21 Emily Murphy, 'A Straight Talk on Courts,' *Maclean's*, 1 October 1920.

22 Emily Murphy, 'The Woman's Court,' *Maclean's*, 19 June 1920.

23 'Administration of Criminal Justice in Canada,' typescript of a speech, no date, Deacon Papers, Folder 12.

24 Murphy, 'A Straight Talk on Courts.'

25 Murphy to Deacon, 9 June 1924, Deacon Papers, Folder 4.

26 J. McLaren, 'Maternal Feminism in Action – Emily Murphy, Police Magistrate' (1988) 8 *Windsor Yearbook of Access to Justice* 249.

27 Murphy, 'The Woman's Court.'

28 See Annual Report Re Dependant and Delinquent Children, Alberta, 1921, Murphy, Emily and Arthur Clipping File, City of Edmonton Archives.

29 Murphy, 'The Woman's Court.'

30 Emily Murphy to A.G. Browning, 18 September 1922, Murphy Papers Edmonton, Box 1, File 20.

31 Murphy, 'The Woman's Court.'

32 Ibid.

33 Murphy, 'A Straight Talk on Courts.'

34 Ibid.

35 See letters in Box 1, File 6, Murphy Papers Edmonton.

36 Emily Murphy, 'Companionate Marriage,' *Chatelaine*, May 1928.

37 Undated MS, 'About Marriage Settlements,' Murphy Papers Edmonton, Box 1, File 33.

38 Ibid.

39 Murphy, 'The Woman's Court.'

40 Undated MS, 'Partnership in Marriage,' Murphy Papers Edmonton, Box 1, File 50.

41 See Cavanaugh, 'The Women's Movement in Alberta,' 78.

42 Undated MS, 'About Marriage Settlements,' Murphy Papers Edmonton, Box 1, File 33.

43 Cavanaugh, 'The Women's Movement in Alberta,' 88–9.

44 See, for example, Murphy Papers Edmonton, Box 1, File 6, and the correspondence in October 1920 with Mrs John Kaplun.

45 2 January 1920, Murphy Papers Edmonton, Box 1, File 17.

46 Ibid.

47 Ibid.

48 'Married Women and School Teachers,' *The Western Home Monthly*, September 1925, Murphy Papers Edmonton, Scrapbook 4.

49 'Obedience in Marriage,' *The Western Home Monthly*, n.d. 1927, Murphy Papers Edmonton, Scrapbook 4.

50 'Law, Love, and Laggards in Love: Should Breach-of-Promise Actions Be Abolished?' *Canadian Home Journal*, n.d. 1927, Murphy Papers Edmonton, Scrapbook 1.

51 Undated MS, 'Mothers and Birth Control,' Murphy Papers Edmonton, Box 1, File 47. See also 'Over Population and Birth Control,' 8 October 1932, Murphy, Emily and Arthur Clipping File, City of Edmonton Archives.

52 'Birth Control: Its Meaning,' *Vancouver Sun*, 27 August 1932, Murphy Papers Edmonton, Box 1, File 31.

53 Murphy, 'The Woman's Court.'

54 Clipping, no date, Re Child Welfare Conference, Ottawa, Murphy Papers Edmonton, Scrapbook 4.

55 Murphy, 'The Woman's Court.'

56 'The Grave Drug Menace,' *Maclean's*, 15 February 1920; 'The Underground System,' *Maclean's*, 15 March 1920; 'Fighting the Drug Menace,' *Maclean's*, 15 April 1920; 'The Doctor – and the Drug,' *Maclean's*, 15 May 1920; 'What Must be Done,' *Maclean's*, 15 June 1920.

57 Published under the name 'Emily F. Murphy, "Janey Canuck," Police Magistrate and Judge of the Juvenile Court, Edmonton, Canada' (Toronto: Thomas Allen, 1922).

58 Sanders, *Emily Murphy: Crusader*, 192.

59 Murphy, *The Black Candle*, 17.

60 Ibid., 16.

61 Ibid., 47.

62 Ibid., 210.

63 Ibid., 96.

64 Howard Palmer, *Patterns of Prejudice: A History of Nativism in Alberta* (Toronto: McClelland and Stewart, 1982), 85.

65 Murphy, *The Black Candle*, 187–8.

66 Ibid., 198.

67 Ibid., 367.

68 For example, *Saturday Night* magazine deemed *The Black Candle* 'more important than any other Canadian book of the season.' The *Winnipeg Tribune* said, '*The Black Candle* is a book to make one's very soul dissolve from the shock.' Toronto's *Globe* urged its readers to take in the book's message of 'mighty import.' Collected in Deacon Papers, Folder 18.

69 See, for example, her 'Drug Menace to Anglo-Saxon Race,' *Toronto Daily Star*, 21 October 1922, reporting on a speech by Murphy in Toronto.

70 Michael Bliss, *The Discovery of Insulin* (Toronto: McClelland and Stewart, 1982), 225.

71 Brian Anthony and Robert Solomon, introduction to the reprint of *The Black Candle* (Toronto: Coles Publishing Company, 1973), 3, writing as researchers for the LeDain Commission of Inquiry into the Non-Medical Use of Drugs. See also Melvyn Green and Ralph Miller, 'Cannabis Use in Canada,' in Vera Rubin, ed., *Cannabis and Culture* (The Hague: Moulton Publishers, 1975), 499–500; P.J. Giffen, *Panic and Indifference: The Politics of Canada's Drug Laws* (Ottawa: Canadian Centre on Substance Abuse, 1991), 150–61, describing Murphy as 'Canada's most ardent moral crusader for narcotic drug prohibition' (151). Compare, however, Catherine Carstairs, *Jailed for Possession: Illegal Drug Use, Regulation and Power in Canada, 1920–1961* (Toronto: University of Toronto Press, 2006), 21–3, 31, arguing that Murphy's influence has been overstated.

72 Anthony and Solomon, Introduction to *The Black Candle*.

73 Undated newspaper clipping, Murphy Papers Edmonton, Scrapbook 4.

74 Ibid.

75 Murphy, 'The Woman's Court.'

76 Ibid.

77 Ibid.

78 Reports on Murphy's speech at Child Welfare Conference in Ottawa, October 1925, Murphy, Emily and Arthur Clipping File, City of Edmonton Archives.

79 Undated Report of 1925 Child Welfare Conference, Murphy Papers Edmonton, Scrapbook 4.

80 Murphy to Deacon, 26 August 1922, Deacon Papers, Folder 2.

81 Emily Murphy to Eleanor Patterson, 10 January 1920, Murphy Papers Edmonton, Box 1, File 7.

82 Emily Murphy to Eleanor Patterson, 4 April 1920, Murphy Papers Edmonton, Box 1, File 7.

83 Editorial, *Canadian Home Journal*, March 1916, Murphy Papers Edmonton, Scrapbook 4.

84 Murphy, 'A Straight Talk on Courts.'

85 Emily Murphy to Mr Mclean, 5 July 1918, Murphy Papers Edmonton, Box 1, File 18.

86 Emily Murphy to A.G. Browning 17 April 1918, Murphy Papers Edmonton, Box 1, File 18.

87 Murphy, 'The Woman's Court.'

88 Editorial, *Canadian Home Journal*, March 1916, Murphy Papers Edmonton, Scrapbook 4.

89 Emily Murphy to William Arthur Deacon, 24 August 1924, Deacon Papers, Box 28, Folder 4.
90 Emily Murphy to William Lyon Mackenzie King, 2 January 1923, quoted in McLaren, 'Maternal Feminism in Action,' 244.
91 See, generally, Angus McLaren, *Our Own Master Race: Eugenics in Canada, 1885–1894* (Toronto: McClelland and Stewart, 1990).
92 Murphy, 'A Straight Talk on Courts.'
93 Emily Murphy to Dr Cook, 27 January 1926, Murphy Papers Edmonton, Box 1, File 1.
94 Emily Murphy, 'The Case for Sterilization,' *Winnipeg Tribune*, 16 January 1932, Murphy, Emily and Arthur Clipping File, City of Edmonton Archives.
95 Ibid.
96 Ibid.
97 Ibid.
98 Emily Murphy, 'Sterilization of the Insane,' *Vancouver Sun*, n.d. September 1932, Murphy, Emily and Arthur Clipping File, City of Edmonton Archives.
99 Emily Murphy, 'Should the Unfit Wed?' *Vancouver Sun*, 10 September 1932, Murphy, Emily and Arthur Clipping File, City of Edmonton Archives; 'The Case for Sterilization,' *Winnipeg Tribune*, 16 January 1932, Murphy, Emily and Arthur Clipping File, City of Edmonton Archives.
100 After her retirement from the bench, Murphy collected and expanded her various writings on sterilization and birth control into a book she called 'Pruning the Family Tree.' She kept this project a 'dead secret,' but told a close friend that it would be controversial: 'I won't have any friends when it comes out.' She submitted the manuscript to several publishers in Canada and England, but none accepted it. The book never saw the light of day and there is no trace of the manuscript in Murphy's papers. Murphy to Deacon, 10 September 1932; Murphy to Deacon, 12 September 1933, Deacon Papers, Folders 7 and 8.

2: The Other Four

1 Undated clippings, Edwards Papers, File 19.
2 Maureen Lux, *Medicine That Walks* (Toronto: University of Toronto Press, 2001), 43–5, 166–8, provides an account of Edwards' medical work with Aboriginal communities.
3 Patricia Roome, 'From One Whose Home Is among the Indians: Henrietta Muir Edwards and Aboriginal Peoples,' in Sarah Carter, Lesley Erickson,

Patricia Roome, and Char Smith, eds., *Unsettled Pasts* (Calgary: University of Calgary Press, 2005), 47–78.

4 Edwards, Speech to National Council of Women, September 1906, Edwards Papers, File 21.

5 Lux, *Medicine That Walks*, 167.

6 Henrietta Edwards, *Legal Status of Canadian Women* (Calgary: National Council of Women of Canada, 1908).

7 Henrietta Edwards, *Legal Status of Canadian of Women in Alberta* (Edmonton: Attorney General of Alberta, 1921).

8 Randi Warne, 'Nellie McClung's Social Gospel,' in Elizabeth Muir and Marilyn Whiteley, eds., *Changing Roles of Women within the Christian Church in Canada* (Toronto: University of Toronto Press, 1995), chap. 17.

9 Veronica Strong-Boag, Introduction to Nellie McClung, *In Times Like These* (1915; reprint, Toronto: University of Toronto Press, 1972), p. xiv.

10 Mary Hallett and Marilyn Davis, *Firing the Heather: The Life and Times of Nellie McClung* (Saskatoon: Fifth House, 1993), 137.

11 8 March 1916, Edwards Papers, File 25.

12 'Alberta Women Moving Along Political Lines,' *Edmonton Bulletin*, 17 March 1916, 'Provincial Committee on Laws for Women Formed,' *Calgary Herald*, 16 March 1916.

13 Nellie McClung, *In Times Like These* (1915; reprint, Toronto: University of Toronto Press, 1972).

14 Strong-Boag, Introduction to McClung, *In Times Like These*, xiv.

15 Roome, 'From One Whose Home Is among the Indians,' 49–51; Janice Fiamengo, 'Rediscovering Our Foremothers Again: The Racial Ideas of Canada's Early Feminists 1885–1945' (2002) 75 *Essays in Canadian Writing* 85.

16 'Speaking of Women,' *Maclean's*, May 1916, at 26 quoted in Hallett and Davis, *Firing the Heather*, 118.

17 McClung, *In Times Like These*, 43.

18 Ibid., 52.

19 *The Manitoba Election Act*, S.M. 1916, c. 36.

20 *The Equal Suffrage Statutory Law Amendment Act*, S.A. 1916.

21 *An Act to Amend the Statute Law*, S.S. 1916, c. 37, s. 1(3).

22 *Woman Suffrage Act*, S.B.C. 1916, c. 76.

23 'Hon. Irene Parlby Visiting Scotland Tells of Women's Political Status in Canada,' *Edmonton Journal*, 9 October 1928.

24 *The Ontario Franchise Act 1917*, S.O. 1917, c. 5.

25 *The Nova Scotia Franchise Act*, S.N.S. 1918, c. 2.

26 *Act to Extend the Electoral Franchise to Women and to Amend the New Brunswick Electors Act*, S.N.B. 1919, c. 63.

27 *The Election Act*, R.P.E.I. 1922, c. 5.

28 *An Act Granting to Women the Right to Vote and to be Eligible as Candidates*, S.Q. 1940, c. 7.

29 *War-time Elections Act*, S.C. 1917, c. 39.

30 Undated newspaper clipping, quoted, in Hallett and Davis, *Firing the Heather*, 152.

31 *Dominion Elections Act*, 1920.

32 McClung and Murphy to R.L. Borden, 11 February 1918, cited in Candice Savage, *Our Nell: A Scrapbook Biography of Nellie McClung* (Saskatoon: Western Producer Prairie Books, 1979), 135; R.L. Borden to McClung, 16 February 1918, McClung Papers, Box 1, File 3.

33 Telegram from N.W. Rowell to McClung, 19 February 1918, McClung Papers, Box 1, File 3; Telegram from N.W. Rowell to Emily Murphy, 21 February 1918, Murphy Papers Edmonton, File 29; Telegram from Newton Rowell to Henrietta Edwards, 20 February 1918, Edwards Papers, File 23.

34 Rowell to Borden, 8 March 1918, Borden Papers, R.L.B. Series, Folder 2534.

35 William Lyon Mackenzie King, *Industry and Humanity: A Study in the Principles Underlying Industrial Reconstruction* (Toronto: Macmillan, 1935).

36 Veronica Strong-Boag and Michelle Lynn Rosa, eds., *Nellie McClung, The Complete Autobiography: Clearing the West and The Stream Runs Fast* (Toronto: Broadview, 2003), 441.

37 Ibid., 440.

38 Ibid.

39 Louise C. McKinney to McClung, July 1921, McClung Papers, File 5.

40 Strong-Boag and Rosa, eds., *Nellie McClung, The Complete Autobiography* 443–5.

41 Mackenzie King to McClung, 5 June 1930, McClung Papers, Box 1, File 13.

42 Untitled clipping, 8 September 1926, Murphy Papers Edmonton, Scrapbook 4.

43 Pamphlet by Sir John Willison reprinted from the *Ottawa Evening Journal*, copy in Deacon Papers, Folder 11, with Murphy's marginal note, 'This is what is raising the dust.'

44 Untitled and undated clipping, Murphy Papers Edmonton, Scrapbook 4.

45 'Magistrate Murphy Storm Centre in Ontario Politics,' *Edmonton Bulletin*, 26 November 1926, Murphy Papers Edmonton, Scrapbook 4.

46 Murphy to McClung, 9 August 1926, McClung Papers, Box 1, File 9.

47 McKinney, 'The Farmers Opportunity,' Speech to the U.F.A. Convention, 22 January 1919, McKinney Papers, File 2.

48 Speech to a WCTU convention, c. 1910, quoted in Savage, *Our Nell*, 48.

49 McKinney, 'Prohibition,' undated pamphlet, c. 1918, McKinney Papers, File 2.

50 Nancy M. Sheehan, 'Achieving Personhood: Louise McKinney and the WCTU in Alberta, 1905–1930,' *Women as Persons, Proceedings of the Third Annual Meeting (Edmonton, AB) of the Canadian Research Institute for the Advancement of Women (CRIAW), November 9–11, 1979* (Toronto: Resources for Feminist Research, 1980).

51 McKinney, 'Prohibition.'

52 Hilda Ridley, 'Pen Portraits of Progressive Women,' *Christian Guardian*, 16 February 1921.

53 'History of the Late Louise (Crummy) McKinney,' quoting Dr Willard McKinney, McKinney Papers, File 5.

54 McKinney, 'The Farmers Opportunity'; Anthony Mardiros, *William Irvine: The Life of a Prairie Radical* (Toronto: James Lorimer, 1979), 61–5.

55 Nanci Langford, '"All That Glitters": The Political Apprenticeship of Alberta Women, 1916–1930,' in Catherine Cavanaugh and Randi Warne, eds., *Standing on New Ground: Women in Alberta* (Edmonton: University of Alberta Press, 1993), 79.

56 Sheehan, 'Achieving Personhood,' 107.

57 *Dower Act*, S.A. 1917, c. 14, discussed in chapter 2 of this volume.

58 Franklin Foster, *John E. Brownlee: A Biography* (Lloydminister, AB: Foster Learning, 1996), 47.

59 Barbara Villy Cormack, *Perennials and Politics* (Sherwood Park, AB: Professional Print, 1968), 63.

60 Undated, untitled MS of speech, Parlby Papers, microfilm.

61 'A While Ago – and Today! Part 2,' undated speech, marked 'July 1928 Canadian Magazine,' Parlby Papers, microfilm.

62 'What Business Have Women in Politics?' undated speech, Parlby Papers, microfilm.

63 'A While Ago – and Today! Part 2.'

64 Ibid.

65 Quoted in Cormack, *Perennials and Politics*, 90.

66 Irene Parlby, 'The Great Adventure,' *The Guide*[?], 1 April 1927, Parlby Papers, microfilm.

67 'What Business Have Women in Politics?'

68 *The Minimum Wage Act*, S.A. 1922, c. 81; *The Minimum Wage Act, 1925*, S.A. 1925, c. 23.

69 *The Children of Unmarried Parents Act Amendment Act, 1928*, S.A. 1928, c. 20, s. 3.

70 *The Dower Act Amendment Act, 1926*, S.A. 1926, c. 9.

71 *The Mothers' Allowance Amendment Act, 1923*, S.A. 1923, c. 51; *The Mothers'*

Allowance Amendment Act, 1927, S.A. 1927, c. 33; *The Mothers' Allowance Amendment Act, 1930,* S.A. 1930, c. 9.

72 *Official Guardian Act,* S.A. 1917, c. 19; *An Act to Amend the Official Guardian Act,* S.A. 1922, c. 45.

73 *The Domestic Relations Act, 1927,* S.A. 1927, c. 5, ss. 53–5; *The Legitimation Act,* S.A. 1928, c. 30, s. 2.

74 *Sterilization Act,* S.A. 1928, c. 37. See Timothy Christian, *The Mentally Ill and Human Rights in Alberta: A Study of the Alberta Sexual Sterilization Act* (Edmonton: Alberta Law Foundation, 1974).

75 *Edmonton Bulletin,* 8 June 1926, Murphy Papers Edmonton, Scrapbook 4.

76 *Buck v. Bell,* 274 U.S. 200 (1927) 207.

77 Sharon Carstairs and Tim Higgins, *Dancing Backwards: A Social History of Canadian Women in Politics* (Winnipeg: Heartland Associates, 2004), 70.

78 See, for example, McClung to Della Jones, 27 June 1935, McClung Papers, Box 1, File 17.

79 Parlby to McClung, 14 February, no year, McClung Papers, Box 12, File 10. Emphasis in original.

80 Undated clipping, 'Greatest Enemy to Progress is the Comfortable Woman,' McKinney Papers, File 7.

81 'What Have We Gained in Sixty Years?' *Canadian Home Journal,* n.d. 1927, quoted in Margaret MacPherson, *Nellie McClung: Voice for the Voiceless* (Montreal: XYZ Publishing, 2003), 125–6.

82 Veronica Strong-Boag, 'Canadian Feminism in the 1920s: The Case of Nellie L. McClung' (1977) 12 *Journal of Canadian Studies* 66.

3: Women and the Law

1 Murphy to Mrs J.F. Hynes, 20 December 1932, Murphy Papers Waterloo, File 5.

2 Murphy to E.E.A.H. Jackson, 25 October 1917, Murphy Papers Edmonton, Box 1, File 26.

3 Emily Murphy, *The Black Candle* (Toronto: Thomas Allen, 1922), 369.

4 Murphy to Alice McCallum, 29 Sept 1918, Murphy Papers Edmonton, Box 1, File 21.

5 Murphy to Mrs J.F. Hynes, 20 December 1932, Murphy Papers Waterloo, File 5.

6 Byrne Hope Sanders, *Emily Murphy: Crusader* (Toronto: Macmillan, 1945), 144.

7 See David Bright, 'The Other Woman: Lizzie Cyr and the Origins of the "Persons Case"' (1998) 13 C.J.L.S. 99, for a detailed account of the case.

8 *Criminal Code*, s. 238.
9 *R. v. Cyr*, [1917] 2 W.W.R. 1185 at 1186. Emphasis in original.
10 David Bright, '"Go Home, Straighten Up, Live Decent Lives": Female Vagrancy and Social Responsibility in Alberta, 1918–1993' (2003) 28 *Prairie Forum* 161.
11 Murphy to A.G. Browning, Deputy Attorney General for Alberta, 16 April 1917, Murphy Papers Edmonton, Box 1, File 21.
12 Bright, 'The Other Woman,' 110.
13 Ibid., 102.
14 [1917] 2 W.W.R. 1185.
15 Louis Knafla and Richard Klumpenhouwer, *Lords of the Western Bench: A Biographical History of the Supreme and District Courts of Alberta, 1876–1900* (Edmonton: Legal Archives Society of Alberta, 1997), 163–4.
16 Ibid., 1187.
17 *R. v. Cyr*, [1917] 3 W.W.R. 849.
18 These cases are discussed in greater detail below.
19 Knafla and Klumpenhouwer, *Lords of the Western Bench*, 176–8.
20 George Ross to William Harcourt, quoted in M.L. Friedland, *The History of the University of Toronto* (Toronto: University of Toronto Press, 2002), 163.
21 *The International Coal and Coke Co. v. Trelle*, [1907] 1 A.L.R. 170.
22 *R. v. Trainor*, [1917] 1 W.W.R. 415. See Jonathan Swainger, 'Wagging Tongues and Empty Heads: Seditious Utterances and the Patriotism of Wartime Central Alberta, 1914–18,' in Louis Knafla and Susan W.S. Binnie, eds., *Law, Society, and the State: Essays in Modern Legal History* (Toronto: University of Toronto Press, 1995).
23 Ibid., 422.
24 Ibid., 423.
25 *R. v. Stoney Joe*, [1981] 1 C.N.L.R. 117, discussed in Knafla and Klumpenhouwer, *Lords of the Western Bench*, 178.
26 *R. v. Hartfeil*, [1920] 16 A.L.R. 19.
27 [1917] 3 W.WR. 857.
28 Ibid., 858–9.
29 Bright, 'The Other Woman'; John McLaren and John Lowman, 'Enforcing Canada's Prostitution Laws, 1867–1917: Rhetoric and Practice,' in M.L. Friedland, ed., *Securing Compliance: Seven Case Studies* (Toronto: University of Toronto Press, 1990); J. McLaren, 'Chasing Social Evil: Moral Fervour and the Evolution of Canada's Prostitution Laws, 1867–1917' (1986) 1 *C.J.L.S.* 125.
30 Albie Sachs and Joan Hoff Wilson, *Sexism and the Law: A Study of Male Beliefs and Legal Bias in Britain and the United States* (New York: Free Press, 1978), 22–66.

31 *Chorlton v. Lings* (1868), L.R. 4 C.P. 374.

32 *Interpretation Act ('Lord Brougham's Act')*, UK 13–14 Vict., c. 21, s. 4.

33 See Sachs and Wilson, *Sexism and the Law*, 23–5, for a discussion of the case and its background.

34 *Chorlton v. Lings* (1868), L.R. 4 C.P. 386.

35 Ibid., 392.

36 Ibid., 396–7.

37 *Municipal Elections Act*, 1869, 32 & 33 Vict., c. 55.

38 *Beresford-Hope v. Lady Sandhurst* (1889), 23 Q.B.D. 79.

39 *The Municipal Corporations Act*, 1882, s. 73.

40 Ibid., s. 41.

41 *De Souza v. Cobden*, [1891] 1 Q.B. 687.

42 Sachs and Wilson, *Sexism and the Law*, 27, citing the Annual Reports of the National Union of Women's Suffrage Societies.

43 *Jex-Blake v. Senatus of University of Edinburgh* (1873), 11 M. 784.

44 *Nairn v. University of St. Andrews*, [1909] A.C. 147.

45 Ibid., 160.

46 In 1903, a panel chaired by the Lord Chancellor refused to accept Bertha Cave as a member of Gray's Inn. See Sachs and Wilson, *Sexism and the Law*, 28.

47 *Bebb v. Law Society*, [1914] 1 Ch. 286.

48 Sachs and Wilson, *Sexism and the Law*, 94–125, 189–97.

49 See, for example, *Minor v. Happersett*, 88 U.S. 162 (1874).

50 *In re Lockwood*, 154 U.S. 116 (1893).

51 Mary Jane Mossman, *The First Women Lawyers* (Oxford: Hart Publishing, 2006), chap. 2. Canada's first female lawyer, Clara Brett Martin, admitted to practice in 1897, did not go to court to challenge the decision of the Law Society of Upper Canada to refuse her admission as a student. Martin took the more direct route of convincing the Ontario legislature to amend the law, first to admit her as a student and then as a practising lawyer: *An Act to Provide for the Admission of Women to the Study and Practice of Law*, S.O. 1892, c. 32; S.O. 1895, c. 27.

52 *Re French* (1905), 37 N.B.R. 359 (S.C.).

53 *Re French* (1911–2), 17 B.C.L.R. 1 (C.A.).

54 37 N.B.R. 361–2.

55 17 B.C.L.R. 8.

56 *Langstaff v. Bar of Quebec* (1915), 47 R.J.Q. 131 (C.S.) 145; aff'd (1916), 25 R.J.Q. 11 (B.R.).

57 *An Act to Remove the Disability of Women so far as relates to the Study and Practice of Law*, S.N.B. 1906, c. 5; *An Act to Remove the Disability of Women so far as*

relates to the Study and Practice of Law, S.B.C. 1912, c. 18.

58 U.K. 9 & 10 Geo.V., c. 71, s. 1.

59 *Viscountess Rhondda's Claim (Committee for Privileges)*, [1922] 2 A.C. 339.

60 Ibid., 365.

61 Ibid., 375.

62 Virginia Woolf, *A Room of One's Own* (1929; reprint, Oxford: Oxford Univeristy Press, 1992), 68–9.

63 U.K. 6 & 7 Eliz. 2, c. 21, s. 1(3).

64 U.K. 1963, c. 48, s. 6.

65 Quoted in J.L. Granatstein et al., *Nation: Canada Since Confederation*, 3rd ed. (Toronto: McGraw-Hill Ryerson, 1990), 241.

66 Ibid., 250.

67 Louise McKinney, 'Where Are Canadian Women Going – Back to Their Homes or Continue in Business Life?' *Canadian Home Journal*, August 1919.

4: Emily Murphy's Senate Campaign

1 In February 1919, the Senate had 50 Conservatives, 40 Liberals, 1 National Conservative, and 3 Liberal Conservatives.

2 Emily Murphy interview, 25 April 1928, *Edmonton Bulletin*, Murphy Papers Edmonton, Scrapbook 3.

3 Byrne Hope Sanders, *Emily Murphy: Crusader* (Toronto: Macmillan, 1945), 216.

4 Ibid.

5 Ibid.

6 Ibid., 217.

7 Price to Doherty, 21 February 1921, Justice File, Vol. 2524, File C-1044.

8 House of Commons, *Debates*, 28 February 1921, Vol. 1, 389.

9 There is no copy in the Department of Justice file with the Edwards opinion, but an incomplete nine-page copy is in the Borden Papers: O'Connor, 'The Effect of Women Suffrage Acts of Certain Provinces as Respects the Exercise of the Dominion Electoral Franchise Within these Provinces,' 3 October 1916, Borden Papers, OC Series, Folder 304.

10 O'Connor to Borden, 16 October 1911, Borden Papers, OCA Series, folder 230.

11 O'Connor later served as parliamentary counsel to the Senate. In 1938, the speaker of the Senate appointed O'Connor to chair a committee to assess the extent to which the JCPC had deviated from the original interpretation of the division of powers set out in the *BNA Act*, comparing the records of constitutional conferences prior to Confederation to the judgments of the

Judicial Committee. O'Connor was asked to determine whether constitutional amendment was required to bring the *BNA Act* into accord with the original intentions of its framers. In determining that a constitutional amendment was unnecessary, O'Connor concluded, 'I think that the failure of the Act fully to achieve the intent of those who framed it has not been owing to any defect in draftsmanship, but has been caused by demonstrable error in the interpretation of its terms.' He explained, 'I think that not amendment of the Act, but enforced observance of its terms is the proper remedy.' *Report Pursuant to Resolution of the Senate to the Honourable Speaker by The Parliamentary Counsel Relating to The Enactment of the British North America Act, 1867, any lack of consonance between its terms and judicial construction of them and cognate matters* (the 'O'Connor Report'), 17 March 1939, 11, 13.

12 *Dominion Elections Act*, R.S.C. 1906, c. 6.

13 O'Connor opinion.

14 Ibid.

15 Memorandum for the Deputy Minister from W.S.E., 18 May 1921, Justice File, Vol. 2524, File C-1044.

16 Memorandum from W.S.E., 2 March [1921], Justice File, Vol. 2524, File C-1044.

17 House of Commons, *Debates*, 1917, Vol. 2, 1495.

18 Gisborne Memorandum, 31 December 1918, Borden Papers, RLB Series, Folder 2236.

19 Doherty to Price, 1 March [sic] 1921, Justice File, Vol. 2524, File C-1044.

20 W.N. Ferguson to Emily Murphy, 18 March 1921, Meighen Papers, Vol. 48, File 192.

21 *Interpretation Act*, R.S.C. 1906, c. 1, s. 31(i).

22 Mrs H. Milton Budd to Prime Minister Arthur Meighen, 13 May 1921, Meighen Papers, Vol. 48, File 192.

23 Veronica Strong-Boag and Michelle Lynn Rosa, eds., *Nellie McClung, The Complete Autobiography: Clearing the West and The Stream Runs Fast* (Toronto: Broadview Press, 2003), 450

24 Price to Doherty, 18 June 1921, Justice File, Vol. 2524, File C-1044.

25 Doherty to Price, 22 June 1921, Justice File, Vol. 2524, File C-1044.

26 Memorandum for the Deputy Minister from W.S.E., 18 May 1921, Justice File, Vol. 2524, File C-1044.

27 Memorandum for W. Stuart Edwards for the Prime Minister, 6 June 1921, Meighen Papers, Vol. 48, File 192.

28 Clipping, n.d. 1921, *Grain Growers' Guide*, Murphy Papers Edmonton, Scrapbook 4.

29 *Journal Society*, 27 September 1921, Emily and Arthur Clipping File, City of Edmonton Archives

30 Sanders, *Emily Murphy: Crusader*, 221–2, quoting editorials from the Halifax *Canadian Morning Chronicle*, the London *Advertiser*, the Fort William *Times Journal*, and the *Toronto Daily Star*.

31 McClung to Senator W.H. Sharpe, May 1921, quoted in Sanders, *Emily Murphy: Crusader*, 221.

32 7 September 1921, quoted in R.G. Marchildon, 'The "Persons" Controversy: The Legal Aspects of the Fight for Women Senators' (1979) 6, no. 2 *Atlantis* 102.

33 1921 n.d., clipping in Murphy Papers Edmonton, Scrapbook 4.

34 Deacon to Murphy, 9 February 1925, Deacon Papers, Folder 5.

35 'The Essayist,' *National Pictorial*, February 1922, vol. 2, no. 3.

36 Murphy to Deacon, 3 September 1921, Deacon Papers, Folder 1.

37 Ibid.

38 Ibid.

39 Murphy to Deacon, 20 September 1921, Deacon Papers, Folder 1.

40 Deacon to Murphy, 23 September 1921, Deacon Papers, Folder 1.

41 David Ricardo Williams, *Just Lawyers: Seven Protraits* (Toronto: Osgoode Society, 1995), 24.

42 Eugene Lafleur, *The Conflict of Laws in the Province of Quebec* (Montreal: C. Theoret, 1898).

43 Williams, *Just Lawyers*, 51.

44 Lafleur was so highly regarded that Mackenzie King pleaded with him to become Chief Justice of Canada in 1924. Lafleur refused. Williams, *Just Lawyers*, 45–9.

45 Williams, *Just Lawyers*, 31. The Lord's Day Alliance retained Newton Rowell to argue the case but, as Lafleur predicted, the appeal was dismissed. See chapter 5 in this volume.

46 E. Lafleur, 'Opinion: Appointment of Women to the Senate of Canada,' 9 December 1921, Murphy Papers Waterloo, File 16. All quotations in reference to his opinion are quoted from this document.

47 *Interpretation Act*, UK 13–14 Vict., c. 21, s. 4.

48 *Chorlton v. Lings* (1868), L.R. 4 C.P. 374, discussed in chap. 3.

49 *Nairn v. the University of St. Andrews*, [1909] A.C. 147.

50 Ibid., 160.

51 Ibid., 163.

52 *Beresford-Hope v. Lady Sandhurst* (1889), 23 Q.B.D. 79.

53 *R. v. Cyr*, [1917] 3 W.W.R. 849, discussed in chapter 3.

54 W.N. Ferguson to Murphy, 20 January 1922, Murphy Papers Waterloo, File 4.

55 McClung to King, 30 December 1921, King Papers, quoted in Mary Hallett and Marilyn Davis, *Firing the Heather: The Life and Times of Nellie McClung* (Saskatoon: Fifth House, 1993), 208.

56 Gertrude E. Budd to Murphy, 13 March 1922, Murphy Papers Waterloo, File 2.

57 'Local Council Would Have Mrs. O.C. Edwards Appointed as Canada's First Woman Senator,' *Calgary Daily Herald*, 8 February 1923.

58 Murphy to Mrs J.P. Hynes, 20 December 1932, Murphy Papers Waterloo, File 5.

59 Quoted by Sanders, *Emily Murphy: Crusader*, 218–19 (no date).

60 Murphy to Mrs Reynolds, 16 March 1933, Murphy Papers Waterloo, File 8.

61 McGregor to Murphy, 9 July 1923, Murphy Papers Waterloo, File 7.

62 Gertrude E. Budd to Meighen, 13 June 1923, Murphy Papers Waterloo, File 7.

63 See, for example, Telegram to Emily Murphy, 24 June 1924, Murphy Papers Edmonton, Box 1, File 26.

64 King Papers, J 3, Vol. 108, File 2.

65 Murphy to Deacon, 5 October 1922, Deacon Papers, Folder 2.

66 King Diary, 26 October 1922.

67 Murphy to McClung, 19 November 1925, McClung Papers, Box 1, File 8.

68 Murphy to King, 15 April 1924, Murphy Papers Waterloo, File 7.

69 *Edmonton Bulletin*, 11 October 1924.

70 King to Murphy, 23 July 1925, King Papers, J 1, Vol. 121: 103155.

71 1925 n.d., *Ottawa Journal* clipping in Murphy Papers Edmonton, Scrapbook 4.

72 'Is Active in Public Life,' *Calgary Herald*, 8 September 1925.

73 'Albertan Since 1898,' *Calgary Herald*, 8 September 1925.

74 'The New Senators,' *Edmonton Journal*, 8 September 1925.

75 House of Commons, *Debates*, 9 March 1925, 911.

76 'Senate Reform to Come From Within, Says King,' *Calgary Herald*, 8 September 1925.

77 'Calls Liberal Senate Reform Talk "Moonshine,"' *Calgary Herald*, 9 September 1925.

78 McClung to King, 4 November 1925, quoted in Hallett and Davis, *Firing the Heather*, 208.

79 Murphy to King, 26 May 1926, King Papers, J 2 Vol. 46, File S-1308 M.

80 W.L. Morton, *The Progressive Party in Canada* (Toronto: University of Toronto Press, 1950), 259.

81 Murphy to King, 2 Sepember 1926, King Papers, J 3, Vol. 108, File 2.

82 Murphy to King, 14 September 1926, King Papers, J 3, Vol. 108, File 2.

83 M. Ollivier, *The Colonial and Imperial Conferences from 1887 to 1937*, Vol. 3, *Imperial Conferences Part II* (Ottawa: Queen's Printer, 1954), 137. See also A. Berriedale Keith, *The Governments of the British Empire* (London: Macmillan, 1935), 254.

84 See Lita-Rose Betcherman, *Ernest Lapointe: Mackenzie King's Great Quebec Lieutenant* (Toronto: University of Toronto Press, 2002).

85 Ollivier, *Colonial and Imperial Conferences*, 138.

86 Ibid., 147.

87 Ibid., 145–6.

88 Ibid., 146.

89 'Inter-Provincial Conference Agenda,' *Manitoba Free Press*, 18 October 1927.

90 Peter Oliver, *G. Howard Ferguson: Ontario Tory* (Toronto: University of Toronto Press, 1977), 302–3.

91 'Ferguson Stands Against Amending the BNA Act,' *Manitoba Free Press*, 20 October 1927.

92 'Amending the Constitution' *Manitoba Free Press*, 28 October 1927.

93 'The Conference Assembles,' *Gazette* (Montreal), 3 November 1927.

94 'Senate Mortality and Senate Reform,' *Manitoba Free Press*, 26 October 1927.

95 See, for example, 'Senate Reform,' *Gazette* (Montreal), 27 October, 1927.

96 See, for example, 'Where Reform Should Begin,' *Manitoba Free Press*, 29 October 1927.

97 'Senate Reform Was Discussed at Conference,' *Gazette* (Montreal), 4 November 1927; Press Release, 4 November 1927, Justice File, Vol. 2525, File C-1044.

98 'Spokesmen Favour Senate Reform,' *Globe* (Toronto), 4 November 1927.

99 'Manitoba Takes Lead in Urging Reform of Senate,' *Manitoba Free Press*, 4 November 1927.

100 Senate Reform Was Discussed at Conference,' *Gazette* (Montreal), 4 November 1927.

101 Robert MacGregor Dawson, *Constitutional Issues in Canada, 1900–1931* (Toronto: Oxford University Press, 1933), 282; Report of Dominion–Provincial Conference, 1927, Canadian Sessional Papers, 1928, No. 69.

102 'Spokesmen Favour Senate Reform,' *Globe* (Toronto), 4 November 1927.

103 'Women as Senators Becoming Inevitable is Belief of Lawyer,' *Globe* (Toronto), 24 November 1927.

104 Dawson, *Constitutional Issues in Canada*, 22; Report of Dominion–Provincial Conference, 1927, Canadian Sessional Papers, 1928, No. 69, 11–12.

105 Dawson, *Constitutional Issues in Canada*, 15–16; House of Commons,

Debates, 18, 19 February 1925.

106 Ibid.

107 Ibid.

108 See H.A. Smith, *Federalism in North America – A Comparative Study of Institutions in The United States and Canada* (Boston: The Chipman Law Publishing Company, 1923), 22–3; Norman Rogers, 'Compact Theory of Confederation' (1931) 10 *Can. Bar. Rev* 395.

109 Dawson, *Constitutional Issues in Canada*, 23; Report of Dominion-Provincial Conference, 1927, Canadian Sessional Papers, 1928, No. 69.

5: Going to Court

1 See T.A. Cromwell, *Locus Standi* (Toronto: Carswell, 1986). Even under expanded modern standing rules, it is doubtful that a private citizen would have standing to challenge a legal opinion of this nature. See, for example, *Thorson v. Canada (Attorney General)*, [1975] 1 S.C.R. 138.

2 *An Act to Establish a Supreme Court, and a Court of the Exchequer, for the Dominion of Canada*, S.C. 1875, c. 11, s. 52; *Supreme Court Act*, R.S.C. 1906, c. 139, s. 60 (now *Supreme Court Act*, R.S.C. 1985, c. S-26, s. 53).

3 See B.L. Strayer, *The Canadian Constitution and the Courts: The Function and Scope of Judicial Review*, 3rd ed. (Toronto: Butterworths, 1988), 73–86; R. Sharpe and K. Roach, *The Charter of Rights and Freedoms*, 3rd ed. (Toronto: Irwin Law, 2005), 107–10.

4 *Reference re British North America Act, 1867 (UK), s. 91(27) (Eskimo Reference)*, [1939] S.C.R. 104; *Reference re Jurisdiction of Tariff Board of Canada*, [1934] S.C.R. 538; *Reference re Timber Regulations*, [1933] S.C.R. 616; *Reference re Constitutional Creditor Arrangement Act*, [1934] S.C.R. 659; *Reference re Dominion Constitutional Act, s. 110*, [1934] S.C.R. 653; *Reference re Canada Temperance Act, Part II*, [1935] S.C.R. 494; *Reference re Royal Prerogative of Mercy upon Deportation Proceedings*, [1933] S.C.R. 269; *Reference re Regulation and Control of Radio Communication*, [1931] S.C.R. 541.

5 *Reference re Amendment to the Constitution of Canada*, [1981] 1 S.C.R. 753.

6 *Reference re Secession of Quebec*, [1998] 2 S.C.R. 217.

7 See, for example, Nancy Millar, *The Famous Five: Emily Murphy and the Case of the Missing Persons* (Cochrane, AB: Western Heritage Centre, 1999), 34–5; Thérèse Casgrain, *A Woman in a Man's World* (Toronto: McClelland and Stewart, 1972), 63; Una MacLean, 'The Famous Five' (1962) 10 *Alberta Historical Review* 1.

8 Murphy to Mrs J.P. Hynes, 20 December 1932, Murphy Papers Waterloo, File 5.

9 Ian Bushnell, *The Captive Court: A Study of the Supreme Court of Canada*

(Montreal: McGill-Queen's University Press, 1992), 219: 'Such a procedure has never been described in any other context, and hardly seems possible. It had never been tried before, nor since, as far as is known.'

10 Ibid.

11 The minutes of the Privy Council directing the refence is dated 19 October 1927, Justice File, Vol. 2524, File C-1044; 'Women If "Persons" May Grace Senate,' *Gazette* (Montreal), 20 October 1927; 'Supreme Court Is to Be Asked for Ruling,' *Manitoba Free Press*, 20 October 1927.

12 King Diary, 20 October 1927.

13 Murphy to Mrs J.P. Hynes, 20 December 1932, Murphy Papers Waterloo, File 5.

14 Ibid.

15 Murphy to McClung, 5 August 1927, McClung Papers, File 10.

16 Murphy to McClung, 2 Dec. 1927, McClung Papers, File 10.

17 Murphy to McClung, 5 August 1927, McClung Papers, File 10.

18 Murphy to McClung, 2 Dec. 1927, McClung Papers, File 10.

19 Ibid.

20 Nellie McClung, 'The End of the Circle,' typed MS, 18 June 1938, McClung Papers, Box 13.

21 Justice File, Vol. 2524, File C-1044.

22 'Judge Murphy Explains,' 1 October 1927, *Gazette* (Montreal).

23 Edwards to Lapointe, 14 November 1927; Lapointe to Edwards, Justice File, Vol. 2524, File C-1044.

24 Edwards to Rowell, 29 November 1927, Justice File, Vol. 2524, File C-1044.

25 Ibid.

26 Murphy to Edwards, 9 November 1927, copy in McClung Papers, Box 1, File 10.

27 Murphy to McClung, 5 November 1927, McClung Papers, Box 1, File 10.

28 See 'Lobby and Gallery,' *Saturday Night*, 29 October 1927; 'Women if "Persons" May Grace Senate'; 'Supreme Court Is to Be Asked for Ruling.'

29 Murphy to McClung, 26 October 1927, McClung Papers, Box 1, File 10.

30 'Woman's Place in the Senate,' *Manitoba Free Press*, 22 October 1927.

31 'Lobby and Gallery.'

32 'Government Asked to Name Women to Upper Chamber,' *Globe* (Toronto), 6 October 1927.

33 'Lady Senators,' *Family Herald*, 2 November 1927.

34 Murphy to McClung, 4 November 1927, McClung Papers, Box 1, File 10.

35 *Supreme Court Act*, ss. 55 (4) and (5).

36 Murphy to W.R. Shibley, 4 November 1927, Justice File, Vol. 2524, File C-1044.

37 As a man of strong Christian beliefs who faithfully observed the Sabbath, Rowell was no doubt disappointed when he failed to persuade the Privy Council to strike down a Manitoba law that would have permitted running Sunday excursions to resorts. *Reference re Act to Amend the Lord's Day Act (Manitoba)*, [1925] A.C. 384. The other cases were *Reference re Judicature Act, 1924 (Ontario)*, [1925] A.C. 759, and *Re Toronto Railway Co. and City of Toronto*, [1925] A.C. 177.

38 M. Prang, *N.W. Rowell: Ontario Nationalist* (Toronto: University of Toronto Press, 1975), 448–51.

39 Ibid., 68–9, 129.

40 Ibid., 33.

41 Ibid., 135.

42 Rowell to Borden, 23 December 1919, Borden Papers, OC Series, Folder 485.

43 Borden to Rowell, 1 January 1920, Borden Papers, OC Series, Folder 485.

44 Prang, *N.W. Rowell*, 110.

45 Sylvia Bashevkin, *Toeing the Lines: Women and Party Politics* (Toronto: Oxford University Press, 1993), 116.

46 Rowell, 'Military Service to Ensure the Vigorous Prosecution of the War,' n.d., Borden Papers, OC Series, Folder 485.

47 King Diary, 9 December 1925, 20 September 1926, 21 September 1926.

48 Ibid., 2 February 1928.

49 Murphy to McClung, 5 November 1927, McClung Papers, MS 0010, File 10.

50 Murphy to McClung, 2 December 1927, McClung Papers, Box 1, File 10.

51 Thomas Mulvey to Murphy, 8 November 1927, Justice File, Vol. 2524, File C-1044

52 Murphy to Edwards, 9 November 1927, Justice File, Vol. 2524, File C-1044.

53 Murphy to McClung, 2 December 1927, McClung Papers, Box 1, File 10.

54 Ibid.

55 Edwards to Murphy, 30 November 1927, Justice File, Vol. 2524, File C-1044.

56 Edwards to Murphy, 14 December 1927, Justice File, Vol. 2524, File C-1044.

57 Rowell to Edwards, 22 November 1927, Justice File, Vol. 2524, File C-1044.

58 Plaxton to Edwards, 30 November 1927, Justice File, Vol. 2524, File C-1044.

59 Murphy to Edwards, 28 December 1927, Justice File, Vol. 2524, File C-1044.

60 Order, 29 October 1927, Supreme Court of Canada File.

61 Philip Girard, 'Edmund Leslie Newcombe,' *Dictionary of Canadian Biography* (forthcoming).

62 Newcombe to Edwards, 1 February 1928, Justice File, Vol. 2524, File C-1044.

63 C.P.P. to Newcombe, 2 February 1928, Justice File, Vol. 2524, File C-1044.

64 Newcombe to Plaxton, 4 February 1928, Justice File, Vol. 2524, File C-1044.

65 Note to Plaxton, n.d., Justice File, Vol. 2525, File C-1004.

66 Edwards to Lafleur 2 February 1928, Justice File, Vol. 2524, File C-1044.
67 The province did not grant women the right to vote until 1940 and maintained its bicameral legislature with an appointed legislative council as its upper house until 1968.
68 Petitioners' Factum, Supreme Court of Canada File.
69 *Interpretation Act, 1850* ('*Lord Brougham's Act*'), 13–14 Vict., c. 21, s. 4.
70 *Dominion Elections Act*, S.C. 1920, c. 46, s. 38.
71 Petitioners' Factum.
72 See Edwards to Cannon and Lafleur, 3 February 1928, Justice File, Vol. 2524, File C-1044.
73 Factum of the Attorney General of Canada, Supreme Court of Canada File.
74 Plaxton to Cannon, 27 February 1928, Justice File, Vol. 2524, File C-1044.
75 Rowell to Edwards, 10 March 1928, Justice File, Vol. 2524, File C-1044.
76 Factum of the Attorney General of Quebec, Supreme Court of Canada File.
77 The following account of the oral argument is derived from 'Right of Women to Senate Seats Is before Court,' *Toronto Daily Star*, 14 March 1928; 'Says Women Only Vote by Legislative Power,' *Toronto Daily Star*, 15 March 1928; 'Women's Right to Enter Senate Is Argued by Rowell,' *Gazette* (Montreal), 15 March 1928; 'Judgment Reserved on Right of Women to Sit in the Senate,' *Globe* (Toronto), 15 March 1928.
78 Ibid.
79 'Hinchcliffe Opposed Women on Flights,' *Toronto Daily Star*, 15 March 1928.
80 'Woman Suffrage Is Defeated in Quebec,' *Manitoba Free Press*, 15 March 1928.
81 See note 77.
82 Ibid.
83 This case discussed in chapter 3 of this volume.

6: The Supreme Court of Canada Decides

1 Ian Bushnell, *The Captive Court: A Study of the Supreme Court of Canada* (Montreal: McGill-Queen's University Press, 1992), describes the period from 1903 to 1929 as 'The Sterile Years.'
2 See Mary Jane Mossman, 'Feminism and Legal Method: The Difference It Makes' (1986) 3 *Aust. J. of Law and Soc.* 30, where she discusses this point in relation to the *Persons* case.
3 'The Modern Evolution of Civil Responsibility' (1927) 5 *Can. Bar Rev.* 1 at 4, quoted in Bushnell, *The Captive Court*, 235–6.
4 Bushell, *The Captive Court*, 18.

5 James G. Snell, 'Frank Anglin Joins the Bench: A Study of Judicial Patronage, 1897–1904' (1980) 18 *Osgoode Hall Law Journal* 664.

6 See, for example 'Mortgagee, Mortgagor and Assignee of the Equity of Redemption' (1894) 14 *Canadian Law Times* 57, 98.

7 Frank Anglin, *Limitation of Actions Against Trustee and Relief from Liability for Technical Breaches of Trust* (Toronto: Canada Law Book, 1900).

8 Bushnell, *The Captive Court*, 56.

9 'Some Differences between the Law of Quebec and the Law as Administered in the Other Provinces of Canada' (1923) 1 *Can. Bar Rev.* 33 at 43–4, quoted in Bushnell, *The Captive Court*, 56.

10 *Reference re the Meaning of the Word 'Persons' in Section 24 of the British North America Act*, [1928] S.C.R. 276 at 281.

11 Ibid., 282.

12 Ibid., 285.

13 Ibid.

14 Ibid., 290.

15 Quoted in James G. Snell and Frederick Vaughan, *The Supreme Court of Canada: History of the Institution* (Toronto: University of Toronto Press, 1985), 129.

16 [1928] S.C.R. 303.

17 Ibid.

18 Snell and Vaughan, *The Supreme Court of Canada*, 122.

19 Bushnell, *The Captive Court*, 215; David Ricardo Williams, *Duff: A Life in the Law* (Vancouver: UBC Press, 1984), 90.

20 King Diary, 12 September, 1924, quoted in Snell and Vaughan, *The Supreme Court of Canada*, 123.

21 Snell and Vaughan, *The Supreme Court of Canada*, 124.

22 *Supreme Court Act*, S.C. 1927, c. 38, s. 1 (number of judges) and s. 2 (duration of service). This amendment applied to sitting judges and thus affected Duff despite his earlier appointment. Section 99 of the *BNA Act* gave superior court judges lifetime tenure until it was amended in 1960 to impose mandatory retirement at age seventy-five, but section 99 did not apply to the judges of the Supreme Court of Canada whose tenure is fixed by the *Supreme Court Act*.

23 *An Act to Amend an Act Respecting the Chief Justice of Canada*, S.C. 1943, c. 1, s. 1.

24 Canadian Bar Association *Report* (1915), 56, quoted in Williams, *Duff: A Life in the Law*, 146.

25 [1928] S.C.R. 291.

26 Ibid., 294.

27 Ibid., 298.
28 Ibid., 297.
29 Ibid., 301.
30 Williams, *Duff: A Life in the Law*, 147.
31 Ibid., 148.
32 'If any question arises respecting the qualification of a Senator or a Vacancy in the Senate the same shall be heard and determined by the Senate.'
33 [1928] S.C.R. 302
34 Bushnell, *The Captive Court*, 226.
35 Ibid., 218. See also Snell and Vaughan, *The Supreme Court of Canada*, 141.
36 Bushnell, *The Captive Court*, 226. Compare Geo. H. Ross, 'Interpreting the BNA Act' (1929) 7 Can. Bar Rev. 704, favouring a more progressive interpretation: 'When the Fathers of Confederation drafted [the *BNA Act*], they did not contemplate amending it from time to time. They drafted it so that it might endure for all time. They endowed it with capacity for expansion so that its principles might be adapted to new and developing conditions.'
37 *Ottawa Evening Journal*, 25 April 1928, quoted in Williams, *Duff: A Life in the Law*, 146.
38 'Women Liberals Become Indignant at Ottawa Ruling,' *Globe* (Toronto), 25 April 1928.
39 'Federal Women to Ask Change in Act Wording,' *Toronto Daily Star*, 24 April 1928.
40 Agnes Macphail, 'Seek Way to Admit Women to Senate,' *Toronto Daily Star*, 25 April 1928.
41 Undated clipping, Deacon Papers, Folder 19.
42 *Gazette* (Montreal), 25 April 1928.
43 'Persons But Unqualified,' *Citizen* (Ottawa), 26 April 1928.
44 House of Commons, *Debates*, 1928, 2311; 'Plans Reform in Senate to Admit Women,' *Gazette* (Montreal, 25 April 1928.
45 'Women Elated Over Plan to Admit Them to Senate,' *Toronto Daily Star*, 26 April 1928.
46 Murphy to Mrs Edwards, n.d. May 1928, Justice File, Vol. 2524 File C-1044.
47 Murphy to Deacon, 19 September 1928, Deacon Papers, Folder 6.
48 'Coming Change B.N.A. Welcome to Women,' *Globe* (Toronto), 26 April 1928.
49 25 April 1928, *Edmonton Bulletin*, Murphy Papers Edmonton, Scrapbook 4.
50 Murphy to Reynolds, 16 March 1933, Murphy Papers Waterloo, File 8.
51 Editorial, *Citizen* (Ottawa), 24 April 1928.
52 'Women Lose Their Fight,' *Globe* (Toronto), 25 April 1928.

53 'The End of the Circle,' McClung Papers, Box 13, File '1938 Newspaper articles.'

54 Ibid.

55 Murphy to Governor General in Council, n.d. May 1928, Justice File, Vol. 2524 File C-1044.

56 Murphy to Mrs Edwards, n.d. May 1928, Justice File, Vol. 2524, File C-1044.

57 Murphy to Edwards, 26 July 1928, Justice File, Vol. 2524, File C-1044.

58 Edwards to Murphy, 10 August 1928, Justice File, Vol. 2524, File C-1044.

59 Edwards to Charles Russell, 19 October 1928, Justice File, Vol. 2524, File C-1044.

60 Murphy to Rowell, 15 August 1928, McClung Papers, Box 1, File 11.

61 Murphy to Edwards, 22 October 1928, Justice File, Vol. 2524, File C-1044.

62 Murphy to Edwards, 5 November 1928, Justice File, Vol. 2524, File C-1044.

63 Murphy to Edwards, 17 October 1928, Justice File, Vol. 2524, File C-1044.

64 McBride to Edwards, 18 October 1928, Justice File, Vol. 2524, File C-1044.

65 Charles Stewart to Edwards, 20 October 1928, Justice File, Vol. 2524, File C-1044.

66 Edwards to Murphy, 9 November 1928, Justice File, Vol. 2524, File C-1044.

67 Charles Russell to Edwards, 16 November 1928, Justice File, Vol. 2524, File C-1044.

68 Murphy to Edwards, 10 December 1928, Justice File, Vol. 2524, File C-1044.

7: The JCPC and the Canadian Constitution

1 John T. Saywell, *The Lawmakers: Judicial Power and the Shaping of Canadian Federalism* (Toronto: University of Toronto Press, 2002), 150–86.

2 Ibid., 150–86; Richard Risk, 'The Scholars and the Constitution: P.O.G.G. and the Privy Council' (1996) 23 *Man. L.J.* 496–523, reprinted in Richard Risk, *A History of Canadian Legal Thought: Collected Essays* (Toronto: University of Toronto Press, 2006), 233–70. H.A. Smith, 'Residue of Power in Canada' (1926) 4 *Can. Bar Rev.* 432, was among the first outspoken critics in the 1920s to complain about the JCPC and its construction of the *BNA Act*. Others followed suit, but primarily in the 1930s. See Risk, *A History of Canadian Legal Thought*, 241.

3 *Judicial Committee Act*, 3 & 4 Will. 4, c. 41. For the history of the Judicial Committee from a Canadian perspective, see Coen G. Pierson, *Canada and the Privy Council* (London: Stevens and Sons, 1960).

4 Richard Haldane, 'The Work for the Empire of the Judicial Council of the Privy Council' (1923) 1 *Cambridge L.J.* 143 at 144.

5 Ibid., 144–5.

6 Ibid., 145. After 1966, the practice changed and dissents were allowed.

7 Human Rights Act Implementation Division (HRAID), *The Law Lords and the Lord Chancellor: Historical Background* (London: Department of Constitutional Affairs, 1999), 6, available online from www.dca.gov.uk/constitution/reform/lawlords-and-lc-history.pdf.

8 Ibid., 8.

9 The proposal would also require Lords of Appeal to attend all appeals, and would include life peers and privy counsellors. In addition, this new court of appeal would hear cases throughout the year. Appeals below a certain value would require leave from the Lords of Appeal. Ibid.

10 Ibid., 9.

11 Ibid.

12 Ibid., 10.

13 *Appellate Jurisdiction Act, 1876,* 39 & 40 Vict. c. 59. The act came into force in 1877.·

14 *The Law Lords and the Lord Chancellor,* 18.

15 *Appellate Jurisdiction Act, 1876; The Law Lords and the Lord Chancellor,* 19.

16 *The Law Lords and the Lord Chancellor,* 18.

17 Ibid.

18 *Proceedings of the Imperial Conference,* Cd. 5745, 222–23 (1911), quoted in Robert Stevens, *Law and Politics: The House of Lords as a Judicial Body, 1800–1976* (Chapel Hill: University of North Carolina Press, 1978), 186, note 3.

19 *Appellate Jurisdiction Act, 1876;* Stevens, *Law and Politics,* 187.

20 Stevens, *Law and Politics,* 187.

21 *The Law Lords and the Lord Chancellor,* 19.

22 Doherty Memorandum, 21 December 1918, Borden Papers, OC Series, Folder 575.

23 For instance, in 1927, the Legislative Assembly of India barely agreed to pay Indian judges for participating on the Judicial Committee. That same year, the JCPC's decision in *Wigg v. Attorney General of the Irish Free State,* [1927] A.C. 674 inspired the judges who sat on that very case to question publicly the correctness of their decision. The case had to be reheard, though the new panel reached the same conclusion. In 1933, the Irish Parliament passed legislation abolishing appeals to the JCPC. *The Law Lords and the Lord Chancellor,* 19.

24 Stevens, *Law and Politics,* 187.

25 Ibid., 188.

26 *The Appellate Jurisdiction Act, 1929,* 19 Geo. V. c. 8.

27 Quoted in Ian Bushnell, *The Captive Court: A Study of the Supreme Court of Canada* (Montreal: McGill-Queen's University Press, 1992), 209.

28 Saywell, *The Lawmakers*, 150–86. For discussion of Haldane's views, see David Schneiderman, 'Harold Laski, Viscount Haldane, and the Law of the Canadian Constitution in the Early Twentieth Century' (1998) 48 *U.T.L.J.* 521; Jonathan Robinson, 'Lord Haldane and the British North America Act' (1970) 20 *U.T.L.J.* 55.

29 *Re Board of Commerce Act 1919 and the Combines and Fair Prices Act 1919*, [1922] 1 A.C. 191.

30 *Combines and Fair Prices Act*, 1919, 9 & 10 Geo. V. c. 45.

31 *Board of Commerce Act*, 1919, 9 & 10 Geo. V. c. 37.

32 As Viscount Haldane explained, the JCPC 'was to have power to state a case for the opinion of the Supreme Court of Canada upon any question which, in its own opinion, was one of law or jurisdiction. It was given the right to inquire into and determine the matters of law and fact entrusted to it, and to order the doing of any act, matter, or thing required or authorised under either Act, and to forbid the doing or continuing of any act, matter or thing which, in its opinion, was contrary to either Act. The Board was also given authority to make orders and regulations with regard to these, and generally for carrying the Board of Commerce Act into effect. Its finding on any question of fact within its jurisdiction was to be binding and conclusive. Any of its decisions or orders might be made a rule or order or decree of the Exchequer Court, or of any Superior Court of any Province of Canada.' [1922] 1 A.C. 194–5.

33 Joined by Lord Buckmaster, Viscount Cave, Lord Phillimore, and Lord Carson.

34 [1922] 1 A.C. 197–8.

35 Ibid., 197.

36 Ibid., 200.

37 [1923] A.C. 695 per Viscount Haldane, Lords Buckmaster, Sumner, Parmoor, and Phillimore.

38 Ibid., 703–4.

39 [1925] A.C. 396.

40 *Industrial Disputes Investigation Act*, 1907 (Can.), c. 20; am. 1910 (Can.), c. 29; 1918 (Can.), c. 27; 1920 (Can.), c. 29. The act applied to public utilities and mines, and required that disputes in these industries be referred to a three-person board of conciliation before a strike or lockout could be declared legally. The board was composed of representatives from each of the interested parties – that is, employer, employee, and the public – and employer

and employees chose their own representatives and agreed to the third, who served as the chair of the board. If the parties could not agreed on the third member, the minister of labour would be responsible for making the appointment. The board itself was designed to have significant powers; it could compel the testimony of witnesses and order the production of documents and was able to take evidence under oath. The purpose of the act was conciliation, and there was no outright ban on the ability of employees to strike or on the employer's ability to lockout his workers; all that was required was that the parties attempt conciliation prior to these actions. In essence, the right to strike or to lockout was not precluded, merely delayed.

41 *Toronto Electric Commissioners v. Snider*, [1924] 2 D.L.R. 761.

42 [1925] A.C. 415.

43 (1882), 7 A.C. 829.

44 [1925] A.C. 412.

45 Ibid.

46 (Editorial), 'Judicial Committee Differences' (1925) 3 *Can. Bar Rev.* 135; G.F.H. (Editorial), 'Comment on *Snider*' (1925) 3 *Can. Bar Rev.* 141; (Editorial) '*Russell, Snider, and Hodge*' (1925) 3 *Can. Bar Rev.* 212.

47 [1925] S.C.R. 434.

48 Ibid., 438.

49 'Drunkenness in Canada' (1925) 3 *Can. Bar Rev.* 256.

50 H.A. Smith, 'Residue of Power in Canada' (1926) *Can. Bar Rev.* 432. On Smith, see Risk, *A History of Canadian Legal Thought*, 241–2; Richard Risk, 'Here be Cold and Tygers: A Map of Statutory Interpretation in Canada in the 1920s and 1930s' (2000) 63 *Sask. L. Rev.* 195 at 198–9.

51 Smith, 'Residue of Power in Canada,' 433.

52 Ibid.

53 Ibid.

54 Ibid., 433–4.

55 Ibid., 434. Despite his concerns, Smith did not conclude on a negative note. With resignation, he conceded that the JCPC's constitution was neither better nor worse than what the framers had intended, just different.

56 *Nadan v. The King*, [1926] A.C. 482.

57 'Notwithstanding any royal prerogative, or anything contained in the Interpretation Act or in the Supreme Court Act, no appeal shall be brought in any criminal case from any judgment or order of any Court in Canada to any court of appeal or authority by which in the United Kingdom appeals or petitions to His Majesty in Council may be heard.' R.S.C. 1906, c. 146, s. 1025.

58 3 & 4 Will. IV, c. 41.

59 *Judicial Committee Act*, 7 & 8 Vict. c. 69.

60 *Colonial Laws Validity Act*, 28 & 29 Vict. c. 63, s. 2.

61 [1926] A.C. 482 at 491.

62 Ibid., 492.

63 Quoted in James G. Snell and Frederick Vaughan, *The Supreme Court of Canada: History of the Institution* (Toronto: University of Toronto Press, 1985), 183.

64 Rowell to King, 11 March 1926, quoted in M. Prang, *N.W. Rowell: Ontario Nationalist* (Toronto: University of Toronto Press, 1975), 441.

65 Rowell to Lapointe, 11 March 1926, quoted in Prang, *N.W. Rowell*, 441–2.

66 M. Ollivier, *The Colonial and Imperial Conferences from 1887 to 1937*, Vol. 3, *Imperial Conferences Part II* (Ottawa: Queen's Printer, 1954), 150.

8: Waiting to be Heard

1 In the summer of 1924, Rowell had argued the *Lord's Day Alliance v. A.G. Manitoba*, [1925] A.C. 384, an appeal from the Manitoba Court of Appeal, before Viscount Cave LC, Lord Dunedin, Lord Carson, Lord Blanesburgh, and Justice Duff, and *Re Toronto Railway Co. and City of Toronto*, [1925] A.C. 177 before Vicount Cave LC, Lord Dunedin, Lord Shaw, Lord Carson, and Lord Blanesburgh. Earlier that year, in February, Rowell had argued another reference, *Attorney General for Ontario v. Attorney General for Canada*, [1925] A.C. 750, an appeal from the Supreme Court of Ontario Appellate Division, before Viscount Cave LC, Viscount Haldane, Lord Dunedin, Lord Shaw, and Lord Phillimore.

2 Margaret Bondfield served as minister of labour.

3 'The King: Date of Return to London,' *Times* (London), 22 June 1929.

4 'A Day of Restoration,' *Times* (London), 22 June 1929.

5 'The King X-Rayed This Afternoon,' *Evening Standard* (London), 8 July 1929.

6 'Manchurian Crisis,' *Times* (London), 22 July 1929.

7 'Reparations,' *Times* (London), 25 June 1929; 'Rhineland and Reparations,' *Times* (London), 8 July 1929.

8 'Afgan War,' *Times* (London), 2 July 1929.

9 'Fascism and Education,' *Times* (London), 25 June 1929.

10 'Mussolini Warns the Modern Woman,' *Evening Standard* (London), 22 June 1929.

11 'Miss Sidney: Murder Verdict,' *Evening Standard* (London), 29 July 1929.

12 See, for example, *Godfrey v. Godfrey and Frankiss*, *Times* (London), 22 June 1929.

13 Rowell to Nell Rowell, 20 June 1929, Rowell Papers, Vol. 89, File 'Correspondence, 1922–28.'

14 Ibid.

15 *Canadian General Electric Company Ltd. v. Fada Radio Ltd.,* [1930] A.C. 97.

16 *Berthiaume v. Dastos,* [1930] A.C. 79.

17 *D.E. Lecavalier v. City of Montreal,* [1930] A.C. 152.

18 *Dominion Building Corporation Ltd. v. The King,* [1930] A.C. 90.

19 *Attorney General for Canada v. Attorney General for British Columbia,* [1930] A.C. 111.

20 *Erie Beach Company Ltd. v. Attorney General for Ontario,* [1930] A.C. 161.

21 *Royal Trust Co. v. Attorney General for Alberta,* [1930] A.C. 144.

22 Murphy to Edwards, 4 January 1929, Rowell to Edwards, Justice File, Vol. 2524, File C-1044.

23 Edwards to Murphy 12 January 1929, Justice File, Vol. 2524, File C-1044.

24 Rowell to Edwards, 25 February 1929, Justice File, Vol. 2524, File C-1044.

25 Edwards to Rowell, 28 February 1929, Justice File, Vol. 2524, File C-1044.

26 *Erie Beach Company, Ltd. v. Attorney General for Ontario,* [1930] A.C. 161, a case involving succession duties, which was heard on 15 and 16 July.

27 *Attorney General for Canada v. Attorney General for British Columbia,* [1930] A.C. 111; *Eugène Berthiaume v. Dame Dastous,* [1930] A.C. 79.

28 *Bethiaume; D.E. Lecavalier v. City of Montreal,* [1930] A.C. 152; *Dominion Building Corporation Ltd. v. The King,* [1930] A.C. 90.

29 *Dominion Building Corporation Ltd. v. The King,* [1930] A.C. 90.

30 *Attorney General for Canada v. Attorney General for British Columbia,* [1930] A.C. 111.

31 *Attorney General for Canada v. Attorney General for British Columbia,* [1930] A.C. 111; *Berthiaume v. Dastous,* [1930] A.C. 79; *Royal Trust Company v. Attorney General for Alberta,* [1930] A.C. 144; *D.E. Lecavalier v. City of Montreal,* [1930] A.C. 152

32 Rowell to Nell Rowell, 20 June 1929, Rowell Papers, Vol. 89, File 'Correspondence 1929–1930.'

33 'General Booth Funeral Pageant in London,' *Times* (London), 25 June 1929.

34 Rowell to Nell Rowell, 25 June 1929, Rowell Papers, Vol. 89, File 'Correspondence 1929–1930.'

35 Ibid.

36 Rowell to Nell Rowell, 28 June 1929, Rowell Papers, Vol. 89, File 'Correspondence 1929–1930.'

37 Ibid.

38 'Are Women Persons,' *Daily Telegraph* (London), 24 June 1929.

39 'Mr. Churchill's Criticisms,' *Daily Telegraph* (London), 4 July 1929.

40 M. Prang, *N.W. Rowell: Ontario Nationalist* (Toronto: University of Toronto

Press, 1975), 453.

41 'The King: Thanksgiving at the Abbey,' *Times* (London), 8 July 1929.

42 Diary, 7 July 1929, Sankey Papers, e.283.

43 Rowell to Nell Rowell, 14 July 1929, Rowell Papers, Vol. 89, File 'Correspondence 1929–1930.'

44 Prang, *N.W. Rowell*, 454. Rowell had also written about the British Empire and international affairs. See Newton W. Rowell, *The British Empire and World Peace: Being the Burwash Memorial Lectures, Delivered in Convocation Hall, University of Toronto, November, 1921* (Toronto: Victoria College Press, 1922).

45 Rowell to Nell Rowell, 14 July 1929, Rowell Papers, Vol. 89, File 'Correspondence 1929–1930.'

46 Rowell to Nell Rowell, 17 July 1929, Rowell Papers, Vol. 89, File 'Correspondence 1929–1930.'

47 Rowell to Nell Rowell, 20 July 1929, Rowell Papers, Vol. 89, File 'Correspondence 1929–1930'

48 Rowell to Nell Rowell, 17 July 1929, Rowell Papers, Vol. 89, File 'Correspondence 1929–1930'

49 Theatre listings, *Times* (London), 16 July 1929.

50 R.F.V. Heuston, *Lives of the Lord Chancellors, 1885–1940* (Oxford: Claredon Press, 1964), 509.

51 There were twenty-two Lord Chancellors appointed between 1852 and 1939. Of that number, only two had no experience in the House of Commons: Lord Sankey (1929–35) and Lord Maugham (1938–9). See *The Law Lords and the Lord Chancellor*, 27.

52 [1935] A.C. 462.

53 Ibid., 481.

54 Heuston, *Lives of the Lord Chancellors*, 525.

55 Robert Stevens, *Law and Politics: The House of Lords as a Judicial Body, 1800–1976* (Chapel Hill: University of North Carolina Press, 1978), 201.

56 The first Canadian case that Lord Sankey heard as Lord Chancellor was *D.E. Lecavalier v. City of Montreal*, an action for nuisance from Quebec heard 1, 2, 4, and 5 July 1929, [1930] A.C. 152. However, his first constitutional case was the fisheries dispute between British Columbia and Ottawa: *Attorney General for Canada v. Attorney General for British Columbia*, [1930] A.C. 111, heard 9, 11, 12, and 15 July 1929.

57 Heuston, *Lives of the Lord Chancellors*, 502.

58 Diary, 26 April 1916, Sankey Papers, e.270.

59 Diary, 28 July 1916, Sankey Papers, e.270.

60 Barry Supple, *The History of the British Coal Industry*, Vol. 4, *1913–1946: The Political Economy of Decline* (Oxford: Clarendon Press, 1987), 126.

61 Diary, 18 March 1919, Sankey Papers, e.273.

62 Ibid.

63 Diary, 6 May 1919, Sankey Papers, e.273.

64 Heuston, *Lives of the Lord Chancellors*, 505.

65 Ibid.

66 Diary, 16 June 1919, Sankey Papers, e.273.

67 Diary, 17 June 1919, Sankey Papers, e.273.

68 Coal Industry Commission, *Reports and Minutes of Evidence*, Vol. 2, cmd. 360 (London: H.M. Stationery Office, 1919), vi–viii.

69 Sydney Webb to Sankey, 26 October 1926, Sankey Papers, c. 505, f. 187.

70 Mark De Wolfe Howe, ed., *Holmes – Laski Letters* (New York: Atheneum, 1963), 383, quoted in Heuston, *Lives of the Lord Chancellors*, 506.

71 8 July 1925, quoted in Heuston, *Lives of the Lord Chancellors*, 506.

72 'The Principles and Practice of the Law To-day,' *The Solicitors' Journal*, 14 March 1928, 11.

73 24 September 1925, quoted in Heuston, *Lives of the Lord Chancellors*, 507.

74 David Marquand, *Ramsay MacDonald* (London: Richard Cohen Books, 1997), 230.

75 Diary, 31 December 1923, Sankey Papers, e.270; see also Stephen R. Ward, *James Ramsay MacDonald: Low Born among High Brows* (New York: Peter Lang, 1990), 124.

76 Diary, 23 January 1924, Sankey Papers, e.278.

77 Diary, 15 January 1924, Sankey Papers, e.278.

78 Diary, 13 December 1926, Sankey Papers, e.280.

79 Laski to Sankey, 1 March 1926, Sankey Papers, c. 505, f. 179.

80 7 February 1928, quoted in Heuston, *Lives of the Lord Chancellors*, 507.

81 25 February 1928, quoted in ibid., 508.

82 Diary, 5 June 1929, Sankey Papers, e.283.

83 'The Law and the Public,' *Times* (London), 6 July 1929.

84 Heuston, *Lives of the Lord Chancellors*, 520–3.

85 *The Solicitors Journal*, 14 March 1928.

86 Compare Gordon Hewart, *The New Despotism* (London: E. Benn, 1929).

87 *The Solicitors' Journal*, 1 September 1928.

88 Holmes to Laski, 8 May 1928, in Howe, ed., *Holmes – Laski Letters*, 1052–3.

89 Diary, 9 and 10 July 1929, Sankey Papers, e.283.

90 'The University Match,' *Times* (London), 11 July 1929.

91 Diary, 8 July 1929, Sankey Papers, e.283.

92 Ibid., 23 July 1929.

93 Obituary, *Times* (London), 30 May 1936.

94 Ibid.

95 L.G. Wickham Legg, ed., *Dictionary of National Biography (1931–1940)* (London: Oxford University Press, 1949), 211.

96 *Times* (London), 26 October 1897, quoted in *Dictionary of National Biography*, 211.

97 Quoted in Walker-Smith, Derek, *The Life of Lord Darling* (London: Cassell and Company, 1938), 93.

98 Ibid., 93–4.

99 See Dudley Barker, *Lord Darling's Famous Cases* (London: Hutchinson, 1936).

100 Legg, ed., *Dictionary of National Biography*, 211.

101 *Huntley v. Simmons* (unreported), referred to in Walker-Smith, *The Life of Lord Darling*, 116–17.

102 *R. v. Upton*, (1899, unreported), referred to in ibid., 117–18.

103 Walker-Smith, *The Life of Lord Darling*, 154.

104 Ibid., 303.

105 *Times* (London), 30 May 1936.

106 Walker-Smith, *The Life of Lord Darling*, 301.

107 'Lord Darling,' Borden Papers, Post 1921 Series, Folder 87.

108 Diary, 15 July 1929, Sankey Papers, e.283.

109 Legg, ed., *Dictionary of National Biography*, 243–5.

110 Ibid., 244.

111 *Times* (London), 22 May 1939.

112 *Matrimonial Causes Act*, 1923 (U.K.), 13 & 14 Geo. 5, c. 19.

113 *Times* (London), 14 August 1935.

114 *Dictionary of National Biography*, 866.

115 *Times* (London), 11 March 1944.

116 Sanderson to Sankey, 14 May 1914, Sankey Papers, Vol. 503.

117 'Sir L. Sanderson to Lunch,' Diary, 3 July 1925, Sankey Papers, e.279.

118 *Viscountess Rhondda's Claim (Committee for Privileges)*, [1922] 2 A.C. 339, discussed in chapter 3 of this volume.

119 See chapter 3 of this volume.

120 *Daily News*, 20 November 1929, Sankey Papers, e.506.

121 Diary, 31 December 1921, Sankey Papers, e.275.

122 Diary, opening page for 1929, Sankey Papers, e.283.

123 Heuston, *Lives of the Lord Chancellors*, 533.

124 House of Lords, *Debates*, 17 July 1924, Vol. 58, 711.

125 House of Lords, *Debates*, 25 May 1925, Vol. 61, 465.

9: The JCPC Decides

1 Case of the Appellants, Privy Council Archives.
2 Sections 11, 14, 42, 63, 75, 83, 84, 93, 127, 128, and 133.
3 Case of the Attorney General of Canada, Privy Council Archives.
4 Ibid.
5 Catherine Cleverdon, *The Woman Suffrage Movement in Canada*, 2nd ed. (Toronto: University of Toronto Press, 1974), 152.
6 Ibid.
7 The JCPC listened to argument in this case on 22, 23, 25, and 26 July.
8 'Privy Council Is Puzzled Whether Women "Persons,"' *Toronto Daily Star*, 25 July 1929.
9 Ibid.
10 'Women in Senate,' *Daily Telegraph* (London), 24 July 1929.
11 'Women and Senate,' *Daily Telegraph* (London), 26 July 1929.
12 David Ricardo Williams, *Just Lawyers: Seven Portraits* (Toronto: Osgoode Society, 1995), 51.
13 'Women and Senate.'
14 'Women's Ability to Keep Secret Raised on Appeal,' *Toronto Daily Star*, 27 July 1929.
15 Ibid.
16 Ibid.
17 'Women and Senate.'
18 Ibid.
19 Diary, 31 July 1929, Sankey Papers, e.283.
20 Ibid., 1 August 1929.
21 Charles Russell to Minister of Justice, Justice File, Vol. 2524, File C-1044,
22 Rowell to Murphy, 3 August 1929, Murphy Papers Waterloo, File 10.
23 Murphy to Rowell, 12 August 1929, Murphy Papers Waterloo, File 10.
24 *Edwards v. Attorney General for Canada*, [1930] A.C. 128.
25 Ibid., 134.
26 Ibid.
27 Ibid., 134–5.
28 Ibid., 138.
29 Ibid.
30 Ibid., 136.
31 Ibid., 143.
32 Peter Russell, *Constitutional Odyssey: Can Canadians Become a Sovereign People?* 3rd ed. (Toronto: University of Toronto Press, 2004), 9–11.
33 *Gompers v. United States*, 233 U.S. 604 at 610 (1914).

34 William Whiting, *War Powers of the President* (Boston: John L. Shorey, 1862), 11.

35 [1930] A.C. 143.

36 'Woman, As Person, May Sit in Senate Says Privy Council,' *Globe* (Toronto), 19 October 1929.

37 Diary, 18 October 1929, Sankey Papers, e. 283.

38 *Toronto Daily Star*, 18 October 1929.

39 *Edmonton Journal*, 19 October 1929, Murphy Papers Edmonton, Scrapbook 4.

40 'Woman, As Person, May Sit in Senate Says Privy Council,' *Globe* (Toronto), 19 October 1929.

41 *Daily Express* (London), 19 October 1929.

42 'Court Decides Women Are Persons,' *Daily Mail* (London), 19 October 1929; 'Women Become Persons,' *Daily Express* (London), 19 October 1929.

43 'A Woman's Big Victory in Privy Council,' *Evening Standard* (London), 18 October 1929.

44 Editorial, *Daily Telegraph* (London), 19 October 1929.

45 See, for example, 'There Will Be No Sex War – If Men Are Strong Enough to Lead,' *Daily Mail* (London), 24 October 1929; 'Women Are Growing More and More Beautiful,' *Daily Mail* (London), 27 October 1929; 'This "Sex Equality" Foolishness,' *Daily Mail* (London), 28 October 1929; 'The Woman Driver,' *Daily Express* (London), 19 October 1929.

46 See 'A Motion in the Lords,' *Times* (London), 24 July 1929.

47 'Temporary Peers Plan Explained,' *Evening Standard*, 8 July 1929.

48 Editorial, 'Women in Senate and Lords,' *Manchester Guardian*, 19 October 1929. The same day, the *Manchester Guardian* carried a story about the claim of the National Union of Women Teachers under the headline 'Equal Pay for Equal Work.'

49 Editorial, *Daily Telegraph* (London), 19 October 1929. Women were not admitted to the House of Lords until the 1960s. See chap. 3 in this volume.

50 'Canadian Women Win Right to Sit in Senate; Law Lords Call Ban Relic of Barbarous Days,' *New York Times*, 19 October 1929; 'Canadian Senate Bows to Ruling on Women,' *New York Times*, 20 October 1929; 'Women Win Another Fight for Full Political Equality,' *New York Times*, 3 November 1929.

51 'Say Women Will Win House of Lords Seats,' *New York Times*, 20 October 1929.

52 'Senate Fight Leaders Acclaim Peers' Verdict,' *Toronto Daily Star*, 19 October 1929.

53 Ibid.

54 'Senate Fight Leaders Acclaim Peers' Verdict,' *Toronto Daily Star*, 19 October 1929.

55 'Woman, As Person, May Sit in Senate Says Privy Council,' *Globe* (Toronto), 19 October 1929.

56 'Mrs. Parlby Pleased,' *Citizen* (Ottawa), 18 October 1929.

57 'Women Are Eligible for Upper Chamber Privy Council Rules,' *Toronto Daily Star*, 18 October 1929.

58 H.C. Hocken, MP, quoted in 'Women Are Eligible for Upper Chamber Privy Council Rules.'

59 'Women are Eligible for Upper Chamber Privy Council Rules.'

60 'Mr. Mackenzie King Comments,' *Manchester Guardian*, 19 October 1929.

61 Sir Robert Laird Borden, *Canadian Constitutional Studies* (Toronto: University of Toronto Press, 1922), 55: 'Like all written constitutions it has been subject to development through usage and custom,' quoted in [1930] A.C. 136.

62 'Women Are Eligible for Upper Chamber Privy Council Rules.'

63 *Edmonton Journal*, 18 October 1929, Murphy Papers Edmonton, Scrapbook 3.

64 'Women Are Persons,' *Citizen* (Ottawa), 21 October 1929.

65 'Privy Council Finding Leaves Capital Cold,' *Toronto Daily Star*, 19 October 1929.

66 'Women Are Eligible for Upper Chamber Privy Council Rules,' quoting Wilfred Heighington.

67 'Women Are Eligible for Upper Chamber Privy Council Rules.'

68 'A Retrospect,' *The Country Guide*, 2 December 1929, quoted in Candice Savage, *Our Nell: A Scrapbook Biography of Nellie McClung* (Saskatoon: Western Producer Prairie Books, 1979), 178–9, and in Margaret MacPherson, *Nellie McClung: Voice for the Voiceless* (Montreal: XYZ Publishing, 2003), 137.

69 22 January 1930, quoted in MacPherson, *Nellie McClung*, 129–30.

70 King Diary, 27 September 1926.

71 See Bank of Canada, 'Rates and Statistics: Inflation Calculator,' online at www.bankofcanada.ca/en/rates/inflation_calc.html.

72 M. Prang, *N.W. Rowell: Ontario Nationalist* (Toronto: University of Toronto Press, 1975), 445–6.

73 Rowell to Murphy, 6 January 1930, Justice File, Vol. 2524, File C-1044.

74 PJC to Edwards, 30 January 1930, Justice File, Vol. 2524, File C-1044.

75 For a more restrained but still sceptical view of the decision, see W.P.M. Kennedy, 'The Judicial Interpretation of the Canadian Constitution' (1930) 8 *Can. Bar Rev.* 703.

76 George Henderson, 'Eligibility of Women for the Senate' (1929) 7 *Can. Bar Rev.* 617.

77 Ibid., 617.

78 Ibid., 619, 625.

79 Ibid., 628.

80 'The Privy Council Decisions: A Comment from Great Britain' (1937) 15 *Can. Bar Rev.* 428 at 429.

81 'The Statute of Westminster and Appeals to the Privy Council' (1936) 53 *LQR* 173 at 181–2.

82 *Montreal West (Town) v. Hough*, [1931] S.C.R. 113.

83 Ibid., 128.

84 Ibid.

10: The Legacy

1 Murphy to King, 19 October 1929, King Papers J1, reel C2312, p. 141348.

2 King to Murphy, 26 October 1929, King Papers J1, reel C2312, p. 141353.

3 Quoted in Byrne Hope Sanders, *Emily Murphy: Crusader* (Toronto: Macmillan, 1945), 256.

4 *Parliament of Canada*, 'Senators and Members: Women in the Senate,' retrieved 26 March 2007 from www.parl.gc.ca/information/about/people/key/ bio.asp?Language=E&query=2282&s=F.

5 Sylvia Bashevkin, *Toeing the Lines – Women and Party Politics* (Toronto: Oxford University Press, 1993), 117. See also Library and Archives Canada, 'Celebrating Women's Achievements: Government,' www.collectionscanada.ca/women/ 002026–825–e.html.

6 12 February 1930, quoted in Franca Iacovetta, 'A Respectable Feminist: The Political Career of Senator Cairine Wilson 1921 – 1962,' in Linda Kealey and Joan Sangster, eds., *Beyond the Vote: Canadian Women in Politics* (Toronto: University of Toronto Press, 1989), 63.

7 Unidentified clipping, n.d., McClung Papers, Vol. 17.

8 Murphy to McClung, 4 March 1930, McClung Papers, Box 1, File 13.

9 Ibid.

10 Ibid.

11 Senate, *Debates*, 21 February 1931, quoted in Iacovetta, 'A Respectable Feminist,' 63.

12 Ibid.

13 King Diary, 5 May 1931.

14 Iacovetta, 'A Respectable Feminist'

15 Library and Archives Canada, 'Celebrating Women's Achievements: Government.'

16 Edwards Papers, File 15.

17 Byrne Hope Sanders, *Emily Murphy: Crusader*, 258; 'Five Are Mentioned by Rumors in City for Seat in Senate,' *The Albertan*, 4 May 1931.

18 'Pat Burns Appointed to Canadian Senate,' 17 *The Albertan*, July 1931.

19 'Five Are Mentioned by Rumors in City for Seat in Senate' does not mention Murphy as a possible contender and suggests that women's groups were promoting the appointment of Mrs P.J. Nolan.

20 Murphy to King, 8 September 1933, King Papers, J 3, Vol. 108, File 2.

21 Kenwood to McClung, 15 March 1939, McClung Papers, box 12, File 3.

22 Untitled speech, Parlby Papers, microfilm.

23 Mackenzie King to McClung, 5 June 1930, McClung Papers, Box 1, File 13. Emphasis in original.

24 *Parliament of Canada*, 'About Parliament, History of Federal Ridings since 1867, Calgary West, 17th Parliament,' retrieved 27 March 2007 from www.parl.gc.ca/information/about/process/house/hfer/ hfer.asp? Language=E&Search=Det&rid=103&txtComments=calgary

25 'Canadian Women Honored,' *Winnipeg Free Press*, 13 June 1938.

26 'What Do Women Want?' MS version, *Edmonton Bulletin*, 11 June 1938, McClung Papers, Box 13, File '1938 Newspaper articles.'

27 Nellie McClung, *Clearing the West: My Own Story* (Toronto: Thomas Allen, 1935).

28 H.W. Wood to Parlby, 28 April 1930, Parlby Papers, File 1.

29 McClung to Parlby, 1 May 1930, Parlby Papers, File 1.

30 Murphy to Parlby 30 May 1930, Parlby Papers, File 1.

31 'Hon. Irene Parlby Not to Stand for Nomination Again' *The Albertan*, 11 November 1934.

32 See Patrick Brode, *Courted and Abandoned: Seduction in Canadian Law* (Toronto: University of Toronto Press, 2002), chap. 10.

33 *Edmonton Bulletin*, 1 March 1939.

34 'Advocating Independent Citizen's Coalition,' 1940, Parlby Papers, Speeches.

35 Quoted in Stephen R. Ward, *James Ramsay MacDonald: Low Born Among High Brows* (New York: Peter Lang, 1990), 259.

36 Frankfurter to Sankey, 17 June 1930, Sankey Papers, e.270, File 80.

37 R.F.V. Heuston, *Lives of the Lord Chancellors, 1885–1940* (Oxford: Claredon Press, 1964), 525.

38 Robert Stevens, *Law and Politics: The House of Lords as a Judicial Body, 1800–1976* (Chapel Hill: University of North Carolina Press, 1978), 201.

39 *Reference re Regulation and Control of Aeronautics*, [1932] A.C. 54.

40 *Reference re Regulation and Control of Aeronautics*, [1930] S.C.R. 663.

41 *Aeronautics Act*, R.S.C., 1927, c. 3.

42 *BNA Act*, s. 132: 'The Parliament and Government of Canada shall have all powers necessary or proper for performing the obligations of Canada, or of any Province thereof, as part of the British Empire, towards foreign countries arising under treaties between the Empire and such foreign countries.'

43 [1932] A.C. 70–1.

44 *British Coal Corporation v. The King*, [1935] A.C. 500.

45 *Reference re Supreme Court Act Amendment Act*, [1940] S.C.R. 49, aff'd *Attorney General of Ontario et al. v. Attorney General of Canada et al. and Attorney General of Quebec*, [1947] 1 D.L.R. 801.

46 See, for example, *Reference re the Combines Investigation Act, s. 36*, [1931] A.C. 310; *Consolidated Distilleries Ltd. v. Canada*, [1933] A.C. 508.

47 *Proprietary Trade Association v. Attorney General for Canada*, [1931] A.C. 310.

48 *Reference re Weekly Rest in Industrial Undertakings Act, Minimum Wages Act and Limitation of Hours of Work Act*, [1936] S.C.R. 461, aff'd [1937] 1 D.L.R. 673 (P.C.); *Reference re Employment and Social Insurance Act*, [1936] S.C.R. 427, aff'd [1937] 1 D.L.R. 684 (P.C.); *Reference re Section 498A of the Criminal Code*, [1936] S.C.R. 363, aff'd [1937] 1 D.L.R. 688 (P.C.); *Reference re Dominion Trade and Industry Commission Act*, [1936] S.C.R. 379, varied [1937] 1 D.L.R. 702 (P.C.); *Reference re Natural Products Marketing Act*, [1936] S.C.R. 398, aff'd [1937] 1 D.L.R. 691 (P.C.); *Reference re Farmers' Creditors Arrangement Act*, [1936] S.C.R. 384, aff'd [1937] 1 D.L.R. 695 (P.C.)

49 M. Prang, *N.W. Rowell: Ontario Nationalist* (Toronto: University of Toronto Press, 1975), 485.

50 Ibid.

51 See V.C. MacDonald, 'The Canadian Constitution Seventy Years After,' (1937) 15 *Can. Bar Rev.* 401 at 426; W.P.M. Kennedy, 'The British North America Act: Past and Future' (1937) 15 *Can. Bar Rev.* 393 at 398–9; F.R. Scott, 'The Consequences of the Privy Council's Decisions' (1937) 15 *Can. Bar Rev.* 485 at 493–4.

52 Prang, *N.W. Rowell*, 86.

53 Ibid., 496.

54 Ian Bushnell, *The Captive Court: A Study of the Supreme Court of Canada* (Montreal: McGill-Queen's University Press, 1992), 268.

55 King Diary, 30 June 1936.

56 In the five years between 1930 and 1935, one woman was among R.B. Bennett's thirty-three Senate picks. Louis St Laurent, serving as prime minister from 1948 to 1957, appointed four women to the Senate out of fifty-five opportunities. John Diefenbaker, with two minority governments and the largest majority to that time in Canadian history, appointed thirty-seven senators over the course of six years in office, two of whom were women.

Lester B. Pearson, who never achieved a majority in Parliament despite serving as prime minister from 1963 to 1968, appointed a single woman to the Senate, although he had thirty-nine opportunities to appoint more.

57 See *Library and Archives Canada*, 'Famous Five,' at www.collectionscanada.ca/famous5/index-e.html.

58 See, for example, Hal Joffe, 'Flawed Record Follows Revered Famous Five,' *Calgary Herald*, 21 February 1998; Janice Fiamengo, 'Rediscovering Our Foremothers Again: The Racial Ideas of Canada's Early Feminists, 1885–1945,' (Winter 2002) 75 *Essays on Canadian Writing* 85.

59 Nancy Millar, *The Famous Five: Emily Murphy and the Case of the Missing Persons* (Cochrane, AB: Western Heritage Centre, 1999).

60 'Famous Five Woman a Creature of Her Culture,' *Calgary Herald*, 1 November 1999.

61 Quoted in 'Owl Takes Flight to Make Way for Famous Five on $50 Bill,' *Calgary Herald*, 4 June 2000.

62 *Reference re Regulation and Control of Radio Communication*, [1931] S.C.R. 541 at 546–7; *Montreal West (Town) v. Hough*, [1931] S.C.R. 113.

63 More supportive was Justice Ivan Rand, a judge on the Supreme Court from 1943 through 1959, who referred approvingly to the living tree approach in *Winner v. SMT (Eastern) Ltd.*, [1951] S.C.R. 922.

64 *Quebec (Attorney General) v. Blaikie*, [1979] 2 S.C.R. 1029. The case did not end there, however. The litigants asked the court to define the scope of section 133 of the *BNA Act* with respect to delegated legislation. Submitted to a rehearing in November of 1980, the Court announced in the spring of 1981 that section 133 applied to regulations and rules of practice enacted by the courts and administrative. The by-laws of municipalities and school bodies were, however, excluded. It did so without further reference to the *Persons case* or the constitutional living tree. *Blaikie v. Quebec (Attorney General)*, [1981] 1 S.C.R. 312.

65 *British Columbia (AG) v. Ellett Estate*, [1980] 2 S.C.R. 466 at 478; see also *Reference re Residential Tenancies Act 1979 (Ontario)*, [1981] 1 S.C.R. 714 at 723 per Dickson J.

66 *Hunter v. Southam Inc.*, [1984] 2 S.C.R. 145 at 155–6.

67 See also *Law Society of Upper Canada v. Skapinker*, [1984] 1 S.C.R. 357 at 365 per Estey J.

68 In 1985, Edwin Meese III, the Attorney General of the United States, called for the courts to return to a jurisprudence of original intention. On this subject, see a series of articles re-published in Jack N. Rakove, ed., *Interpreting The Constitution: The Debate Over Original Intent* (Boston: Northeastern University Press, 1990).

69 *Reference re Motor Vehicle Act (British Columbia) s. 94(2)*, [1985] 2 S.C.R. 486.

70 Ibid., para 53.

71 *Reference re Electoral Boundaries Commission Act (Saskatchewan)*, [1991] 2 S.C.R. 158 at 180.

72 See, *Charter Politics* (Scarborough, ON: Nelson Canada, 1992); F.L. Morton and Rainer Knopff, *The Charter Revolution and the Court Party* (Peterborough, ON: Broadview, 2000); Rainer Knopff, *Judicial Power and the Charter: Canada and the Paradox of Liberal Constitutionalism* (Toronto: Oxford University Press, 2001).

73 *Reference re Secession of Quebec*, [1998] 2 S.C.R. 217, para 52.

74 *Reference re Same-Sex Marriage*, [2004] 3 S.C.R. 698, para 22.

75 See *Winnipeg Child and Family Services (Northwest Area) v. G. (D.F.)*, [1997] 3 S.C.R. 925, para 118, per Major J. (dissenting): 'Precedent that states that a foetus is not a "person" should not be followed without an inquiry into the purpose of such a rule. In the well-known case of *Edwards v. Attorney General for Canada*, [1930] A.C. 124, the Privy Council overruled precedent and a unanimous Supreme Court of Canada, [1928] S.C.R. 276, and held that women were "persons" with respect to s. 24 of the *British North America Act, 1867*. Rigidly applying precedents of questionable applicability without inquiry will lead the law to recommit the errors of the past.'

76 *British North America Act*, s. 91(26).

77 [2004] 3 S.C.R. 698, para 29.

78 Ibid., para 27.

79 In a 1984 criminal law decision, Dickson J. refused to limit the very specific language of criminalizing anti-drug legislation in light of changed scientific knowledge, in *R. v. Perka*, [1984] 2 S.C.R. 232 at 265. See also *R. v. Prosper*, [1994] 3 S.C.R. 236, per L'Heureux-Dubé J. (dissenting) at para 70: '... the "living tree" theory has its limits and has never been used to transform completely a document or add a provision which was specifically rejected at the outset. It would be strange, and even dangerous, if courts could so alter the constitution of a country.'

80 *R. v. Big M Drug Mart Ltd.*, [1985] 1 S.C.R. 295, para 117.

81 *R. v. Blais*, [2003] 2 S.C.R. 236, para 40.

82 *Gosselin v. Attorney General (Quebec)*, [2002] 4 S.C.R. 429, paras 82 and 317.

Archival Sources

These are the archival sources we have used in the preparation of this book. In the footnotes, we use the abbreviated references for these materials.

Borden Papers: The Borden Papers, 1893–1937, Library and Archives Canada, Microfilm copy, Robarts Library, University of Toronto.

Deacon Papers: William Arthur Deacon Papers, MS 160 Box 28, Thomas Fisher Rare Book Library, University of Toronto.

Edwards Papers: Edwards/Gardiner Family Fonds, Glenbow Archives, Calgary, M7 283

Justice File: Department of Justice File, Library and Archives Canada, Ottawa, RG 13, Vol. 2524, Vol. 2525, File C-1004.

King Diary: William Lyon Mackenzie King Diary, Library and Archives Canada, Ottawa. Available online at http://king.collectionscanada.ca.

King Papers: William Lyon Mackenzie King Papers, Library and Archives Canada, Ottawa, MG 26.

McClung Papers: Nellie McClung (Mooney) Papers, British Columbia Archives, Victoria, MS 0010.

McKinney Papers: Louise McKinney Fonds, Glenbow Archives, Calgary, M-8138-2.

Meighen Papers: Arthur Meighen Papers, Library and Archives Canada, Ottawa, Series 2, MG 26, 1.

Murphy Papers Edmonton: Emily Murphy Collection, MS2, City of Edmonton Archives.

Murphy Papers Waterloo: Emily Ferguson Murphy Papers, University of Waterloo, Doris Lewis Rare Book Room, WA 13.

Parlby Papers: Irene and Walter Parlby fonds, Glenbow Archives, Calgary, M938.

Privy Council Archives: Privy Council Archives, London, No. 121 of 1928.

Rowell Papers: Newton Wesley Rowell Papers, Library and Archives Canada, Ottawa, MG 27 II D 13.

Sankey Papers: John Sankey Papers, Bodleian Library, Oxford, MSS. Eng. hist.

Supreme Court of Canada File: Supreme Court of Canada, Library and Archives Canada, Ottawa, RG 125, Vol. 563.

Facsimile of the Amended Petition – November 1927

IN THE SUPREME COURT OF CANADA.

In the matter of a reference as to
admission of women to the Senate of Canada.

The humble petition of Mrs. Henrietta Muir Edwards,
Mrs. Nellie L.McClung, Mrs. Emily F.Murphy, Mrs. Louise C.McKinney
and the Honorable Irene Parlby, sheweth as follows:

1. That your petitioners are respectfully referring
to this Honourable Court, through His Excellency the Governor General,
for hearing and consideration, pursuant to Section 60 of the Supreme
Court Act, the three following questions upon constitution :-

    (a) Is power vested in the Governor General of Canada,
or the Parliament of Canada, or either of them, to
appoint a female to the Senate of Canada ?

    (b) Is it constitutionally possible for the Parliament
of Canada, under the provisions of the British North
America Act, or otherwise, to make provision for the
appointment of a female ~~person~~ to the Senate of
Canada ?

    (c) If any statute be necessary to qualify a female
to sit in the Senate of Canada, must this statute be
enacted by the Imperial Parliament, or does power
lie with the Parliament of Canada or the Senate of
Canada ?

2. That the questions so referred are questions of general
public importance and your petitioners, as representatives of a class
of persons interested and affected by these questions, are desireous
of being represented by Counsel upon the hearing of argument of the
questions so referred.

-2-

3.   That your petitioners having regard to the special
.ture of the questions so referred, consider that they ought not,
.s individuals, to be required to bear the expense of retaining
counsel to prepare and present the argument on their behalf upon
the said question.

Your Petitioners therefore humbly pray that this
Honourable Court will be graciously pleased, in its discretion,
in pursuance of the provisions of section 60, sub-section 5, of
the Supreme Court Act, to request the Honourable Newton W.Rowell to
appear on their behalf on the hearing of argument of this reference
and to argue the case as to their interests therein; the reasonable
expenses thereby occasioned to be paid by the Minister of Finance
as by the statute in that behalf provided.

And your petitioners will ever pray etc., etc.

Illustration Credits

Malak Photographer: The Right Honourable Lyman Poore Duff

National Portrait Gallery, London: Viscount John Sankey, by Olive Edis (NPG x7207)

Supreme Court of Canada: The Right Honourable Frank Anglin

Index

Robert Fraser, ed., *Provincial Justice: Upper Canadian Legal Portraits from the Dictionary of Canadian Biography*

1991 Constance Backhouse, *Petticoats and Prejudice: Women and Law in Nineteenth-Century Canada*

1990 Philip Girard and Jim Phillips, eds., *Essays in the History of Canadian Law: Volume III – Nova Scotia*

Carol Wilton, ed., *Essays in the History of Canadian Law: Volume IV – Beyond the Law: Lawyers and Business in Canada 1830–1930*

1989 Desmond Brown, *The Genesis of the Canadian Criminal Code of 1892*

Patrick Brode, *The Odyssey of John Anderson*

1988 Robert J. Sharpe, *The Last Day, the Last Hour: The Currie Libel Trial*

John D. Arnup, *Middleton: The Beloved Judge*

1987 C. Ian Kyer and Jerome Bickenbach, *The Fiercest Debate: Cecil A. Wright, the Benchers, and Legal Education in Ontario, 1923–1957*

1986 Paul Romney, *Mr Attorney: The Attorney General for Ontario in Court, Cabinet, and Legislature, 1791–1899*

Martin L. Friedland, *The Case of Valentine Shortis: A True Story of Crime and Politics in Canada*

1985 James Snell and Frederick Vaughan, *The Supreme Court of Canada: History of the Institution*

1984 Patrick Brode, *Sir John Beverley Robinson: Bone and Sinew of the Compact*

David Williams, *Duff: A Life in the Law*

1983 David H. Flaherty, ed., *Essays in the History of Canadian Law: Volume II*

1982 Marion MacRae and Anthony Adamson, *Cornerstones of Order: Courthouses and Town Halls of Ontario, 1784–1914*

1981 David H. Flaherty, ed., *Essays in the History of Canadian Law: Volume I*